HAROLD H. BLOOMFIELD, M.D., is an eminent Yale-trained psychiatrist and bestselling author of *How to Survive the Loss of a Love, Making Peace with Your Parents, Making Peace with Yourself, TM,* and *Inner Joy.* His books have sold over four million copies in twenty languages. **SIRAH VETTESE, Ph.D.,** is a counselor and leading educator of love fitness and relationship skills. Prominent for her work in self-hypnosis and visualization, Dr. Vettese has produced a bestselling audiocassette series. Drs. Bloomfield and Vettese appear regularly on national television and are among the most sought-after speakers and seminar leaders in the world on self-improvement, marriage, and family. They have three children and a psychotherapy practice in Del Mar, California. **ROBERT KORY** is a writer and entertainment lawyer in Los Angeles.

LIFEMATES

The Love Fitness Program for a Lasting Relationship

Harold H. Bloomfield, M.D.
and Sirah Vettese, Ph.D.
with Robert B. Kory

A SIGNET BOOK

SIGNET
Published by the Penguin Group
Penguin Books USA Inc., 375 Hudson Street,
New York, New York 10014, U.S.A.
Penguin Books Ltd, 27 Wrights Lane,
London W8 5TZ, England
Penguin Books Australia Ltd, Ringwood,
Victoria, Australia
Penguin Books Canada Ltd, 10 Alcorn Avenue,
Toronto, Ontario, Canada M4V 3B2
Penguin Books (N.Z.) Ltd, 182–190 Wairau Road,
Auckland 10, New Zealand

Penguin Books Ltd, Registered Offices:
Harmondsworth, Middlesex, England

Published by Signet, an imprint of Dutton Signet,
a division of Penguin Books USA Inc. Previously published in
NAL Books and Plume editions.

First Signet Printing, February, 1992
10 9 8 7 6 5 4

Contents

AUTHORS' NOTE

Anyone with a history of psychiatric disorder, who feels emotionally unstable, or is taking major tranquilizers or antidepressant medication should not do the exercises in this book without first consulting a qualified mental health professional.

To protect confidentiality, the names and identifying details in case histories have been changed.

Chapter 1

Love Fitness:
A Personal Challenge

Few people recognize how out of shape they are when it comes to intimate communication and, therefore, their ability to love. Most of us are afraid of letting others know who we really are and what we really feel, and yet we also expect that a great relationship should be easy to achieve. Couples in terrific relationships often evoke comments such as "They are so lucky," or "Of course they've got a super relationship. They were made for one another." The implication is that great relationships are found, not created. Question those couples, however, and you will discover their secret to lasting, passionate love: overcoming their fears of heart-to-heart communication.

You don't need to be a psychiatrist to diagnose the discouragement and frustration that abound in relationships today. Many women are angry at men who don't listen or can't express feelings. Many men remain fearful of self-disclosure and do not understand what women want. It seems to be the rule for relationships to begin with stars and rockets, only to fizzle in boredom and resentment. Many people who were once deeply in love eventually give up on one another—through either divorce or resignation to a relationship devoid of passion. Although the primary cause of this frustration is an unacknowledged fear of sharing deep feelings, we remain optimistic. We believe you and your lover can initiate a breakthrough in your relationship by learning to open up to one another as never before.

As therapists and personal growth seminar leaders,

we have witnessed the pain of broken or passionless relationships. We understand how people resist change, particularly when it comes to revealing their deepest feelings. For most people, however, we do not recommend lengthy therapy as an antidote. Rather, we offer a new approach to creating, building, and sustaining relationships that not only last but thrive: the Lifemates' Love Fitness program.

Communication problems in most relationships stem from emotional habits learned in childhood from parents who themselves had difficulty expressing feelings. Unfortunately, mere understanding of how you were emotionally programmed by your parents is usually not enough to precipitate a change in your emotional behavior. To overcome this limitation, we have developed a series of "emotional workouts" to retrain emotional responses. This book presents a program of these exercises to develop love fitness—the psychological strength and communication skills to sustain a close, passionate love relationship.

Over the past decade, there has been a resurgence of interest in fitness. Many people now recognize that the rewards of getting in shape, improving diet, and giving up destructive habits, such as excessive drinking or smoking, far outweigh the effort and sacrifice required. So too, we are confident that the time has come for people to apply the same principles of self-improvement to their love relationships. Mere wishing won't bring you a lifemate or enliven an established relationship. There is much you can accomplish with the right emotional workouts to make the changes you desire, both in how you respond to your lover and how he or she responds to you. Great relationships are created, not simply found!

Most people are accustomed to treating problems in their relationships with emotional Band-Aids. Sex may go flat, resentments may develop as blaming and criticism become predominant, one or both love partners may be holding back so much anger that the relationship resembles a seething volcano, and yet both may unconsciously conspire to ignore or deny the mounting problems. A shopping spree substitutes for expressing hurt feelings, fatigue becomes an excuse for a diminished sex life, work develops into an escape from the problems of living together, and quarreling becomes the mode of maintaining emotional contact without addressing the real issues. Even worse, both singles and couples tend to repeat these emotional mistakes with all the attendant turmoil in their relationships. Freud called this process "repetition compulsion," a tendency to unconsciously re-create emotional conflict. It is as if people repeat the same problems in their relationships until they finally force themselves, out of desperation, to learn key emotional lessons.

It is tragic that many troubled couples seek help when it is too late to heal their emotional wounds. Couples typically avoid facing problems in a relationship for the same reasons they avoid sharing their deepest feelings—fear. The emotional cost of coping honestly with intense feelings often seems too high. Rage, rejection, loss, jealousy, and sexual impotence all may appear overwhelming. Psychological resistances naturally come into play. If one person takes the initiative to confront emotional issues in the relationship, the other person is likely to resist. Typical avoidances include: "I don't have time for this [exchange of feelings]," "Talking [about our real feelings] won't get us anywhere," "This [confronting our real feelings] could destroy our relationship [what we have left]," "Let's forget it and make the best of what we have [and hide from the real problems]."

When communication in a relationship begins to sour, bigger problems are not far off. The Love Fitness program helps you avoid or reverse emotional damage that erodes love. The key is to stop repeating emotional mistakes from the past. With this program you can prevent further problems in a relationship just as a physical fitness program can prevent chronic disease. Of course, it can be difficult to stick to a regimen of physical fitness exercises. Since that same lack of willpower can also limit what you gain out of the Love Fitness program, we have included throughout this book plenty of tips for overcoming resistances and enjoying your emotional workouts.

The Challenge of Love

We know well the trap of ignoring communication problems in a relationship because we almost let it destroy our marriage. Surprised to hear a psychiatrist and psychotherapist making such a statement? We believe it is important to begin this book with the truth about our own marriage because nothing else illustrates so well what the Love Fitness program is intended to accomplish and how it differs from traditional therapy. Today we have a marriage that is more intimate, passionate, and rewarding than either of us thought possible. People often comment on the overflowing love between us. What they don't realize, however, is the turmoil we went through and the hard work and personal commitment it took to become true lifemates.

Most of us did not learn much from our parents about how to build a great love relationship, and we are no exception. You might also be interested to know that very few psychiatry and psychotherapy training programs teach any more about creating great relationships than medical schools teach about creating peak health and fitness. We had a particularly difficult time addressing the communication problems that developed early in our marriage because we thought our expertise in helping others solve emotional problems should insulate us from our own. As a result, when we began to have serious problems in our marriage, we tried more than most to pretend to our families, friends, and to ourselves that everything was fine. Fortunately, however, we found the strength to face the truth, and out of that experience we not only achieved a personal breakthrough in our marriage but also discovered the seeds of the Love Fitness program that we subsequently developed through work with thousands of clients and seminar participants.

Our story is quite ordinary to begin with. When we met ten years ago, we quickly became enraptured with the magic of romance. The attraction was so strong that we, like almost every romantic couple, believed destiny was unfolding before our eyes, and past frustrations were merely stepping-stones toward final culmination in this perfect relationship. We spent every moment we could together; sex was fantastic; and our disagreements seemed minor and had a natural resolution. We moved in together, sure that we had finally found the perfect lover.

What neither of us understood at the time was the enormous challenge of becoming true lifemates and creating a relationship that allowed for the full, free, and flowing expression of intimate feelings—good and bad, loving and angry, enthusiastic and depressed, confident and fearful, passionate and bored. Nor did either of us fully understand the enormous impact our parents had had, simply by way of example, on how we handled our own feelings in an intimate relationship. Theoretically, yes, we knew how childhood traumas affected adult psychology, but we hadn't considered how the modeling of communication (or noncommunication) in our parents' marriages impacted our own communication skills and patterns of expressing our feelings. As a result, when the magic of romance began to wear thin and serious problems emerged, we experienced the same surprise, disappointment, and despair that we had heard time and time again from our clients in similar emotional straits.

Our marriage problems and our initial responses were both typical. We quarreled frequently, but avoided sitting down to find out why. Sirah felt hurt and resentful, but didn't make her feelings known. Harold began to feel trapped, but found no outlet to vent his frustration. As tension grew in the relationship, sexual passion diminished, and we both struggled to put on a happy face and pretend to one another that we were still soul mates.

Little did we know, despite all our training, that we were caught in a repetition compulsion: each of us acting out core conflicts and maladaptive habits internalized from our childhood conflicts and our parents' unhappy marriages. Our romantic fantasy was shattered; we were shocked and deeply disappointed. The painful crisis we created would either destroy our marriage or compel us to develop new emotional strengths never learned from parents, previous relationships, or previous psychological training. A brief look into our backgrounds sheds light on the dynamics of our love crisis.

Sirah: "Fleeing the Tyrant"

My earliest memory was being awakened in the middle of the night by screams and banging in the kitchen. I was three years old. As I ran into the hall, I saw my father holding a large kitchen knife in one hand, my mother by the hair with the other. She was sobbing, "Please, don't." His eyes were filled with rage as he screamed, "You bitch; you deserve it." I remember calling out to her, and he yelled, "Get out of here."

I am the oldest girl in an Italian family of seven children. At least three times a month my Mom and Dad had violent fights where my mother would come out of her room with a black eye and bruises. I remember one time we children huddled together crying, and my older brother said, "I'm going to get back at him some day." I recall myself saying, "I hate his guts; I wish he was dead," and my sister sobbing, "Let's all run away and never come back."

My father controlled us with emotional abuse and constant threats. Swearing and degrading comments, such as "stupid, ugly, no good," were the norm. I remember him telling me when I was twelve, "You are nothing and never will amount to anything." Sometimes, he disappeared for up to a week and in the meantime we would run out of food. When we asked for money for school supplies, shoes, and so on, he wouldn't give it to us. In a rare good mood he would throw a hundred-dollar bill on the table and say, "Go out and buy yourselves something."

Despite my father's temper, I longed for his love and respect. One night I heard him hitting my mother, and I couldn't stand it any longer. I ran to him and said, "You don't love anyone but yourself; you're selfish and mean, and I hate you." He ripped off the bedpost, and struck me with it saying, "I'm going to teach you a lesson you'll never forget." From that time on I experienced bouts of depression and would lock myself in my room. Eventually I became self-supporting and although I withdrew from my family, I found new hope in work, school, and creative endeavors.

At eighteen, I married a man who, unlike my father, was a kind, loving gentleman. Nevertheless, in our ten years together, life was an endless struggle—raising two children, attending college, and then completing graduate school. Constantly short of money and time, we often bickered. Unfortunately, we never learned to acknowledge our hurts or release our anger toward each other. I was afraid of my feelings, and yearned to share them, but couldn't. The unfinished business in my relationship with my father finally reared its ugly head. I felt more and more rage, but didn't know how to release it. Lacking love fitness skills, we got caught in bitter silence and grew further and further apart. Eventually, our marriage became so painful that we divorced.

When I met Harold, I was sure that I had left the problems of my past behind me. Little did I know that the tyrant inside my own head would reappear to create a new love crisis for me.

Harold: "A Prisoner of War"

In the first year of my life, I received support and nurturance from my mother. We got into serious difficulties, however, when I voiced my first independent thought! Our estrangement grew rapidly—by the time I was in my last year of high school, the rage and hostility between us was overpowering. I recall feeling more than once, "I'm so mad at my mother I could kill her." As a result I felt very guilty, trapped and frightened by intimate feelings.

During my childhood, my parents either argued or maintained a hostile silence. The tension was so great that I remember thinking, "God, just help me survive now; I'll heal later." While I loved my mother and father, I also resented them for never raising themselves out of bitterness and mutual contempt.

My mother expressed her despair and hopelessness by: (1) threatening emotional illness: "You're driving me crazy"; "You're going to give me a nervous breakdown"; "I'm going to kill myself, and it's all your fault"; (2) threatening physical illness: "I'm going to have a heart attack because you're upsetting me so"; "I'll probably get ulcers and have to go to the doctor just because you won't listen to me"; (3) threatening disapproval: "Wait until the neighbors/your friends hear about this"; "God will punish you"; "If you don't listen to me, you won't have any success in life" and (4) guilt-inducing comments: "I gave up everything for you"; "You don't care about anyone; you're so selfish"; "If you loved me, you'd do what I say"; "The only reason I stayed with your father was because of you."

Years later, despite my psychiatric training at Yale, I still acted like a rebellious child ten minutes after stepping into my mother's home. Even though she had softened over the years and become less controlling, her slightest inquiry would prompt me to yell at her for treating me like a child. Of course, I was still behaving like one!

To cope with my mother, my father became depressed, passive, and emotionally withdrawn. Sometimes, however, he would explode in violent rage, screaming out in frustration and shaking his fists. With this model, I grew up perceiving marriage and long-term love relationships as soul-destroying traps. Falling in love was a signal for me to flee rather than face imprisonment in a lifetime of endless demands and a futile struggle to please. I was determined to avoid any situation remotely similar to the ball and chain of my father's distress. I feared that my love relationships would emulate my parents' embittered marriage. Hiding my fears, I took pride in becoming an arrogant, wild, and single Don Juan. My game was typical. If a woman became too close, I would soon find fault with her, and quickly move on. While on the surface I felt triumphant for escaping my fears, deep inside, I yearned for everlasting love but was terrified of feeling trapped.

When I met Sirah, I was bored with being single but still highly phobic about marriage. To my surprise, Sirah seemed to understand me as no woman had before. Although frightened of the risk, I proposed marriage because I finally had met a woman I didn't want to lose. Despite my hopes, as our relationship developed I began to feel trapped, bitter, and resentful. Eventually I made every attempt to drive Sirah away. Although I felt compelled to punish her in order to survive emotionally, I hated myself for hurting her and depriving myself of her love.

After we got engaged and set a marriage date, my marriage phobia intensified. In a vain effort to assert my freedom, I contacted old lovers and created a series of affairs. I also started picking fights with Sirah, and blamed her for making me upset. I literally made Sirah's life miserable as I struggled with my compulsive "acting out" of my own conflicts. A week prior to the wedding, when we went to apply for a marriage license, I created a vicious fight in the parking lot as a last attempt to drive Sirah away. Sirah finally said that perhaps we should call off the wedding. Feeling helpless and in deep despair, I broke down and cried. Sirah comforted me and we went on with the wedding as scheduled. I thought I had come to grips with my conflicts, but only later did I recognize how much more growth was necessary to create the quality marriage I was desperately seeking.

Our Love Crisis

Our subsequent love crisis grew out of the feelings that we each feared most. Sirah's biggest complaint was feeling dominated and manipulated. Growing up in a household where only her father could get angry, Sirah never learned to express her anger and consequently found herself incapable of expressing her needs to Harold. She grew resentful as the major decisions in the relationship seemed always to go Harold's way. Harold, on the other hand, felt trapped. Having been single for many years, he was accustomed to getting his way and was not particularly open to listening to Sirah. As a result, Sirah began seeing Harold in some ways acting out the worst characteristics of her father and Harold saw Sirah acting out what he thought to be the most oppressive characteristics of his mother.

Anger became a major problem in the relationship. Harold, who hated the memories of his father flying into a rage with fists raised at his mother, now found himself overwhelmed with similar feelings. To his horror, he felt his marriage was unleashing the same repressed dark forces that in childhood he had witnessed between his mother and father. Sirah, who despised the brutality in her father, now found herself once again cowering in the face of angry outbursts, just as her mother had been meek and subservient. Neither of us could rise above these old patterns as our quarreling grew more frequent and hostile. It took a major crisis for us to confront the severity of our problems.

One afternoon Sirah had complained that Harold was not paying enough attention to her. For Harold, who had been extremely pressured by clients and speaking engagements, it was the last straw. Almost unconsciously he found himself screaming at Sirah, fists raised, wanting to destroy not so much her but the woman controlling him, a repressed image of his mother. Sirah was terrified, having seemingly created a nightmare. All of a sudden, however, she recognized that she was re-creating for herself the same timid, compliant stance her mother had always taken. Reaching deep within herself, Sirah found the courage to yell back, "I'm not going to take this. Show me the respect I deserve." She too raised her voice and her fists. We were both terrified and stunned. Here we were, the perfect couple, soul mates, now at each other's throats.

It is surprising that we didn't recognize the extent of our problems earlier. In retrospect, the signs were everywhere. For example, our bickering had become characterized by constant blaming and complaining—a classic symptom of a relationship in trouble. Whenever one of us felt frustrated, we made it an opportunity to unload on the other. Neither of us was taking responsibility for bringing our own satisfaction and positive energy to the relationship. Rather, we each let ourselves focus on the other's demands, and we both felt we were giving more than we were getting.

Sex too became a cause for intense anxiety. The passion that we thought would never end disappeared in the face of resentment and rage. Harold was oppressed with memories of his mother chastising his father for his lack of sexual interest in her. As the relationship deteriorated, Harold became impotent, resentfully fantasizing how great a lover he had been as a Don Juan. His previous love relationships were based on pseudo-intimacy—getting close enough to a woman for a sexual conquest but not so close as to reveal genuine feelings. Struggling to please Sirah, he became increasingly angry, depressed, and guilt-ridden. The harder Harold thought he tried, the worse he felt about himself and the relationship.

For Sirah the loss of sexual interest made her feel even less powerful in the relationship—sex, her ability to control through passion, had evaporated. She had learned to use her sexual charms to attract and manipulate Harold. She used seduction to win affection, admiration, and appreciation. When the sexual energy in the relationship diminished, Sirah too felt impotent—but in her case, deeply emotionally impotent. Her power was gone; she felt defeated and hopeless about ever changing the relationship; because of her rage and disappointment, she hardly had the energy to try.

Both of us became terribly disheartened about the marriage and even started to talk about giving up. Our relationship, once "made in heaven," had become filled with resentment and pain. We seemed to be acting out some primordial struggle between the sexes—Sirah trying to lead Harold into submission and Harold struggling to escape the "tender trap." We couldn't go on pretending, so we finally acknowledged that we were creating a relationship that was making us both miserable, and that neither of us really knew what true intimacy was all about.

Emotional Workouts: The Habits of Love

In the midst of this relationship nightmare, we began the search for a light to guide us out of the hostility and conflict. Although we recognized that we didn't have immediate answers, we at least had the courage to ask questions. Each of us had helped other couples through marital crises, so we had faith that an honest effort to identify and solve relationship problems was of value in a troubled relationship.

What surprised and confused us initially was the

very fact that our relationship had become so fraught with tension. Each of us was strong in his and her own right, and there was no doubt that we shared a deep and abiding love. In fact, that is where we began to assess our relationship. We each asked ourselves whether we still loved the other and how much we wanted the relationship to work. On both counts, we got positive answers. From this reaffirmation of basic commitment, we felt safe enough to conduct an honest evaluation of the relationship and discuss what each of us wanted to change. There also emerged a new concept of what it takes for a relationship to remain passionate and fully rewarding. We later coined the term "love fitness" to describe this concept.

We began an intensive effort to solve the communication problems in our relationship, and over the next eighteen months, each of us, and our relationship, under went a profound transformation. We didn't start with a detailed analysis of how our parents' marriages influenced our relationship because we knew that intellectual insight alone would not help us make significant changes. Instead, we started by identifying the specific emotional habits we wanted to alter, and to develop step-by-step exercises to increase emotional strengths and communication skills. For example, we were both caught in the habit of blaming each other for our frustration in the relationship. Once we realized what we were doing, it was obvious that this destructive emotional behavior had to stop. We then developed a simple exercise called "Heart Talks" to achieve this change. We also recognized that Sirah felt defeated about trying to get through to Harold when she was hurt or angry. Again, it was clear that emotional habits on both sides had to change. The emotional workout called "Tell Me More" helped modify that pattern. Our sex life, once passionate and vibrant, was in real trouble; performance anxieties, resentment, and rejection made us feel bored and impotent. So, we created several emotional workouts to improve our sexual communication.

Here are ten exercises we have found essential to enjoy a strong and lasting relationship:

1. "Tell Me More," Chapter 2, p. 57
2. "Heart Talks," Chapter 3, p. 89
3. "Renewing Your Love" Chapter 3, p. 101
4. "Having an A.F.F.A.I.R. with Your Spouse," Chapter 4, p. 132
5. "Anger with Heart" Chapter 5, p. 150
6. "Writing the Wrong," Chapter 6, p. 197
7. "Heart Letter," Chapter 6, p. 201
8. "Habits of the Heart," Chapter 7, p. 243
9. "Rephrasing with Love," Chapter 7, p. 259
10. "Transforming Expectations into Preferences," Chapter 7, p. 261

These exercises are the core of the Love Fitness program.

As we created these emotional workouts, we developed a new perspective on our work with clients. Rather than struggle to gain more and more insight as to why a relationship was in trouble, we concentrated on the specific changes each couple wanted and needed to make. Once old communication habits were broken, new ways of expressing underlying love began to emerge. We found for ourselves and our clients that these emotional workouts created unanticipated benefits. For example, "Tell Me More" helped Sirah to overcome the timidness and compliance learned from her tyrannical father; "Heart Talks" allowed Harold to overcome his fears of a controlling mother.

Most relationships between healthy people fall short of expectations because most people are unprepared for the demands of a deeply loving communication process. They lack either the commitment or the emotional skills to become true lifemates. When people initially "fall in love," they discover a wide-open channel of expression with one another. What people often fail to recognize, however, is that this initial romantic rush of energy and excitement is a phenomenon of contrasts. Soon, couples adapt, emotional habits develop, and the initial energy goes flat. The intense communication of courtship loses vibrancy and becomes routine. The flow of vital information is then limited and the process of loving diminished. Couples perceive this change in the intensity of their emotional communication as a "falling out of love."

Love Fitness: A New Paradigm

We believe that increasing numbers of people are trying to create relationships based on more full and honest communication than they have previously witnessed in their own lives or between their parents. To achieve this goal, it is not enough for men merely to become more sensitive and women more assertive. Relationships often end in disappointment because couples never really examine what is necessary for their love to thrive. What often passes for love is a form of infatuation—the desire to find totality in another. From that perspective, disappointment is inevitable as each lover discovers that the other cannot meet expectations.

Relationships flourish when couples begin with a commitment to their own growth as individuals and as a couple. Love alone is not enough because love fades in the face of inevitable misunderstandings, small hurts, repressed anger, and resentment. In order to create and sustain a lasting love relationship, you must become a skillful communicator in the complex language of emotion. We have coined the term "lifemates" to denote those characteristics of a couple committed to developing those skills and creating a relationship that truly thrives.

For us, the journey of becoming lifemates has involved a new understanding of love. We have discovered an unprecedented freedom to share our deepest feelings—even hidden fears and dark secrets—and both healed and energized one another as a result. We have learned to support one another in pursuit of our separate goals without fear of competition or a struggle of wills. Each of us has learned to trust our own needs and our mutual commitment to fidelity, intimacy, and honesty. We have also acknowledged the need to challenge each other regularly. There is no "taking each other for granted," but instead, we regularly savor the mystery of discovering new thoughts, feelings, ideas, and visions that lie within us. We have also learned that becoming lifemates is a spiritual adventure of the heart. When love unfolds to unprecedented depths, we believe it awakens the senses, enlivens peak experiences, and opens horizons of psychic powers. By nurturing love, lifemates start to feel bonded to the whole of life.

This vision of what a relationship can be is not an idealization. Every person has an enormous ability to love, and our own discoveries have been repeated by our clients. The key is developing the communication skills necessary to share feelings fully and honestly in a committed relationship. The Love Fitness program teaches those skills that are essential for a lasting relationship to truly flourish.

The Love Fitness program begins with three building blocks. The first is recognizing that almost everyone is out of shape when it comes to the process of loving. We introduced this idea earlier, but it is worth reexamining in more detail. It has become commonplace to hear complaints about how men are incapable of sustaining relationships or communicating feelings. The fact is, men and women are equally out of shape when it comes to the process of loving. They each possess certain emotional strengths and communication skills but lack others that are critical to a vibrant love relationship. Generalities in this regard are not very helpful. Rather, to become lifemates, each person must acknowledge the emotional habits that may be impeding communication and practice key emotional workouts to develop new skills.

Second, just as modern medicine has come to recognize degrees of health, the Love Fitness program recognizes that the quality of love relationships also varies. The goal of the Love Fitness program is not just to cope with problems, but rather to develop strengths in heart-to-heart communication that can make a relationship terrific. The Love Fitness program can prevent needless and emotionally draining conflicts, divorce, or your children growing up alienated from you, just as physical workouts help avoid the problems of fatigue, obesity, and disease.

Third, the Love Fitness program involves an ongoing process of development—for you and for your relationship. Love fitness is not a state you achieve once and for all any more than physical fitness is everlasting. Rather, love fitness requires an ongoing commitment to growth and continued development of a relationship. A lasting love relationship will inevitably involve emotional crises associated with ordinary life events—the birth and raising of children, career successes and failures, illnesses, death of parents or loved ones, children growing up and moving away, retirement. All of these events are made sweeter or at least more bearable by the sharing of love. Yet each of these events presents new challenges to sustaining the flowing, heart-to-heart communication necessary to keep love vibrant. The Love Fitness program is a lifelong undertaking to generate intangible rewards of the heart that will vastly exceed the effort required.

There are certain additional parallels worth noting between the Love Fitness program and a physical fitness program. First and foremost, the Love Fitness program is intended to develop emotional strength. Too many people feel defeated and discouraged about their ability to create a vibrant love relationship. The emotional workouts we describe are aimed at enabling each person in a relationship to take 100 percent responsibility for the quality of the relationship. Blaming and complaining are out! The Love Fitness program also develops emotional grace, the ability to accept your lover's strengths and limitations. The intense enjoyment of true heart-to-heart communication replaces the idealized effort to make your lifemate into something he or she is not. The Love Fitness program also develops emotional vitality. If you are bored in your relationship, one of the problems may be that you have let yourself become boring. The same holds true for your lover. We describe emotional workouts to escape from that trap. Finally, the Love Fitness program develops emotional agility and timing. You learn when to confront or when to hold back, and how to express strong feelings, such as anger or rage, in effective rather than destructive ways.

We use the fitness analogy to explain our approach to improving relationships because it best summarizes both the theoretical approach and the practical benefits of our program. Naturally, we do not claim to have developed the Love Fitness program anew. Our approach represents a distillation of certain psychological exercises that stem from dramatic developments in modern psychology.

A revolution has occurred in psychology over the past decade, equivalent perhaps to the potential of the microchip in its impact on the quality of modern living. At the core of this revolution is the discovery that the old model of psychological growth, that is, constantly focusing on past traumas and emotional injuries, is not beneficial for most people. What they really need is insight into which patterns of feeling, thought, and action are not serving them well, and then learning new psychological skills to correct those habits.

This approach requires a new mode of understanding personal growth and psychological change, one that is better compared to a fitness program than to psychotherapy. In the old model, a psychiatrist or psychotherapist is popularly known as a "shrink." In the new model, the more appropriate term would be a "stretch," a psychological coach or guide, assisting people to stretch their psychological capacities to love and be loved.

The Myths of Personal Growth

In creating the Love Fitness program, we uncovered five basic myths about psychotherapy and personal growth, each of which can make the whole process unnecessarily laborious and complicated. Shattering these myths is the first step to taking full charge of your love fitness.

Myth One: Psychological growth is a mysterious process of gaining insight. Perhaps the most common myth about psychological growth is that it is intricate, unconscious, and mysterious. We never cease to be amazed at how pervasive the idea has become that psychological growth requires a search for repressed childhood traumas that, when recognized, will bring sudden insight and transformation. For most people, psychological development just does not happen that way. This myth is often destructive because it reinforces a magical expectation that relationship problems can be solved through a search for a Holy Grail of "in-depth" psychological insight.

The fact is that poor modeling, rather than emotional trauma, is responsible for most problems in relationships. Whether the issue is an inability to make a commitment, express anger, or reveal intimate feelings, the problem can be traced to poor emotional habits developed during childhood. Few people have grown up in families where the basic communication skills necessary for creating vibrant love relationships were modeled. Most people with problems in their love relationships are basically mature and emotionally healthy. We have described our own story to emphasize the point that a love crisis can happen to anyone. The problem is usually not some deep psychological disorder but rather a simple lack of emotional strengths and communication skills necessary for a sustained, passionate love relationship.

There is some good news and some bad news in this new model of personal development. The good news is that the whole process involves self-education and regular emotional workouts that can be entirely under your control. The bad news is that you must surrender the myth that your relationship will start working with one or two blazing insights from a magical therapist. You have to take responsibility for acquiring the information you need and practicing emotional workouts regularly to develop new emotional strengths and communication skills. By doing so, you will discover that deep psychological insight does not have to precede behavior change; on the contrary, behavior change most often precedes greater insight! The whole process can thus be accelerated and you can look back and see why and how you were locked into emotional patterns that were not beneficial.

Myth Two: Psychological development requires lengthy investigation to reveal "What's Wrong." One of the most dangerous myths about psychological development is that a person is more deeply and thoroughly served through three or four sessions of psychotherapy a week. The fact is that such a practice is just as likely to be destructive as it is to be helpful. For most people, a lengthy examination of their personal problems just makes them more preoccupied with those problems and reinforces a fear that there is something deeply wrong with them. Throughout this book, we will emphasize a key principle about psychological development: *What you put your attention on in life grows stronger.* For example, if you place attention on successes rather than failures, your self-esteem will grow stronger. Similarly, placing attention on negative feelings you may have about yourself or problems you may have in your love relationship are likely to cause those bad feelings and problems to dominate your awareness. Spend enough time ruminating about these problems and you are likely to convince yourself and your love partner there is something deeply wrong with you. The more you think there is something deeply wrong, the more your problems will persist. Low self-esteem decreases your capacity to love and be loved, thus perpetuating a vicious cycle.

This is not to say, however, that no diagnosis of relationship problems is necessary. Developing love fitness does require that you assess the emotional habits, beliefs, and attitudes that are ineffective or disabling to you. We have included brief quizzes to help you do so in each chapter. Such self-assessment will help you identify the emotional workouts that are most appropriate to your needs. Of course, we also are not saying that insight into your past is without value. Our point is simply that there will always be "reasons" why you've developed emotional habits that don't serve you, and an inventory of reasons alone will not help empower you to change. In the Love Fitness program, we focus your attention primarily on "stretching"—expanding your emotional strengths and intimacy skills.

Myth Three: The right therapist or seminar will provide the answers. The boom in psychotherapy and personal development seminars has created a new myth. Some people seem to believe that if they just keep hopping from one psychotherapist or personal growth seminar to another, they will eventually find one that gives them the ultimate key to happiness. On the one hand, competent therapy and good seminars can be valuable. On the other hand, becoming a therapy or seminar "junkie" reinforces the myth that someone else can do it for you.

The Love Fitness program is based on the premise that the greatest therapist lies within. You are no doubt aware of your body's enormous physical regenerative abilities. Think of the healing energy your body mobilizes to mend a broken bone. That same healing and regenerative capacity exists emotionally. With the emotional workouts we describe, you put your psychological capacity for growth in high gear. Exercising your emotions can have the same broad beneficial effect as exercising your body.

A fundamental premise of the Love Fitness program is that no one can change your emotional habits but you. Even the most highly skilled therapist, seminar leader, or best-selling book can only assist in identifying what emotional habits are not serving you and suggest appropriate skills and exercises to learn new emotional and communication skills. Ultimately you and you alone are responsible for your personal development. In some cases, this responsibility means finding the right therapist as a consultant. You don't have to look for an "earth mother" or "wise father" and you don't have to spend years in therapy first creating and then unraveling a dependency on your therapist. You may wish to find a therapist who will briefly and effectively, yet compassionately, be your guide. In Chapter 6, we discuss how to choose such a therapist.

Myth Four: You will be happy and successful when therapy is finally over. Many people go into psychotherapy thinking, "I'll be happy when . . ." They expect they will "finally be happy" or "have it all together" when the therapeutic process is over. This attitude often leads to years of effort with few results. People wind up talking about their problems for months and even years, as if in their "last session" they will be awestruck with wisdom and the power to change!

The Love Fitness program utilizes a drastically different approach—personal growth takes place naturally in steady increments. We instruct our clients to look for progress in every session as well as through the emotional workouts they practice on their own. So, too, in reading this book, you should find value on each page and see steady progress as you practice the various emotional workouts that comprise the Love Fitness program.

Myth Five: Psychological growth involves a labor of pain and turmoil. None of the myths about psychological growth is more damaging than this one. Many people will be afraid to try the emotional workouts we describe because they believe that challenging their emotional status quo may involve pain or the risk of unacceptable emotional turmoil. The Love Fitness program will go a long way toward shattering this myth once and for all. Physical fitness workouts can involve some pain, but they can also be a source of fun, excitement, energy, and even pleasure. So, too, many of the emotional workouts that constitute the Love Fitness program will be enjoyable. They will expand your emotional horizons, help you gain a new perspective on yourself and your lifemate and enable you to get in touch with greater sexual energy and passion.

When we work with clients, one of our principal objectives is to help them "lighten up" about the problems in their lives. Most people take themselves far too seriously. With a little perspective and humor, they can find solutions to relationship problems that seemed insurmountable. The Love Fitness program is intended to be fun and enjoyable. You should find many of the workouts not only challenging and informative but also entertaining. Your enlightenment will naturally unfold as your emotional "heavies" become much "lighter."

How Fit for Love Are You? Quiz One

The place to begin the Love Fitness program is with a self-assessment. Just as testing at the outset of a physical fitness program is helpful in understanding your current level of physical fitness and where you need emphasis, initial evaluation in the Love Fitness program is helpful in assessing your current emotional strengths and communication skills.

With the following quiz, you will learn how your feelings, attitudes, and behaviors affect the quality of your love relationship. You will also receive feedback on where you can benefit to develop greater love fitness. Consider each of the following statements.

Mark each statement True or False as it applies to you.

1. My self-esteem has increased since being in this relationship.
2. I can freely express my need for private time.
3. I seem to confide more in friends than in my love partner.
4. I am not afraid to let my lover see me cry.
5. I sometimes feel bullied or manipulated by my love partner.
6. Revealing my innermost feelings is easy for me.
7. When I'm upset, I tend to blame my lover.
8. I feel my love partner truly understands and appreciates me.
9. I get upset when my lover criticizes my shortcomings.
10. I tend to be overly critical or short-tempered with my lovemate.
11. I frequently feel upset or angry with things my partner has said or done.
12. I drink excessively, use drugs, or overeat to mask negative feelings.
13. I am responsive and supportive when my love partner shows signs of vulnerability or insecurity.
14. I often compare my lover unfavorably with other people (less attractive, less sensitive, less successful, etc.).
15. I do not depend on my love partner for constant approval or validation.
16. I feel guilty when my lover feels unhappy, disappointed, or hurt.
17. I have forgiven my love partner for the times he/she has hurt me.
18. I experience great sexual excitement and passion in my love relationship.
19. I often feel my lover's barriers go up when I'm emotionally vulnerable.
20. I spend too much time "working on" and "fixing" my relationship.

21. It irritates me that I'm the one who always has to suggest an intimate dinner or romantic weekend.
22. I enjoy sharing my sexual fantasies with my love partner.
23. My lover and I make all major decisions together.
24. As a relationship continues I tend to feel bored, disillusioned, or trapped.
25. I'm afraid to assert myself because of my love partner's temper.
26. I would feel comfortable revealing anything about my past to my love partner.
27. It is difficult for me to give criticism to my lover.
28. In a love quarrel I am not inclined to give up in frustration.
29. I don't like to admit it, but sometimes I talk down to or patronize my lover.
30. When differences emerge, I'm afraid of being abandoned, rejected, or disapproved of.
31. I feel comfortable asking my love partner for what I truly want and need.
32. My love partner is also my best friend, whom I can always count on.

Now go back over the questions and give yourself one point for each true response to questions 1, 2, 4, 6, 8, 13, 15, 17, 18, 22, 23, 26, 28, 31, and 32; give yourself another point for each false response to questions 3, 5, 7, 9, 10, 11, 12, 14, 16, 19–21, 24, 25, 27, 29, and 30. Add up your score. Here is a summary to help you interpret your results:

0–8   You're probably feeling a good deal of frustration in your relationship. You have obvious difficulty expressing and accepting intimate feelings. You may experience substantial personal growth by working through the exercises in this book. It may also be useful to seek the support of a psychotherapist or a marriage and family counselor to assist in this process.

9–16   Most people score in this range. Relatively low scores are indicative of how badly out of shape the majority of us are at expressing and receiving love. When it comes to love fitness, it's as if we're all on a junk-food diet and have sedentary, stressful jobs. If you've had any experience with the joys of developing physical fitness, you know how rewarding a regular program of physical workouts can be. So, too, if you take the time to practice the exercises in this book, you are likely to discover the joys and rewards of increasing your fitness for love.

17–24   Your fitness for love is above average. In some areas you may be afraid to express your feelings; in others you may be unable to respond with sufficient support to your partner. Focusing on relevant chapters of this book will be particularly helpful.

25–32   You are enjoying a very high level of love fitness. You're comfortable expressing and receiving intimate feelings. You enjoy loving and being loved but you're also independent. You can be open and vulnerable but also enjoy expressing your strength.

How Fit for Love Is Your Relationship? Quiz Two

This test is aimed at assessing the love fitness of your relationship. In answer to each of the following twenty-five questions, give yourself 1, 2, 3, or 4 points: 1 = rarely; 2 = sometimes; 3 = often; and 4 = almost always. If you are not currently in a relationship, answer the questions on the basis of your last significant relationship. The Roman numeral coding in parentheses is explained at the end of the quiz.

1. Are you comfortable with your lover's anger? (V)
2. Do you accept your love partner fully without trying to change him/her? (VII)
3. When it comes to major decisions about careers, children, and lifestyle, do you feel like true partners? (VII)
4. Have you overcome fears of being trapped by a committed love relationship or marriage? (VI)
5. Can you create laughter, fun, and play in your lovemaking? (IV)
6. Are you comfortable saying "no" to your lover? (V)
7. Are you good at letting your lover know when you feel neglected? (II)
8. Do you trust your partner's loyalty and sexual fidelity? (IV)
9. Are you able to express feelings of jealousy without fearing how your love partner will react? (II)
10. Is your lovemaking tender and exciting? (IV)
11. Do you have open, intimate conversations with your lover? (III)
12. Are you good at receiving criticism from your lover? (II)
13. Can you let down your barriers and bare your soul with your lifemate? (III)
14. Can you share your insecurities and failures as openly as your strengths and victories? (III)
15. Do you feel free of resentment and bitterness toward your love partner? (VI)
16. Do you and your lover know how to quarrel and settle disputes effectively? (V)
17. Do you feel that your love partner is also a close friend? (III)
18. Can you express anger appropriately and constructively? (V)

19. Would your love partner join you in counseling at your request? (VI)
20. Have you learned to truly forgive your lover for those times when he/she may have deeply hurt you? (VI)
21. Can you listen receptively to accusations, anger, and hurt without feeling rejected or becoming defensive? (II)
22. Do you respect your love partner's work, values, and opinions? (VII)
23. Can you and your lover be sexually free, spontaneous, and unpredictable? (IV)
24. Do you feel understood, nurtured, and cared for by your love partner? (II)
25. Do you feel supported by your lifemate in achieving your goals? (VII)

Now, add up your score.

85–100   Your relationship is in great shape. You and your lover trust and respect one another. You know how to be both close and autonomous. Your emotional exchange is excellent and you are enjoying a high level of love fitness.

70–84   Your love relationship is in good shape, but there's no reason not to raise the quality of your relationship to a peak level of fitness.

55–69   Your love relationship is probably of average or below-average fitness; it's starting to get flabby and may already be quite out of shape. You may not notice it yet, but there is a significant risk that bigger problems will emerge in your relationship. You've got basically two choices: You can put up with a flabby, out-of-shape love relationship and hope that problems don't arise, or you can work to create a higher level of love fitness.

40–54   Your relationship is badly out of shape. You can't count on getting by without making some improvements. The likelihood is that your relationship will only deteriorate unless you take action now. While you start with the exercises in this book, you might also benefit from a therapist or counselor who could assist you and your lover in making a focused effort to increase your love fitness.

25–39   Crisis. The relationship has deteriorated to the point where it is unlikely that you can solve the problems you face on your own. We recommend that you find an excellent therapist or marriage counselor to assist you in taking appropriate action immediately.

The Roman numeral that follows each question refers to the chapter in which these issues are discussed. By reviewing those questions answered with a 1 or 2, you can see where you need the most exercise and practice, and which chapters (in parentheses) deserve special attention.

Who Can Benefit from This Book

The Love Fitness program has proved enormously valuable already to thousands of people. We have had seminar participants tell us that learning these emotional workouts has been worth thousands of dollars in therapy. This book has been written for anyone who wishes to learn more about how to create and sustain a vibrant, deeply rewarding love relationship. Most of the emotional workouts are intended to be practiced by couples. You do not, however, have to be currently in a relationship to find value in the Love Fitness program. The exercises will help you to attract and sustain a new, more deeply satisfying love relationship. Many of the emotional workouts can also be practiced with a close friend to yield great results.

This book can be extremely helpful for a couple, whether married or simply in a committed relationship, to solve an impending love crisis. Anyone who has gone through the pain of a broken heart knows the suffering involved. Unfortunately, in many cases, couples who deeply love one another give up out of frustration or a feeling of defeat. The relationship fails out of fear and lack of effort to change; each person later regrets the loss. When we look back and realize that we almost lost our own marriage and the opportunity to create a love beyond our greatest expectations, we are both deeply thankful for the Love Fitness program.

We have found the Love Fitness program to be a breakthrough for ourselves and our clients in four principal ways. First, it provides a model: a step-by-step way out of the emotional pit of fear, anger, and hopelessness of a love relationship in trouble.

Second, it develops specific emotional strengths and communication skills in areas where you may feel genuinely uncomfortable or incompetent. It helps you learn how to deal with intense feelings, such as anger, jealousy, and disapproval.

Third, it provides specific exercises to produce results on a daily basis. There is nothing like tangible emotional success to increase confidence in yourself and your love relationship. The emotional workouts are designed to generate personal relationship breakthroughs that soon build to great adventures of the heart.

Fourth, one of the great benefits of the Love Fitness program is prevention. This book should therefore be of tremendous value to any couple considering marriage. The Love Fitness program will assist you in exploring your relationship more deeply before making a further commitment. If you are in a quality love relationship already, the exercises will help you to sustain and enrich it.

Everyone who reads this book is likely to respond differently. Some exercises and ideas may seem more directly useful than others. In working your way through this book, find whatever seems most useful and truthful, then use it and use it well. If a particular emotional workout is inappropriate to your needs at present, set it aside for now. You can trust the therapist within you. By putting these strategies and techniques into practice, you will discover the keys to creating, sustaining, or renewing a great love relationship with your lifemate.

Chapter 2

Exercising Your Love: "Tell Me More"

A major concern of modern medicine and physical fitness programs is arteriosclerosis, a hardening of the arteries from poor diet, stress, and inadequate exercise. There is a parallel psychological process for which we have coined the term "psychosclerosis"—a hardening of the mind, heart, and spirit. Just as arteriosclerosis constricts arteries, causing major disorder and disease, psychosclerosis constricts love, thereby limiting self-expression, eroding communication, and narrowing the capacity for feeling.

The parallels between arteriosclerosis and psychosclerosis are revealing. While arteriosclerosis makes arteries stiff, psychosclerosis makes relationships brittle. Arteriosclerosis takes the joy out of exercise; psychosclerosis takes the passion out of a relationship. The longer arteriosclerosis goes unchecked, the greater the risk of heart attack or stroke. Similarly, the longer psychosclerosis goes unchallenged in a relationship, the greater the chance that love will wither and cause the relationship to end in chronic bitterness, despair, or divorce.

Psychosclerosis develops insidiously, and quite predictably, in relationships. At the outset of every love relationship, communication is supple and vibrant as couples inevitably go through emotional workouts without the specific intention of doing so. The very process of getting to know someone for the first time challenges your feelings and attitudes; you naturally bend to accommodate and learn about another human being. This process is usually exciting, and if it becomes sufficiently charged with emotional energy, you may feel yourself falling in love.

If the relationship endures, however, emotional habits begin to take over. One person may tend to get irritable easily, so the other becomes excessively accommodating. One may only be able to express anger through the "silent treatment," so the other learns to deal with problems in the relationship through emotional withdrawal. One person may harbor sexual performance anxieties, so the other accepts routine sex to allay these fears. Eventually, this system of interlocking emotional habits becomes rigid, and many needs for heart-to-heart communication and self-expression go unmet. Anger, resentment, and frustration are the inevitable consequences.

To some degree everyone suffers from psychosclerosis, as do almost all relationships. Consider how often you think, say, or have heard the following signs and symptoms of psychosclerosis:

"What's the use, he/she will never change . . ."

"I can't get through to him/her . . ."

"Our sex life is boring."

"Nothing goes right for us anymore."

"We don't connect like we used to."

"Nobody understands me."

"Is this all there is to love?"

"I don't know what he/she wants."

"Nothing I say makes any difference."

"We never talk about what is really important."

Psychosclerosis destroys love relationships in three principal ways. First, it causes resistance to personal growth. Feelings stop flowing and emotional habits get carved in psychological stone. Second, it can cause you to feel hopeless about improving a relationship. Inflexibility can make you feel defeated before you even try to evoke change. Third, psychosclerosis impairs your ability to listen to your lover and your lover's ability to listen to you. Given these emotional effects, overcoming psychosclerosis is vital to becoming lifemates.

Overcoming Psychosclerosis

How much freedom do you have in your emotional responses? Can other people provoke or hurt you easily? Or do you choose your emotional responses for most effective communication? The first step in overcoming psychosclerosis is recognizing your power to choose the quality of your experience. Don't think this statement is a simplistic self-help formula. Obviously events happen in people's lives over which they have little or no control. Personal tragedy rightfully begets sadness and tears, just as a great success generates energy and joy. Our point is, however, that emotional responses need not be automatic.

Behavioral psychologists claim that most human interactions are governed by automatic, predictable stimulus-response patterns. Your spouse comes home grieving; you get tense. Your lover gets angry; you feel intimidated. Your lover fails to respond sexually; you feel rejected. These are examples of common stimulus-response patterns in love relationships. But these observations don't go far enough. Remember, the behaviorists developed their theories by observing pigeons. There is obviously something more to consider when talking about humans—and that something more is the essential quality of freedom. People have the ability to choose their responses, even under trying emotional circumstances—as long as psychosclerosis has not made their emotional habits entirely rigid and automatic.

Your ability to choose your emotional responses is absolutely fundamental to love fitness. No doubt you have a certain confidence in your ability to change your body through diet and exercise. So, too, you must develop confidence in your ability to change psychosclerotic patterns in your relationships. The place to begin developing this confidence is with a simple exercise.

You may not know it, but you have the ability to choose to feel joyful and loving almost any time. Of course, we are not talking about self-deception, putting on a happy face when you feel miserable, or acting like a Pollyanna in the face of real tragedy. Most of our lives, however, are neither extremely happy nor deeply tragic. We live in a middle ground where our general feelings about ourselves can go either way. That is the context in which we state that you can choose to feel joyful and abundant or discontented and empty. We have developed a very simple emotional workout to illustrate this point: the "Choosing Joy and Love" exercise.

Choosing Joy and Love

Step 1 Start by evaluating your current state of mind. How are you feeling right now? Take a little time to rate your present mood on the following seven-point scale. Be as honest and objective as you can. Remember, you are doing this in the privacy of your own heart and mind.

Experience Scale 1

TERRIFIC	GOOD	SLIGHTLY UP	MIDDLING	SLIGHTLY OFF	SOMEWHAT BLUE	DEPRESSED
___	___	___	___	___	___	___

Step 2 Now read the following sentences, one at a time, and briefly consider whether you agree or disagree with the statement right now. Don't dwell too long on any sentence, but don't hurry either. Just read

them slowly and gently, and ask yourself for a few seconds, "Do I agree with this right now?"

1. I am feeling about as usual today, neither better nor worse.
2. Still, I've had some special things happen today.
3. I can think of something beautiful about today.
4. Today may not be the very best day of my life, but it's not bad at all.
5. I sometimes feel very happy and in love.
6. I can recall an especially happy and loving experience I've had.
7. My feelings are my own; I can create my own experience.
8. My love partner can be wonderful.
9. When I think of the people who love me, I feel a little surge of happiness and warmth.
10. Maybe the whole world does not admire me, but I have a special feeling for my love partner who looks up to me and respects me.
11. I have confidence in the things I do well.
12. Compared to some years ago, I've grown enormously.
13. When I have doubts, they are often a sign of strength, not weakness.
14. I have a strong commitment to sharing my love.
15. Sometimes I think that I'm really a pretty good person.
16. I forget how fortunate so much of my life is.
17. I like a lot of things about my love partner.
18. I take special pleasure in a nurturing home life.
19. I have a promising future with my lover.
20. Sometimes I can clearly imagine how good things are going to be for us.
21. When I think about how far I've come, I feel a surge of pride and pleasure.
22. I have solved some difficult problems in the past, and I will no doubt do so in the future.
23. I am able to be more self-confident, strong and loving.

24. I have a pervasive sense of well-being.
25. I respect myself a lot.
26. Sometimes I feel joy.
27. My love partner, who really knows me, appreciates and deeply loves me.
28. I have great strength and stability.
29. I can see sunshine and blue skies in our future.
30. It's not wrong to love yourself; in fact, loving yourself makes it possible to give more love to others.
31. I can see a lot of doors opening up for me today and in the future.
32. Sometimes it is soothing just to listen to my love partner.
33. The qualities of my love partner are special to me.
34. He/she supports me in the important areas of my life.
35. I have some really pleasurable experiences.
36. Sometimes I get frustrated about the little things and forget how good things look in the big picture.
37. I am basically a positive, optimistic person.
38. I like to smile with genuine happiness.
39. I have a great sense of humor.
40. I am really a very kind and friendly person.
41. If the whole world were populated with people like me, world peace would be more likely.
42. I sometimes feel like laughing out loud with my love.
43. Joy is not so difficult to achieve.
44. Life has moments of ecstasy.
45. Happiness is just a state of mind.
46. I feel more and more in charge of my experience.
47. I am basically a joyous, loving person.
48. I have a "happy child" inside who is capable of a lot of fun.
49. I can choose my own experience.
50. My life is mostly joyful and filled with love.

Step 3 Now, how do you feel? Once more, rate your mood on the seven-point scale below:

Experience Scale 2

TERRIFIC	GOOD	SLIGHTLY UP	MIDDLING	SLIGHTLY OFF	SOMEWHAT BLUE	DEPRESSED
___	___	___	___	___	___	___

How does your rating on Scale 2 compare to Scale 1? Most people notice a marked improvement in their mood. The more you were able to "get into" the fifty sentences, the more your mood improved. Congratulations! You have just recognized your ability to create more love and joy through a simple exercise.

Notice how simple this process is—what could be more simple than reading some sentences? And yet, doing this exercise can change your experience for the rest of the day. Let's examine the mechanics of this mood-shifting exercise. First, the sentences start from a moderate position, and move to a more positive view. That way, they don't startle you with positive feelings that may not fit your current state of mind. The sentences feel more credible when they fit your mood, so that you don't dispute them mentally or reject them out of hand. If you were able to let the positive words, feelings and mental images come up without disputing them, this exercise worked for you— your mood has probably improved. If you found it impossible to accept any of the sentences, and mentally rejected them, it probably did not work as well.

This Choosing Joy and Love exercise demonstrates two key principles. First, emotional workouts can be as powerful or even more powerful in changing how you feel as physical workouts are in changing your body. Second, whatever you put your attention on will inevitably gain a stronger influence in your life. By simply putting your attention on a series of increasingly uplifting and positive statements, you become more uplifting and positive.

What You Place Your Attention on Grows Stronger

This principle is so fundamental to the Love Fitness program that it requires careful examination. If you allow yourself to be consistently conscious for a brief period of pleasant, constructive, and supportive thoughts, your whole experience will develop in that direction. You have also probably had the experience of an argument with your lover that caused you to feel angry and tense for some period afterward. Between these emotional directions lies your essential freedom, your power to shift your attention, even slightly, in one direction or another. This point may seem so small as to be insignificant. In fact, it is the essence of personal freedom and an essential skill for developing love fitness.

All the emotional workouts in this book depend upon accepting your true feelings and those of your lifemate while at the same time shifting your attention and favoring the positive as those feelings unfold. We do not pretend that this process is easy. Our point is not that you will learn to select the positive and ignore the negative. We are not talking about complimenting your lover on how he or she looks while pretending that your anger, resentment, or hurt does not exist. Rather, we encourage you to identify and favor loving, positive feelings both in yourself and your love partner while fully accepting and acknowledging the negative.

Let's review this core principle of the Love Fitness program, which is often overlooked by some therapists. If you allow your awareness to be dominated

(1) consistently (that is, without inner argument or struggle),
(2) for a brief time (a few minutes is often enough) by either pleasant or unpleasant thoughts or images,

you can shift the direction and quality of your whole emotional experience. Understanding this principle empowers you to take control of your emotional responses, whereas before you may not have exercised a choice. Only *you* should be able to decide what will dominate your conscious experience.

To have a happy, good, or even great relationship is not a static goal. The Love Fitness program does not promise eternal bliss or a love relationship free from problems or pain. A love relationship—even at the peak of fitness—will always have some occasions of hurt, conflict, and loss. The Love Fitness program, however, can maximize the good, heal the pain, and place you more in charge of your love life.

Instead of seeing your love relationship as being either 100 percent happy or else completely disappointing, it's far more productive to see your satisfaction in love on a "10–80–10" spectrum. In a love relationship, 10 percent of the time is naturally joyful: a big promotion, a birth, a given day is perfect. Another 10 percent of anyone's love life is at the opposite end of the spectrum: large or small disasters strike, problems accumulate, people behave in a hurtful way. Generally, events at these two ends of the spectrum will occur no matter what you do. The luck of the draw and inevitable losses are both part of life.

The Love Fitness program focuses on the middle 80 percent of your love relationship—that part in which a mixture of good and bad things happen—in which you can learn to create joy and satisfaction in your love relationship as a result of your own enthusiasm, compassion, and humor. In the middle 80 percent, your love relationship is what you make it; here is where the Love Fitness program makes an enormous difference.

10%	80%	10%

GREAT	WHERE LOVE FITNESS MAKES THE DIFFERENCE	AWFUL

When you lack the emotional skills and relationship habits of growth necessary to create the love relationship you want, your love life can be awful as much as 90 percent of the time. On the other hand, the Love Fitness program can help your love relationship be more intimate and satisfying as much as 90 percent of the time.

Developing love fitness is more than "positive thinking." We are not suggesting that you should force yourself to have only positive thoughts or that you fend off any negative thoughts toward your love partner. Life is not meant just to be a continuous experience of love and joy. Negative thoughts play a very important role; they reveal problems and issues that need attention. Struggling to be positive all the time would mean denying reality. Anger, hurt, sadness, and fear deserve attention when they arise. Losing touch with those feelings, even if that were possible, might be dangerous and would certainly make life shallow. So the point is not to drop all negative thoughts—it is to raise the questions in your life: Do my thoughts and feelings really serve me well? Do they work for or against me? Or have they become psychosclerotic—automatic and mechanical? What does my lover need? What is he/she asking for, and where can I find a common ground for our love?

Fundamental to the Love Fitness program is recognizing that you are the creator of your experience; you are responsible for your life and choices. Not your love partner. Not your parent(s). Not your therapist. Not society. Recognizing and acting upon your capacity to choose your experience is a crucial daily exercise of the Love Fitness program. Every other exercise in this book depends upon your making the decision to use it as a tool to create a more open, vibrant, and fit relationship than ever before.

Listening: A Key to Change

It is easy to feel defeated in a relationship. When we first developed emotional workouts for our clients, one woman replied, "My husband will never do it. He won't make the time." Another said of her lover with whom she had lived for two years, "He'd rather go to the movies, not go through this stuff." A third, who was in a committed relationship, explained, "He'll fear it will ruin the relationship. How can I get him to try it?" We understand these concerns. They are symptoms of psychosclerosis.

Part of the solution is developing an attitude that encourages communication and incremental steps of change. This is a key application of putting your attention on the positive rather than dwelling on the negative. Many of our clients get trapped by the "I'll be happy when . . ." syndrome. They identify an issue—sexual boredom, for instance—and then decide the relationship will be terrific when that problem is solved. Love fitness doesn't develop that way any more than physical fitness ensues from a single workout. Development occurs gradually and builds in small successive steps. If you put your attention on even small positive changes, then you encourage further growth.

One of the most serious effects of psychosclerosis is the loss of the commitment to listen. Early in most relationships, couples tend to hang on each other's every word. The excitement of discovery of another person's feelings, opinions, and needs is so enthralling that most couples can't pay enough attention to one another. Over time, that enthusiasm for listening wears off. Couples tend to think they know one another and tend to lose interest in probing deeper. It becomes easy to pretend to be listening while reading the paper, watching TV, or driving the car. In reality, one or another person may be tuned out. Couples who come for counseling have almost always developed an inability to listen to one another.

Have you ever thought about or complained to your love partner in this manner:

• "I'm not going to tell you how I feel because even when I try to, you don't hear me. You become defensive and angry and jump in with your views and opinions. Whenever we talk about anything really important, I feel like I have to compete to get a word in. It's impossible for me to let you know how I feel because you are so defensive."

• "When you go out of control in an argument, you make it very clear that I'm not allowed to express my true feelings. You'll never change, so why should I bother being open with you?"

• "You do a very good job of pointing out my faults. I think it makes you feel better about yourself. You even joke about it as if you think it's funny. I end up apologizing for my shortcomings just to appease you."

• "I can never tell you how I feel about something without you threatening me or tuning out. You won't let me know what you're really feeling unless you get mad."

• "I agree with you just to keep the peace, so you'll shut up. I've concluded you'll never understand how I feel. I'm going to hold back my affection too. I'll pour my love into other things, the children, my work, not you."

• "I feel like I always have to be on my toes, especially when we disagree—consequently I don't stand up for myself. I allow you to intimidate me, which causes me to feel more hurt and angry. My stinging comments are poison darts from my accumulated inner rage. The situation feels hopeless and I feel powerless."

You may resent not being heard by your lover, yet you may fail to appreciate that he or she also needs to feel understood and appreciated. When this doesn't happen you tend to blame each other. Communication fails because you become each so involved in defend-

ing yourselves, trying to control each other, and proving you are "right," that you can't hear what each
really needs.

Here then is the place to begin practicing a Love
Fitness workout. Rarely have we encountered a relationship that cannot benefit by one or both lovers
renewing the commitment and developing greater ability to listen. There is a simple phrase you can use to
strengthen your listening skills. It's three short words:
"Tell me more." How often have you needed to have
your love partner say those three words and how often
have you instead found yourself frustrated with feelings you really wanted to share but were afraid to
express? How often have you settled for an apology or
a gift, or ignored a problem in hopes it would go
away?

A psychotherapist is, in part, a highly paid listener.
Studies have shown that therapists with the best listening skills usually get the best results with clients. The
essence of listening is giving someone else your undivided attention and respect. We have found the simple
phrase "Tell me more" to be a useful tool in helping
couples achieve a breakthrough in the frequency and
emotional depth of their communication.

By learning to use the phrase "Tell me more," you
can initiate positive emotional exchanges with your
actions alone. When your spouse or lover comes home
exhausted or tense, complaining about the traffic or
some other frustration at work, remember to choose
your experience. Rather than respond with "I've had a
bad day too" or "All you do is complain," which will
only focus both your own and your lover's attention
on mutual frustration, try something positive such as:
"Sweetheart, I can understand; why don't you take a
shower and let's have a cup of tea, I'd like to hear
more." You could accomplish the same result with
something as simple as: "I see you're upset; tell me
more about your day."

This simple phrase "Tell me more" can be useful in
a wide variety of situations. Look for an opportunity

to use it during dinner. It will nurture an emotional need and can make a meal an opportunity for heart-to-heart sharing rather than the same old routine. Another important time to use this phrase is before bed. If your lover seems tense or upset, say to him or her "I can see you're feeling [tense, worried]; please tell me more about it, I'd like to help if I can."

By using the phrase "Tell me more" as a tool to enhance your listening ability and the quality attention you give your lover, you can begin to change psychosclerotic communication patterns in your relationship by your own example. Persistence is necessary, but if you begin listening more to your lover, you are likely to find that your lover will soon begin listening more to you.

The "Tell Me More" Exercise

Sometimes it is extremely difficult to listen to your lover. This is particularly true when your lover needs to express feelings of frustration, anger, or criticism. The natural response to such an emotional onslaught is to become defensive. Although natural, responses such as "Yes, but . . ." or "Listen to me for a moment . . ." prevent you from acknowledging, absorbing, and learning from what your lover has to say. One of the most important skills for healing a love relationship is for you and your lover to learn to hear each other's hurt, anger, or frustration without becoming defensive.

At the height of our own marital crisis, we too found ourselves unable to listen to each other. We each felt hurt and angry, but we each tended to cut the other off in mid-sentence with that old standard, "Yes, but . . ." The more each of us resisted what the other had to say, the more our arguments tended to escalate.

One afternoon we picked up a fight begun the night before on our way home from a party. Sirah was angry because Harold had ignored her, and Harold was upset that he couldn't talk to other women without incurring Sirah's jealous wrath. We each tried to present our own side, but we got nowhere in the face of our "Yes, but . . ." responses. Our argument was heated; we were clearly in trouble.

Suddenly it struck us that we weren't listening to each other at all. Sirah said something like, "Did you hear what I just said?" And Harold, taken aback, found himself answering, "No, but . . . listen to me; I'm pissed off too!" In that moment, we finally realized that we were severely blocked and that we couldn't simply listen to each other. Instead, we needed a structured exercise to change the pattern of communication in our relationship.

Few emotional tasks are more difficult than hearing and accepting a lover's hurt, anger, and criticism without becoming defensive. The inability to communicate openly about difficult emotional issues is among the most common and serious *unrecognized* problems in relationships. We were no exception, and we needed a structured workout that forced us to hear each other's upset feelings without becoming defensive. We later called this structured emotional workout the "Tell Me More" exercise. The basic steps are as follows:

1. Find a room in which you both feel safe and relaxed. This room should be pleasant and comfortable, perhaps decorated with flowers and candles or incense. Unplug the phone and put a "Do Not Disturb" sign on the door.

2. Arrange two chairs so that you and your lover sit facing one another, close enough to feel in contact but not so close that you violate each other's comfort zone. A conversational distance is best.

3. The suggestion to try the Tell Me More exercise is usually made by the person who needs to have some feeling resolved. For example, if Sirah has something bothering her, she will suggest that we take time out for the Tell Me More exercise. Once we are sitting comfortably in our den, Harold may initiate the con-

versation by saying, "Sirah, I see that you've got some feelings that are bothering you and I would like to hear what you have to say." If you notice that your lover is upset, however, you need not wait for him or her to suggest the Tell Me More exercise. Rather, you can initiate this process as a way of clearing the air and reestablishing emotional contact.

4. The listener restricts his or her statements to one simple phrase, "Tell me more." It is critical that this expression, "Tell me more," not be said casually or mechanically. There is a natural rhythm to conversation and particularly to self-revelation. If one of you is courageous enough to sit down and express all of his or her feelings, the other must use the phrase, "Tell me more," as a sincere expression of interest in hearing all the stored feelings your lover wants to express.

5. When one of you has thoroughly expressed his or her feelings, switch roles. The other now has an opportunity to express all of his or her feelings in response to the phrase, "Tell me more." The exercise is not over until both partners feel complete or spent with good feelings. Always finish with a long hug and each say, "I love you."

Breaking the Cycle of Jealousy

Here is the Tell Me More process we did the day after the party. It should give you a better understanding of how this exercise works in practice:

SIRAH: I am *so* angry with you. Last night at the party you didn't pay any attention to me, you kept looking for that brunette in the red dress. You must've gone to the bathroom ten times to walk by her! I felt embarrassed, I felt humiliated. She was an attractive girl, but that was ridiculous. We haven't gone out in such a long time, we've been so busy, and on our one night out . . . what do you do? The whole evening you kept staring at someone else! I feel we can't even go out to a party . . . [Harold *becomes agitated and gets up.*]

SIRAH: Harold, come back and sit down.

HAROLD: Tell me more—just give me a second. Tell me more.

SIRAH: I feel that I can't even go out to a party or a restaurant with you without worrying who you're going to be looking around for. We have so little time together as it is, that when I'm with you I want to feel that you enjoy being with me. I don't mean you should stare at me the entire time, but I want to feel that you've given me some of your attention. Like right now . . . please give me your attention . . . thank you. I want to feel like you really want to be with me. I'm afraid sometimes . . . you're bored with me. After all these years of being together, I'm afraid you're ready to move on, that you want to be with somebody else.

HAROLD: [*Quietly*] Tell me more.

SIRAH: I feel hurt and embarrassed that I even have to tell you this. I feel like I really don't have it together. And I'm afraid it has something to do with the way my father was with my mom and it frightens me. Would you hold my hand. This is difficult and . . . [Harold *sits forward and holds* Sirah's *hands.*] I want to trust you. I don't want to think that your looking at other women might be a reflection on us. I want to be able to trust you.

HAROLD: Tell me more.

SIRAH: I love you and I love being with you. I want us to have some of that romance that we had in the beginning of our relationship. It feels good to be able to tell you this.

HAROLD: Tell me more.

SIRAH: I'm sorry I spoiled our evening last night.

HAROLD: Tell me more.

SIRAH: I love you. I don't feel angry anymore.

HAROLD: I love you, too. [Harold *and* Sirah *get up and embrace . . . long pause.*]

HAROLD: In no way do I want to make wrong what you just shared with me. I'm touched. And I just have to get some of my feelings and perceptions out too.

SIRAH: Of course. Let's sit down.

HAROLD: Can you stay receptive?

SIRAH: Yes.

HAROLD: You're sure?

SIRAH: I'm sure.

HAROLD: I can't take this. I just can't believe you. We go to a party, I have a conversation for twenty minutes with a woman who happens to be attractive, and suddenly I'm betraying you. I mean, I don't think that marriage is a ball and chain where I have to be careful who I have an intimate conversation with. If I meet someone at a party, I can only say, "Hi, how are you? Are you over eighty years old or under eight? Well, I can talk to you for ten minutes, okay? Then, I've got to go back to my wife." I don't have any freedom. Same as my father had in his relationship. There's no space. No freedom at all. And it just pisses me off! I wasn't doing anything so terrible last night, but when you're staring at me all the time, it doesn't make me want to come over to you. It's more like, "Hey, forget this! Let me have some quality attention over here!" You know? I don't need those dagger-eyes of yours. I feel controlled and manipulated by your jealousy.

SIRAH: Tell me more.

HAROLD: It makes me sad. I want to be married to you, I love you, but I also need to feel free. I need to feel that I'm still my own person, like

I can have a conversation with someone even if they are attractive! I need to feel like that's okay.

SIRAH: Tell me more.

HAROLD: You know, I was single for a long time. You just don't suddenly change the habits of a lifetime. [Harold *laughs at himself here and elicits a smile from* Sirah.]

SIRAH: Tell me more, Harold.

HAROLD: It feels good to be able to get out these feelings that I've been stuffing away. I've been feeling trapped, on a leash. The more it makes me angry, the more I want to get away from you. The real truth is, I feel so free right now being able to share these feelings with you. I've never been able to do this with anyone else in my life. It feels really good [*pause*]. It puts me in touch with just how much I love you. I want to be married to you, and I love going out with you. And you're right. I haven't been giving you enough quality attention. I'm going to make more time for you and me. Because you're right, we don't have to let romance dwindle. I don't believe that anymore. We can rekindle it when we choose to. I feel it right now.

This Tell Me More workout was an emotional breakthrough for us. For the first time, we felt safe enough with one another to be totally vulnerable. We saw how we were keeping each other from the innermost regions of our hearts because of our own fears and anger. We also saw there was no greater force to heal ourselves than an open heart-to-heart communication of our feelings. The Tell Me More became the cornerstone of the Love Fitness program. Regular practice of this exercise helped us rid ourselves of suppressed anger and blocks to sexual intimacy. It helped us open up to one another as never before.

Dos and Don'ts
of the Tell Me More Exercise

We usually recommend Tell Me More as the first exercise to start improving love fitness. Our experience indicates that when lovers express their feelings to one another fully and completely, the result is almost always positive. It is critical in this process, however, that you hear your partner's feelings without *in any way* becoming defensive, no matter how much hurt, anger, or resentment may be expressed. The point is to vent pent-up emotion in an atmosphere of safety and trust. Be patient; let the feelings unfold. Underneath anger is hurt, and underneath the hurt is love. Once the underlying love surfaces, it naturally grows, healing the painful feelings and providing a renewed emotional base for correcting problems in the relationship.

Here are additional instructions for the Tell Me More exercise:

1. *Don't start the exercise if you're excessively tired or preoccupied.* In order to practice Tell Me More effectively, you must be reasonably well rested. Remember, this exercise is an emotional workout. It will be demanding on you and your lover. It takes energy and can be emotionally intense. You can't expect an emotional workout to go well if you start it feeling exhausted. Similarly, if either you or your lover are excessively preoccupied with problems about work, money, or children, it may be better to postpone the exercise. Judgment is required here.

Although preoccupation with outside pressures shouldn't become an excuse to avoid intimate communication, be sensitive to this issue. You can use this exercise to share worries and pressures, and the result can be very comforting for the person suffering under the pressure as well as very bonding for the person who may have been ignored or excluded as a result of work or other outside stresses. The key is to use Tell Me More as a tool for emotional release and mutual bonding early, before outside demands leave you completely exhausted and angry.

2. *Don't interrupt.* The key to the Tell Me More exercise is never to interrupt your lover and only to respond with one simple phrase, "Tell me more." When faced with your partner's expressions of anger or criticism, you may feel tempted to interrupt, to deny that his or her views make any sense, to make explanations or excuses or to make your lover feel guilty, stupid, or awkward. In order for the Tell Me More exercise to work, you must guard against these manifestations of the "yes, but" syndrome. The correct response is to pause, breathe deeply, and say "Tell me more."

3. *Don't be impatient.* This exercise cannot be hurried and you shouldn't rush your lover to express his or her feelings. Sitting on the edge of your seat blurting, "Tell me more, tell me more," won't create the feeling of safety and trust necessary for a complete expression of feelings. When your mind is jumping to respond, even with the phrase "Tell me more," you're not listening well and your partner will feel it. Relax and put yourself in as receptive a mode as possible.

4. *Don't be defiant or arrogant.* It is possible to fake participation in the Tell Me More exercise by giving the false impression that you are listening when in fact your mind is tuned out. This attitude of defiance allows you to defend yourself internally from your love partner's hurt, anger, or frustration by silently demeaning his or her words. Arrogance stands in the way of genuine listening. This exercise demands an open mind and heart willing to learn about another's deepest feelings.

5. *Don't jump to conclusions.* Don't assume that you know the outcome when your partner expresses a recurring set of feelings. Rather than jump to conclusions, maintain an attitude of discovery. Show respect

for your lover's intelligence and expression of feelings by listening without preconception.

6. *Give your undivided attention.* Face your lover squarely, maintain eye contact, and keep an open body position. You may tend to cross your arms to defend your heart, or to cross your legs to protect your sexuality. Open body posture is part of being wholly accessible and sensitive to your lover. Listen to your lover's words and the feelings that underlie those words. Your lover may say things that cause you to respond defensively, tighten up, look away, or to say internally, "yes, but." Train yourself to relax, breathe deeply, and if you must, take a few moments to regain your sense of personal safety. By fully accepting your lover's expressions of anger, hurt, and frustration, you are giving your lover and yourself a great gift of freedom and unconditional love.

7. *Develop empathy.* The goal of this exercise is to empathize with your lover and let your lover know that you are acknowledging and accepting exactly what he or she feels. This does not mean you have to agree. Listening from the heart is a skill that helps you transcend your personal boundaries by increasing your capability to empathize with another person's frame of reference. If your love partner is frustrated by his or her inability to express feelings of anger and hurt, the more understanding and open you are, the safer he or she will feel about disclosing intimate thoughts. Instead of trying to convince your lover to feel differently, listen and be patient.

8. *Be committed to understanding.* The reason you use the phrase "Tell me more" is to elicit enough communication from your lover so that you fully understand his or her feelings, what may be behind those feelings, and what your lover may need to heal. It is better to use the phrase "Tell me more" more often than necessary to be sure that you understand your partner's feelings and wants. You may initially be confused by those feelings, but stay committed and a natural resolution will emerge.

9. *Stay calm.* Most people feel tense under criticism. As soon as you notice your pulse rising or your muscles tightening, breathe deeply a few times and consciously focus on relaxing your body. If you feel particularly upset, nonverbally signal that you need a break. Sit quietly with eyes closed for a few minutes until you regain your composure. If tears come, that's okay. Once you release the tears, you will feel lighter and more calm.

10. *Accept your partner's feelings and point of view without judgment.* A major message behind the Tell Me More exercise is that you value your love partner as a unique human being with his or her own wisdom, perceptions and desires. The point of this exercise is not to agree, but to unconditionally accept and support your lover's feelings. Tell Me More is not about who is right and who is wrong, but appreciating your lover's point of view; when it comes to feelings no one is wrong. Even if he or she employs destructive criticism ("You always do this," "You're just like your mother," etc.), somewhere behind those accusations is a clue to a better understanding of your partner's unvoiced fears of losing your love ("I want to love, but I've been hurt; I want to love you, but I'm afraid of what you'll find out if you get too close").

Just as there are dos and don'ts as a listener in the "Tell Me More" exercise, there are precepts to follow as a speaker:

1. *Don't be afraid to say what you feel.* The purpose of this exercise is to communicate your feelings as thoroughly and deeply as possible. Only by expressing your feelings in depth can you achieve true resolution, avoid storing resentment, and discover grounds for better communication between you.

2. *Don't try to make your lover wrong.* There is a fine line between communicating hurt feelings and destructively dumping, berating, and making your lover wrong. You are allowed to get angry and express frustration and pain. But it is not valuable to indulge

in demeaning invectives such as, "You're a liar," "You never do anything right," or "I told you so." This destructive criticism is meant to put down, punish, or manipulate, and the effects are negative and unsupportive. Be specific about exactly what behavior or incident upset you. Avoid global judgments that are merely attacks on self-esteem.

3. *Don't rush yourself.* Feelings unfold gradually. You may begin with feelings of frustration which, when acknowledged, give rise to deeper feelings of hurt, anger or resentment. If you give full expression to those feelings, it is likely that beneath the anger and pain are deeper feelings of care and commitment. Only by following the Tell Me More exercise to its conclusion will those fundamental feelings of love emerge.

4. *Focus on one issue.* There may be many conflicts to address through the Tell Me More exercise. However, the exercise works best if you select one issue at a time and pursue it to resolution. Address a second issue at another time.

5. *Acknowledge your vulnerabilities and weaknesses.* Simple, humble communication is necessary. It is important that you share your weaknesses and your "dark side." Feel free to acknowledge your own demons such as: "It's true. I can be selfish and controlling"; or "I am so full of envy and anger sometimes, I don't know what to do with it"; or "I hate myself for lying." Know that you are in a safe and trusting environment with your love partner.

6. *Share your love.* Throughout this exercise it is critical that you honor your basic commitment of love. This commitment requires communication with no intent to cause harm or seek revenge. Your lover needs support to acknowledge exactly how you feel. It is best not to expect agreement or complete resolution. Be patient. It may take another Tell Me More session and some discussion of what you are each learning in order for forgiveness and reconciliation to evolve fully.

The Greatest Gift

So there you have the Tell Me More exercise. It is extremely simple and perhaps the single most useful emotional workout for keeping a relationship fit and vital. This is no overstatement, because the Tell Me More exercise will allow you to reap two of the greatest emotional rewards of all.

1. You will learn how to GIVE your commitment to acknowledge and accept your lover's hurt, anger, and criticism without becoming defensive. As a result, you and your lover will develop greater emotional strength and freedom to communicate. Paradoxically, overcoming the fear of getting hurt emotionally allows for the blossoming of secure and lasting intimacy.

2. You will RECEIVE quality feedback about your own experiences and behavior. Criticism serves the vital function of allowing you and your lover to learn and for your relationship to grow.

It is precisely because acknowledging and accepting your lover's hurt, anger, and criticism is so difficult— and yet so valuable—that this is one of the greatest gifts you can give and receive. When you hear your lover's hurt, anger and criticism without becoming defensive, you

- Demonstrate unconditional respect and affirm your lover's self-worth by listening to all of his or her feelings
- Help your lover stop hurting by allowing unexpressed feelings to come forth without interruption or comment
- Strengthen the bonds of mutual trust and confidence by listening to painful feelings without running away, blowing up or giving up on the relationship.

The Tell Me More exercise, like all the Love Fitness workouts presented in this book, is likely to have positive effects beyond simply resolving a specific issue or conflict. For us, the Tell Me More exercise precipitated a major breakthrough in our relationship. It enabled Sirah to begin expressing not only her feelings of hurt and resentment but all her feelings more fully and openly. As a result, she no longer felt dominated in the relationship. Tell Me More became a direct experience of equality and true partnership. Harold discovered that he could accept Sirah's intense feelings without feeling threatened. He became more comfortable in acknowledging his own feelings of hurt and anger that he had been so afraid to express. Harold learned to forgive himself—and Sirah— for not being perfect and to accept parts of himself he had been resisting his entire life.

Love Fitness workouts have positive effects beyond the specific exercise in the same way that physical workouts have positive effects beyond strengthening specific muscle groups. For example, it is well established that if you exercise regularly, you may expect lowered blood pressure, higher resistance to disease, and better response to stress than if you aren't physically fit. So, too, we have discovered that regular practice of Tell Me More helps people express and receive hurt, anger, and loving feelings generally, outside the formal exercise. You stop hiding the parts of yourself you fear are unacceptable and you stop worrying about what others might think.

Primary Principles for Developing Love Fitness

Love Fitness workouts are similar to physical fitness exercises in another important respect. They can either be enjoyable and healthy, if you pace yourself, or laborious, or even injurious, if you try to accomplish too much too soon. We have identified below the major principles that apply to all the workouts in this book. The following guidelines will help you use Love Fitness workouts to best advantage:

• *Take the initiative.* It is very easy to let yourself feel defeated when you are unhappy with your love relationship. Until you practice a few Love Fitness workouts, you won't be able to see how much power you really have. No doubt you can think of many reasons why you, your lover, or your relationship can't change, and you can spend hours in therapy talking about all those reasons. The real challenge is to break a few old, negative emotional habits. Don't try for all at once. Start simply by selecting one emotional workout that particularly appeals. Making your love partner responsible for its success won't help, although you have the right to ask his or her participation. Change always begins with you. Don't focus on changing your lover, even "for his or her own good."

• *Reevaluate your "comfort zone."* Many people get comfortable with feeling uncomfortable! Starting to feel more genuinely intimate and loving may initially leave you feeling unusual, fearful or even strange. One of the first things you may experience when you practice a Love Fitness workout is "this isn't me—it doesn't feel natural." We expect this initial response because emotional workouts develop new relationship habits and self-perceptions. Think for a moment how you felt when you first learned to ride a bicycle, ski, or play tennis. You probably felt a little awkward, and the motions involved felt strange and artificial. You may even have felt you would never learn to develop the grace and coordination required. But with practice, hundreds of repetitions later, the new habit became automatic and felt completely natural.

When you practice an exercise intended to expand your behavioral repertoire, or change an emotional response, you should definitely expect to feel some initial awkwardness. As you practice the exercise, you will soon begin to internalize the new information and develop a new and valued way of feeling about yourself or relating to others. Ways of responding that may initially seem mechanical will soon start to feel graceful, particularly as you develop several new heart-to-heart communication skills. Give yourself the time and permission to overcome any initial feelings of discomfort. Your "comfort zone" will stretch to include a whole new experience of the heart.

• *Start simply*. The Love Fitness program addresses many key emotional issues in relationships. Each chapter contains what can be termed elementary, intermediate, and advanced workouts. We don't mean to be mechanical about our instruction, but you will be well served to start with the simplest exercises in each chapter. Our clients have told us that even the simplest workouts have produced wonderful changes in their relationships.

• *Stretch, don't strain*. Growth is a natural process that does not need to be forced. An acorn doesn't strain to become an oak tree; neither must you strain to grow. In a physical fitness program, you would be cautioned against overdoing it, which can lead to loss of motivation, discomfort, or even injury. The same principle applies to the Love Fitness program.

In a Love Fitness program, significant changes are going to occur on very intimate levels of feeling about yourself and your lover. Delicate personal energies are involved. You won't achieve the desired growth if you push yourself into changing by setting up absolute demands and then becoming angry at yourself if you don't meet them. If an exercise doesn't seem to be helping you achieve a result on a particular day, set it aside and try again tomorrow. Be "gently disciplined" and "firmly patient" with yourself, as you would be in starting a Nautilus program or Jazzercise.

• *Accept opposites; welcome paradox*. Psychological growth involves the integration of seemingly opposite values (i.e., strength and tenderness, analysis and intuition, stability and flexibility, maturity and spontaneity, etc.). When it comes to your relationship, accept yourself and your lover as you are, embrace your differences and learn together, rather than strain to be what you are not or what you think you ought to be. Only then will you discover the true emotional freedom with your lover to grow as lifemates.

• *Remember: Humor, forgiveness, and mutual silent comforting are the best emergency procedures.* Sometimes Love Fitness exercises may not be appropriate, particularly in times of extreme emotional stress. For example, Robert, our co-author, and his wife, Anjani, had been using the Tell Me More exercise to their satisfaction. One day, however, Robert had had so much pressure at work that he was forced to cancel a joint meeting critical to Anjani's career without telling her. Anjani, who had prepared a major presentation, arrived for the meeting only to find it was cancelled. Quite naturally, she felt embarrassed and enraged. When Anjani and Robert finally met at home late that evening, she saw that Robert was so drained that he lacked the emotional strength to accept her feelings. Robert recognized Anjani's need to vent her anger and wanted to give her that opportunity, but he also acknowledged his need to defend himself from further emotional stress. He too was stressed and not prepared to use the Tell Me More exercise at that moment.

There are times in every love relationship when one or both people will "blow it." It is important to understand at such moments that love fitness is not some idealized concept. Lifemates do not become disillusioned or cynical when they make "emotional mistakes." Rather, they acknowledge their errors and find a way to reestablish heart-to-heart communication as quickly as possible. The best way to begin is with a simple, direct, and heartfelt apology. By apologizing and asking for forgiveness you heal the emotional breach and learn from your mistakes.

In times of emotional crisis, don't let yourself become disillusioned with your lover's commitment. Part of becoming lifemates is learning to accept each other's emotional emergencies and using good judgment in getting through them. An apology is the first step.

Also important is forgiving yourself and your lover for your mutual hurt or your inability to express your feelings. A little humor can be very helpful, as long as you are laughing with one another or at the situation.

Finally, there is a silent mutual embrace. If you and your lover are both in pain, but neither of you can express it, nothing may be more helpful than a simple, silent hug. Because Anjani and Robert had practiced the Tell Me More exercise, they had learned to acknowledge their hurt and to be patient with each other. Rather than blame or withdraw, they chose to embrace and comfort each other. Later on, they were able to use the Tell Me More exercise to resolve their hurt and vent Anjani's anger. By using Love Fitness workouts regularly, you develop emotional strength and mutual respect that will help you and your lover handle emotional emergencies.

• *Repetition is the key to mastery.* Developing love fitness is a learning process. For that reason, we often describe our role as that of teacher, coach, or guide, rather than doctor, psychiatrist, or therapist. We explain to individual clients and participants in our seminars that to make lasting changes, daily workouts with these exercises are needed. No one is a one-trial learner!

Watching our then one-year-old daughter take her first steps, we learned a powerful fitness lesson: It's not how many times you fall but how many times you get back up. Each person learns to walk by first stumbling thousands of times. Developing love fitness is no different; accept that failure and vulnerability are an essential part of mastering heart-to-heart communication skills.

You can't expect to gain any benefits from this book by rubbing its cover or placing it under your pillow. All psychological growth involves insight and behavior change. You must put the insights and techniques into practice. In learning a musical instrument or athletic skill, repetition is the key to success. So, too, with the Love Fitness program: The exercises must be practiced regularly to achieve the results you desire. Keep in mind, however, that this can also be fun, so enjoy yourself!

• *Difficulties and challenges will always arise.* There is no permanent victory in life; problems and challenges always arise. Growth is never in a straight upward line. It is more often an irregular path, two steps forward and one back. You may reach a new ability to love and respect yourself or a new plateau of understanding with your lover, only to encounter a crisis that sets you back. There is a common tendency to revert to old emotional habits under stress, particularly in love relationships. Don't despair if that happens. Use "backsliding" as a new opportunity to solidify and increase your progress. Crisis is an opportunity for further growth.

• *Above all, the Love Fitness program is an adventure of the heart.* The Love Fitness program is not meant to establish a rigid, monolithic standard. Rather, it is intended to be enjoyable and exciting, an adventure in self-development and mutual discovery with your lover. Once you achieve one or two specific goals, you may experience a shift in the perception of your relationship from one of frustration and problems to one of abundance and joy. Where you felt constricted and stuck, you will start to see new opportunities for exercising your love.

Making the Love Fitness Program Your Own

One final word is necessary about the fundamentals of the Love Fitness program. Some people fear that the Love Fitness program is too mechanical. Others fear that a spouse won't even consider trying one of the exercises. A few people can't see either themselves or their lover actually sitting down to do the exercises exactly as described. Now that we have described several emotional workouts and the basic guidelines of the Love Fitness program, this issue must be addressed.

First, about our guidelines and what may appear to be mechanical rules. On the one hand, it is important to understand the reason for structured exercise and to recognize how Love Fitness workouts can have a powerful impact on you and your relationship. Intense feelings can develop. Though guidelines may seem mechanical, they provide structure, safety, and understanding of what to expect and how to handle unexpected emotional responses. Structured exercises also take you out of your habitual emotional responses and paradoxically allow truly spontaneous, heartfelt expression of feeling. On the other hand, the instructions are not intended to be rigid. Naturally we expect you will adapt phrasing to your own way of speaking. However, we also expect that in adapting the exercises, you will be careful to observe the essential principles of each exercise.

Second, about you and your lover getting started. A simple direct approach is best. You can suggest your lover read this book, one chapter, or even part of one chapter. Make the suggestion in an open, nondemanding way. Offer the possibility of taking a few minutes to try one of the workouts as an experiment; emphasize that the exercise can be a learning experience and an opportunity to draw you closer. Listen to your lover's response; respect his or her point of view and concerns. It is valuable to discuss fears about an exercise before you try it. Discuss your commitment to observe our guidelines for each exercise because these guidelines provide the necessary atmosphere of safety and trust. Also, don't forget that these workouts can be playful.

Finally, it is important to note a difference between the Love Fitness program and a physical fitness program. With Love Fitness workouts you develop emotional skills that eventually become fully integrated with your personality and your relationship. An exercise such as Tell Me More becomes a spontaneous way of responding to your lover when you notice his or her tension, anxiety, or anger. You don't have to sit down and go through the whole exercise, but can start the Tell Me More process in the kitchen, the car, at the beach—wherever it might be appropriate at the time. By developing superb skills of receptive listening, you minimize the likelihood of a major accumulation of tension in the relationship and the long-form Tell Me More exercise becomes a process you save and savor when you need it, although some couples use it as a form of emotional toning. The great value of the Love Fitness program, however, is its cumulative effect—a blossoming of heart and spirit.

Chapter 3

Heart Talks
for Greater Intimacy

Can you and your lover freely reveal to each other
who you really are and what you really want—good
and bad, strengths and weaknesses, hopes and fears,
successes and failures?

For many couples, the answer is at best a qualified
yes, but for others it is no. Most people are afraid to
let others, even a lover, know what they really feel
about important personal issues. For example, sexual
anxiety remains widespread, but most couples rarely
talk about it enough to allay their fears. Although
frustration in achieving personal goals may be discussed, few couples take the time to explore their
deepest hopes. Lack of self-confidence, hidden resentments, painful memories, and secret desires are universal, but few couples know how to help each other
accept and resolve these powerful but hidden feelings.

Most couples spend less than thirty minutes per
week sharing their most intimate feelings. No wonder
relationships go stale. Rather than explore their feelings, many couples assume they know how each other
feels when in reality they are each afraid to ask! For
love to remain exciting and vibrant, intense and deeply
honest communication of feelings is vital. This chapter
is about accepting that challenge and creating an adventure of mutual discovery.

To begin, an assessment of fears which stand in the
way of heart-to-heart communication is helpful. For
some people, a fear of rejection is a primary inhibi-
tion. Almost everyone harbors some anxiety that if a
lover really knew everything, rejection might be the

result. Other people fear their own anger. They resist exposing their deepest feelings because they sense a rage that could lead to violence. Still others fear an encounter with their own self-image. They fear that letting a lover know them will be humiliating or lead them to feel inferior. Those who desperately seek love and find it may discover a new worry—the fear of losing that love and once again being left to face life alone. The persistence of such fears makes creating and sustaining a great love relationship difficult, if not impossible.

The following comments from participants in our seminars illustrate common fears in love relationships:

"Our relationship has gone flat; I feel like you're bored with me."

"If my lover knew the real me, she would leave."

"I get to a certain point in a relationship where I feel blocked. I can't get any closer."

"After we have sex, I feel lonely and disconnected."

"I'm afraid to risk my heart again; I don't want to get hurt."

"We've been living together for two years, but lately we're distant from each other; I escape to aerobics classes and he is glued to the TV."

"I don't feel loved or appreciated; we share the same house, the same bed, yet most of the time we're like strangers."

Withholding such feelings creates a burden on you and your relationship by undermining self-confidence and your ability to give and accept love. When two people hide their deepest feelings, the relationship is doomed to boredom and chronic frustration. Instead of making their needs clear, couples begin to manipulate, intimidate, or induce guilt in each other. Affairs and divorce often follow.

Overcoming Fears of Self-Disclosure

How do you overcome fears of self-disclosure that block heart-to-heart communication with your love partner? We have developed a series of Love Fitness workouts called "Heart Talks," based on the psychological principle that the best way to expand the capacity for love is to let go of fear. Heart Talks establish an emotional environment of care, safety, and trust, allowing both you and your lover to accept and enjoy the risk of self-disclosure, discover hidden parts of yourselves, and develop new emotional connections. Those who learn and practice Heart Talks report that these exercises are exciting, challenging, and often lots of fun.

Heart Talks involve much more than saccharine sentimentality. They are designed to help you discover the courage to be vulnerable, to divulge insecurities and pain, to endure conflict and struggles, and also to share your dreams and hopes. Heart Talks instill the safety and trust necessary to do the psychological house-cleaning that every intimate relationship requires. Even if your lover is uncooperative at first, the more self-disclosing you are, the more open and honest others will be around you. Talk from your heart and soon your lifemate will join you.

Heart Talks can serve to benefit you and your love relationship in the following ways:

1. *Emotional safety.* You and your lover can create safety and trust to talk about whatever might be disturbing you.
2. *Tension release.* Every love relationship will encounter rough points and accumulate frustration; Heart Talks are a way of clearing the air.
3. *Nurturing and connecting.* Heart-to-heart communication nurtures you and your lover in a way that no amount of physical sex alone can provide. Heart

Talks are a means to experience greater intimacy and connectedness on every level of your being.

4. *Learning more about yourself.* Some people shy away from intimacy because they fear going deeper into themselves. A Heart Talk is a personal invitation to allow your lover to get closer to you, and to help you discover more about yourself.

5. *Feeling affirmed, understood, and accepted.* No matter how autonomous and independent you may be, it is important to be fully acknowledged and understood by those to whom you feel closest, particularly your lover. Heart Talks help you and your lover make sure that each of you gets the acceptance and acknowledgment you need.

6. *Fun, play and laughter.* Heart Talks are more than serious emotional conversations; they are also a means of having fun and experiencing the joys of intimacy.

7. *Rediscovering your love partner.* In the business of everyday life, it is easy to take your lover for granted and assume you know how he or she thinks and feels. Heart Talks are a means of rediscovering recent changes in your lover's feelings, ideas, and goals.

8. *Energizing a love relationship.* By strengthening the bonds of intimacy, Heart Talks allow you and your lover to experience new heights of passion. You will discover ways of enjoying one another that you might not have even thought possible.

9. *Healing yourself.* Heart Talks are also an opportunity to heal yourself by reclaiming your "dark side." To love deeply, each of us must accept the feelings of hostility, fear, rage, confusion, and helplessness that lie within. Heart Talks allow for repentance, forgiveness, and understanding the contradictory forces of love and anger. When love partners learn to embrace each other's dark sides, they also become more compassionate with themselves.

Heart Talks can revitalize a long-term relationship, as well as deepen the experience of those newly in love. These exercises will also be valuable for the reader who is not currently in a love relationship to practice with a close friend. Skill at being open yourself, as well as helping others be more open, is one of the fastest ways to ensure a healthy, passionate love relationship.

Heart Blocks

If intimacy is so wonderful, and yields such benefits, why is the fear of self-disclosure so widespread? The primary reason, as we have said, is that most people were exposed to unhealthy emotional habits from early childhood. Since they didn't see their parents as models for intimate conversation, they never learned its value, much less how to do it. On the contrary, most people saw their parents engage in conflict, emotional withdrawal, or both. Another reason is that while new relationships are propelled by the excitement of romance, many couples get so caught up in their everyday lives—career, finances, children—that they stop putting energy into their relationship without even realizing it. When they don't work as hard to maintain intimacy, they allow themselves to get "emotionally flabby" and the relationship suffers.

Before you work out with Heart Talks, insight into your "heart blocks" is helpful. Read the following statements and mark each one true or false as it applies to you:

1. There are some things I'm just too embarrassed or ashamed to admit.
2. If I am open and vulnerable, my love partner will perceive me as weak and will lose respect for me.
3. If I share my true feelings with my lover, he or she will get angry or withdraw.
4. If I am completely open, it will be used against me.

5. As soon as a relationship gets serious, I worry it will end.

6. I want to be more intimate, but I just can't find the right person.

7. I worry that my lover will grow bored with me; familiarity breeds contempt.

8. As I become more emotionally involved, I lose touch with reality; work and other relationships suffer.

9. When it comes to intimacy, I feel that I give too much and get too little in return.

10. After my previous love relationship, I doubt that I can be totally open and intimate with someone again.

11. I'm afraid of getting stuck in an unhappy marriage like my parents had.

12–20. I don't like to admit it, but sometimes when my love partner wants to be close and reach out to me:

- I seem to accept his or her feelings outwardly without really letting them touch me.
- I go into a monologue and become defensive.
- I behave in an arrogant "above-it-all" fashion.
- I become analytical and intellectualize, staying away from my deeper feelings.
- I get irritated, or start a fight.
- I pretend to be confused, saying I don't really understand what's being said or asked for.
- I make jokes to avoid intimate conversation.
- I change the subject or act as if that discussion isn't really important; as if there are responsibilities or "real" business to be attended to.

- I suspect that my partner has hidden motives—wanting sex, permission to buy something, etc.

If you marked three or fewer of the statements as True, you open your heart freely and aren't afraid to be vulnerable. If you marked four to eight of them True, you open your heart halfway, depending on circumstances and whom you are with. If you marked nine to fourteen statements as being True, you open your heart a crack to peek outside, possibly to risk taking a further step. If fifteen or more were True, you keep the door to your heart locked and double-bolted.

Your score on this quiz is helpful in several ways. First, if you are among the high scorers (nine or more True), you can expect exercising with Heart Talks to feel awkward at first. Remember, that is okay. Learning new emotional skills will stretch your comfort zone. Second, the Heart Talk exercises described in this chapter are graded in intensity. The higher your score, the more time you should spend with the easier exercises before going on to more challenging ones. Third, take another look at your answers, paying attention to those marked True. You can gain valuable insight into how you protect your feelings (for example, by withdrawing, changing the subject, becoming intellectual, etc.). Be on the alert to drop these habitual defenses during Heart Talk exercises.

Some Cautions

Several cautions about self-disclosure: Although essential to personal growth and intimacy, self-disclosure is a process to be undertaken carefully. Total openness can impose an unrealistic standard upon love and marriage. To say that husband and wife should keep no secrets from one another and that complete honesty is always the best policy fails to recognize the human need for some zones of privacy. If you don't feel comfortable sharing the sexual details of a past romance, there is no reason to feel as if you must. Also, there is no obligation to reveal a sexual fantasy or secret that you feel is just too personal to share even with your lifemate. Intimacy does not mean you have to tell your lover everything!

Self-disclosure must be done safely, and in measures appropriate to the situation. There are some disclosures that may lead to disabling or even terminating a love relationship, rather than strengthening it. For example, Roger had a one-night stand with a woman he met at a convention. His love relationship with his wife Lisa was basically in good shape, and he thought that brief liaison would have no further impact on their marriage. Yet he also felt troubled by guilt. To use self-disclosure as a means of relieving his feelings of guilt, and to burden Lisa with the news of this brief affair, would be inappropriate for this love relationship. In this case, it was probable that Lisa might not understand or forgive this disclosure were Roger to make it.

Was it worth Roger's taking the risk of destroying his relationship with Lisa so that he could feel cleansed? Did he owe it to Lisa to share, or not to share, this information? There is no easy answer to such a personal decision. We are not condoning affairs, which we see as an emotional escape valve that many resort to as a result of their lack of love fitness. What we are saying is that without a trained counselor in attendance, a confession of this nature may trigger consequences that neither partner anticipates. The revelation of a one-night stand that would have no further consequence can actually lead to serious impairment or destruction of a relationship.

Heart Talks can be misused to psychologize a relationship to its death. Some people enter a relationship with the false assumption that they must expose and analyze every facet of their lifemate's psyche. Heart Talks are never meant for playing armchair psychiatrist with your love partner. If you discuss each other's traits ad nauseum, you may drive each other crazy. When communication is usurped by endless confrontation, introspection, and psyche-searching, it is appropriate to say to your lover, "Tell me less" rather than "Tell me more."

Almost any truth or value taken to an extreme becomes false. So too with the value of openness. Getting to know and be known by a lover is exciting and emotionally enriching. Angrily "letting it all hang out" can be unkind as well as unwise, however. Just as important to intimacy as openness are propriety and good taste. There is no excuse for napalming your spouse's self-esteem: "You are stupid, fat, and worthless. Everyone who meets you despises you. You're a complete bore in and out of bed and you're a rotten parent to boot. I mourn the day I married you." You get the picture. Spontaneity must be balanced with respect. Releasing every destructive thought you ever had about your lifemate without some measure of self-censorship is cruel, hostile behavior and absolutely uncalled for in a love-fit relationship.

One last caution: Heart Talks are not a cure for a relationship on the rocks. If you are in a marital crisis, or feel your relationship is poor or unstable, or that you or your partner will react negatively to intimate sharing, it is best to contact a trained mental health expert or marriage counselor to assist in safely exploring self-disclosure and dealing with the subsequent issues that may emerge.

Heart Talk Agreements

The instructions for Heart Talk exercises are very simple, but strict adherence to the prescribed set of procedures is necessary to ensure correct practice. The first procedure, and one that we insist upon, is also the primary rule for "Tell Me More" as outlined in Chapter 2, and that is never interrupt your lifemate. This is crucial in Heart Talks, since you take turns answering a question or completing a statement.

For many people, the habit of interrupting is so ingrained that it occurs despite their best intentions. To avoid the ensuing irritation and misunderstanding, we suggest passing a small heart-shaped pillow back and forth as a reminder not to interrupt. Whoever holds the Heart Talk pillow may speak without interruption while the other partner communicates "Tell me more." Your Heart Talk pillow will become very special to both of you, a symbol of your love, commitment, and intimacy, and it should only be used for your Heart Talks.

Certain rules are essential to creating the emotional safety and trust to make Heart Talks work. Therefore, before trying a Heart Talk both of you should first agree to the following:

1. I promise not to withdraw emotionally or to leave physically; I will not reject you for anything you wish to share.
2. I will make it safe for you to express your most intimate feelings; I will stay open and vulnerable to you.
3. Nothing you say will be used against you or to provoke an argument later.
4. I will be responsible for my emotions, and I will not blame you for how I feel. If I do blame or complain, I will take immediate responsibility for doing so, and stop.
5. I will share the truth from my heart as caringly, honestly, and respectfully as I can.
6. I will love you unconditionally and use any block or conflict that may arise as a stimulus to more learning and greater love.
7. I will try not to manipulate, defend, or control what you communicate.
8. I commit to dealing with and working through any barriers that come up in our Heart Talks

until there is resolution and we are once again open and loving with each other.

9. I agree that we can disagree. As we may not see eye-to-eye about all issues, we will each allow the other his/her feelings, understanding, and point of view.

10. I agree to finish each Heart Talk session with at least one embracing hug (remember, five hugs a day keeps the marriage counselor away) and a sincere "I love you."

These agreements are so important that we suggest you photocopy them or keep the book open to this page during your Heart Talks. Take turns reading aloud these agreements before you begin your Heart Talks.

Create an appropriate environment for your Heart Talks. Disconnect the phone and take precautions against outside interruption. Also, until you learn to be "in close," it is important to set up a "proper distance." Use comfortable chairs placed three to three and a half feet apart, allowing for eye contact and enough "space" to be able to deal with any difficult feelings that may emerge. As you grow more comfortable, you can move closer together. Some people like to sit cross-legged on the floor or in bed, holding hands while maintaining eye contact. Do what feels best to you and your lover. When dealing with very intense feelings of hurt, pain, or anger, you may want to have a little more distance, but always face each other with an open body position.

Set a time limit at first—at least thirty minutes but not more than one hour per sitting. This will preempt the tendency to "feel like quitting" when resistances come up. Just as with a physical fitness program, three half-hour sessions a week is the minimum necessary for love fitness, while a full one-hour workout once every week or two will allow for even greater intimacy with your lifemate.

Keep in mind that love partners are not alike in

their tolerance of or desire for intimacy. While almost everyone could use more intimacy, people have different paces, styles, and comfort zones that must be respected. To expand your capacity for intimacy, you will need to be more self-disclosing in your most private thoughts, feelings, and fantasies, but you will also need to respect your lover's pace and style of self-disclosure. Both of you must take responsibility for maintaining mutual respect, honoring your Heart Talk agreements, and creating an atmosphere of safety and trust.

Levels of Intimacy

The Heart Talk diagram below depicts four levels of intimacy and personal privacy. Level E covers emotionally neutral information. In this zone, communication consists primarily of explorations and attitudes (e.g., "What I like most about my work is . . ."; "My views on national defense are . . ."; "I participate in environmental preservation by . . .").

Levels F, A, and S represent zones of increasing intimacy, where you either let close friends, confidantes, or lovers into your life or keep them out. It is at these levels that you begin to reveal your true self. At level F, you begin to communicate your feelings and desires (e.g., "I feel frustrated . . ." "I am optimistic . . ." "I hope . . ." "I look forward to . . ."). At level A, you share more intimate and difficult feelings about yourself, your relationship, and what is most important to you. The designation "A" is for ambivalence—the feelings that generate uncertainty (e.g., "I'm confused about"; "Sometimes I wonder if we'll make it . . ."). Level S is the innermost level of intimacy—secrets. This level represents the territory of hidden feelings and buried fears (e.g., "I feel threatened when . . ."; "Ever since I can remember, I've been afraid of . . .").

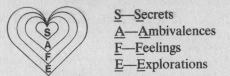

S—Secrets
A—Ambivalences
F—Feelings
E—Explorations

Most people keep the content of levels A and S a wholly private concern. They share these thoughts, feelings, and wishes with no one, thereby severing a crucial link to potential intimacy. If you are somewhat open and courageous, you can share from these innermost levels of the heart with perhaps one or two special people whom you trust completely. Level S allows for the deepest, most rewarding connection, since by definition you trust no one, yet also requires great skill in sharing yourself. Disclosures at level S include those dealing with sex (sexual anxieties, fantasies, desires, and fears), dishonesty, corruption, shame, violence, and rage.

These levels of intimacy form the acronym S.A.F.E., a reminder of the key element of Heart Talks. You and your lover must create an emotional environment of total trust and safety. Once that is established, you can be completely vulnerable, which leads to personal liberation from fear and therefore a higher quality of love.

Heart Talks: Exercises for Intimacy

The following Love Fitness workouts are designed to assist lovers in communicating heart to heart. For each Heart Talk session, choose one exercise from the appropriate level and take turns completing the incomplete sentence. Remember to review your Heart Talk agreements before commencing each workout.

Heart Talks—Level E: Explorations

1. The three people in history I would most like to have as dinner guests in our home are . . .

2. The personal and professional goals I want to accomplish in the next year are . . . in the next five years are . . .

3. A one-month, all-expense paid trip I would like to take anywhere in the world is . . .

4. The three people who have most influenced my values and thinking are . . .

5. My feelings about homosexuality are . . .

6. What I would do to end world hunger is . . .

7. My views on abortion are . . .

8. How I feel about divorce is . . .

9. I think our children should be brought up to . . .

10. What you and I should do in relation to housework and child rearing is . . .

11. What I like best about my work and career is . . .

12. What I like least about my work and career is . . .

13. If I could have three magic wishes, I would wish for . . .

14. My feelings about being/becoming a parent are . . .

15. My religious beliefs are . . .

16. God, in my view, is . . .

17. I would like to spend more of our time . . .

18. It would please me greatly if you were interested in . . .

19. What I have noticed recently about myself is . . .

20. Three objects, representing significant events in our life together, that I value most are . . .

21. What I feel to be crucial to world peace is . . .

22. Why are we here? Does your life, my life, our life, "Life" have a bigger meaning?

Here are some fun yet revealing questions to consider.

23. If your partner were to be an item of food, what would he or she be? Why? Describe why you chose this particular food to represent your love partner.

24. If your partner were to be an animal, what animal would he or she be? Again, describe why.

Many couples find they can dramatically reduce tension as a result of self-disclosure, and with certain exercises it dissolves into laughter and tears of joy. We hope that Heart Talks help you to stop taking yourself so seriously and discover that we human beings all have the same basic fears, needs, and hopes. If Heart Talks do no more than cause you and your love partner to laugh, play, and enjoy yourselves, won't they be worthwhile?

Heart Talks—Level F: Feelings

1. The two biggest personal challenges I am facing in my life at present are . . .
2. What I am most worried/concerned about this week is . . .
3. An important change I would like to see in you is . . .
4. If I could change one thing about the way I was raised, it would be . . .
5. The five specific things I feel most grateful for are . . .
6. Personal living or work habits I would like to change in myself are . . .
7. The reasons I have the "better deal" in our relationship are . . .
8. The reasons you have the "better deal" in our relationship are . . .
9. The kind of funeral I would like to have is . . .
10. The ways I would enjoy being famous are . . .
11. Three specific things that make you a pleasure to live with are . . .
12. Three specific things that make you difficult to live with are . . .
13. What I am most afraid of is . . .
14. The person I most resent is . . .
15. My feelings about my success in life are . . .
16. My greatest anxieties are . . .
17. An unforgettable evening with you would be . . .
18. A perfect weekend with you would consist of . . .

19. An important change I want to see in myself is . . .

Heart Talks—Level A: Ambivalences

1. The best thing about our sex life is . . .
2. The worst thing about our sex life is . . .
3. Parts of my body and appearance I dislike the most are . . .
4. Parts of my body and appearance I feel best about are . . .
5. The most self-destructive behavior pattern I notice in me is . . .
6. The most self-destructive behavior pattern I notice in you is . . .
7. The three things I like least about my life are . . .
8. The three things I like best about my life are . . .
9. The way I would feel more loved by you is . . .
10. What are some major decisions in your life you would change if you could do so?
11. How well do you live up to your moral, spiritual, and ethical values?
12. How would you like to be remembered after you die?
13. What aspects of your personality do you worry about or regard as weaknesses?
14. What would you be willing to die for?
15. What are your three most treasured memories of our love?
16. Have you ever felt hatred for someone in your family? Why?
17. Whom else have you ever hated, and why?
18. What are the five greatest achievements of your life?
19. What do you think are the five greatest achievements of my life?
20. When did you last cry by yourself and why?
21. What do you really think about my family, your in-laws?

22. What do you like and dislike about our children?
23. If you knew that you only had one year to live, what about your life would you change and what would you like to do?
24. If there were three specific qualities or abilities you wanted me to acquire, what would they be?
25. What would you do if you discovered I had contracted AIDS or a similarly life-threatening disease?
26. Is there something you have dreamed about doing for a long time but have not done as yet?
27. Was there ever a time in your life when you had suicidal thoughts? What was going on?
28. If friends and family members gave you the worst possible but honest feedback about yourself, what might they say?

Heart Talks—Level S: Secrets

1. The three most dishonest, dishonorable things I have ever done are . . .
2. Things I have done that I feel most ashamed of are . . .
3. Sometimes when I feel sexually excited, I . . .
4. Fears and inhibitions I have and don't want known are . . .
5. Faults and disabilities I have and don't like to acknowledge are . . .
6. The most magical/mysterious experience I've ever was . . .
7. I've been secretly resentful about . . .
8. Two specific things I don't want you to know about me are . . .
9. If I were to die within the next twenty-four hours, what I would most want to communicate to you is . . .
10. Do you have a secret sexual fantasy that you would like to have fulfilled?
11. What were the most embarrassing moments of your adolescence?

12. What actions have you most regretted in your life and why?
13. What was your worst experience with nonprescribed drugs or alcohol?
14. What specific events in your life have been the most traumatic and emotionally painful?
15. What outrageous things might you do sexually if you were sure no one would hurt or laugh at you?
16. When did you last want to scream or yell at me, and why?
17. What thoughts do you have when you see yourself nude in the mirror?
18. What have been your biggest disappointments in life?
19. What have been your biggest failures?
20. What is your biggest, darkest secret?

Late Night Heart Talks

Some couples prefer to engage in Heart Talks at the end of the day while in bed. Lifemates take turns completing at least one of the statements:

1. "What worked in my relationship with you today is: _____." The purpose is to share specific feelings, events, and observations that contributed in a constructive way to the overall enhancement of the relationship. You may identify something positive that your lover said or did during the day. You might also acknowledge yourself for some contribution to the relationship, such as a new way of behaving or the correction of an emotional habit that had caused problems. Here is an example from one client: "I noticed that when I took a wrong turn on our way to the meeting last night, you did not criticize me as you would have in the past. I asked for your assistance and acknowledged that I was unsure of how to get there. I

felt good about my willingness to acknowledge a mistake and appreciated your understanding.''

2. "What did not work for me in my relationship with you today is: _____.'' Again, the statements which follow may be descriptions of the events, conversations and observations which the speaker perceived as problems in the relationship. As the speaker shares those feelings, the listener does not interrupt or comment, except to say, "Tell me more." The purpose of this exercise is to create an opportunity for regular feedback in the relationship. The more specific the statement, the more easily appropriate adjustments can be made.

3. "What worked in my relationship with me today is: _____.'' This exercise allows you to acknowledge and reinforce desirable habits and achievements. Here is another example from a client: "Although I felt tired at the end of the day, I took the time to walk on the beach and get my exercise. I felt great afterward and I am glad that I took the time in spite of fatigue." Patting yourself on the back in this way will reinforce personal growth. You and your lover can be cheerleaders for each other. It works!

4. "What did not work in my relationship with me today is: _____.'' This exercise is intended to assist lovers in acknowledging and encouraging their respective personal growth. For example, one client noted, "I was really a jerk for not being more assertive in today's presentation to a new customer. I need to improve my sales skills in this business." By inviting your lover to understand what changes you are trying to make in your own life and career, you give your lover an opportunity to understand your weaknesses and to help you develop new strengths. Such mutual disclosure allows you and your lover to better understand each other's personal struggles and feel supported.

These late-night Heart Talks are not for introducing "heavy" issues, but rather to connect emotionally with your lifemate at the day's end. Once both partners have completed the statements, discuss what you shared.

An Adventure of the Heart

Frequently in relationships, one person is more emotionally open and spontaneous, while the other is more constrained and reserved. In the early phases of dating, this match seems to work well. The person who is more emotionally open, usually the woman, finds stability and security in the one who has his feet firmly planted on the ground. The more emotionally closed individual finds fun, joy, and an emotional outlet by vicariously experiencing his lover's emotional intensity. However, opposites not only attract, they can also repel. Either person, or both, can become bored, disappointed, or frustrated. The emotionally open partner may feel controlled and constricted by her lover, who now seems to not just have his feet on the ground but encased in cement. To adjust to his rigidity, she may restrict her desires, inhibit her passion, and feel resentful. The more reserved, emotionally constrained lover may feel threatened and rejected, and further heighten his self-protection. Deep intimacy becomes increasingly difficult at a time in their love relationship when they need it most.

Such was the case for Bill, a corporate vice-president, and Julia, who returned to her job as a city planner once their three-year-old son was enrolled in a day care center. Married for five years, they attended a seminar of ours, and spoke of their success in managing a two-career household. Over the last year, however, Julia and Bill had grown increasingly distant from each other. They bickered frequently over minor matters, and their sex life was practically nonexistent.

The following diagram illustrates how Bill and Julia operated in terms of self-disclosure and fears of intimacy.

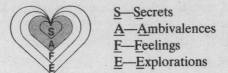

S—Secrets
A—Ambivalences
F—Feelings
E—Explorations

Although both communicated freely at Levels E and F, neither shared his or her innermost world: Levels A and S were almost completely blocked. Bill and Julia had deluded themselves into believing they had a great relationship when, in fact, they kept their most intimate feelings, thoughts, and desires to themselves.

When love partners first invite each other to share deep feelings through Heart Talks, they often try to limit disclosure to feelings that are nonthreatening to each other's self-image or the stability of the relationship. Women encourage men to express hurt and even cry, but are often dismayed by subsequent expressions of rage, sexual boredom, and confusion. Likewise, men may encourage women to be more assertive, but experience great difficulty hearing about their lifemate's fears and resistance to playing the traditional wife/mother role.

Bill and Julia were surprised at how powerful Heart Talks can be. By using Heart Talks to create the necessary environment of emotional safety, they learned that once threatening thoughts and feelings produced no lasting pain. Through these regular sessions of self-disclosure, they overcame deep personal fears, and discovered that they could share painful, suppressed feelings, actually with greater respect, confidence and love for each other than ever before.

Some of the Heart Talks that Bill and Julia found most revealing were the following:

Level A: Ambivalences

10. What are some major decisions in your life you would change if you could do so?
24. If there were three specific qualities or abilities you wanted me to acquire, what would they be?

28. If friends and family members were willing to give you the worst possible but honest feedback about yourself, what might they say?

Level S: Secrets

7. I've been secretly resentful about . . .
8. Two specific things I don't want you to know about me are . . .
16. When did you last want to scream or yell at me, and why?

What follows is an excerpt from Julia and Bill's first session with Heart Talks.

Julia

"You encouraged me to go back to work to help out with expenses and take some of the pressure off you. But now that I'm working full time, you complain that it takes away from the quality time I spend with you and our son. You wanted me to depend on you less and 'earn my own way,' but you don't want my career to interfere with your plans either—I get a week less vacation time than you, yet you expect me to just take three weeks off!

"Sometimes you say to me, 'Please tell me what's upsetting you.' Yet when I try to tell you why I'm angry, you say I'm ungrateful or 'just under a lot of stress.' That infuriates me even more!

"When I do make myself available to pamper and please you, I feel taken for granted or like I'm just complying with your demands. If I take 'too much' time for me, with yoga classes, getting my nails done, or going out with my girlfriends, you accuse me of being selfish and rejecting.

"When I attempt to relate my frustrations about work, you go into a monologue about 'harsh realities' and 'office politics,' and how I should understand now what you've been going through. You want me to not complain and be tough, but not be too tough for you!

"You want me to take more sexual initiative and be more passionate. Yet when I try to be sexually assertive, you feel pressured and intimidated. Either way, I'm frustrated and you seem closed off and bored.

"You still make the rearing of our son my prime responsibility, while you just 'pitch in' and maybe give him a bath or read him a story. You act like Dr. Child Expert, accusing me of being overprotective or ignoring his needs. Why don't you share more of the parenting with me?"

Bill

"You resent having to take prime responsibility for household chores, yet I put in longer hours at work, and I'm still chiefly responsible for our financial support. When I do vacuum or put away the dishes you get super critical and say it's easier to do it yourself.

"You encourage me to have male friends, but when I spend time with them you feel rejected and even jealous. I then feel guilty for neglecting you and our son.

"You say I should work less, but since you've gone back to work we're also spending much more. You think I'm preoccupied with money and my career as a way of avoiding you. That hurts. You want me to be a successful world-beater and yet be completely relaxed, available, and intimate. Well, you've discovered for yourself it's not that easy.

"You want me to be more romantic and sensual, and less sexually driven and goal-oriented. Yet you wonder what's wrong if I do relax but occasionally lose my erection. You want me to be a great sexual performer 'your way'; I feel confused and manipulated.

"When I want to be nurtured and cared for, you say I'm demanding. I'm reluctant to ask for a backrub or request a special meal. If I don't share my feelings and needs you say I'm closed off from you. If I do express them, you think I'm selfish and needy.

"I resent that you don't appreciate how much I love our son. You accuse me of only having fun times with him if I buy him a toy. No matter what I do, it's never enough. You play the martyr and I can't please you."

Julia and Bill were troubled by conflict and expectations common among two-career couples. They found it difficult to break away from the old dominant-male/submissive-female relationship, and become true lifemates. Julia's Heart Talks were signaling, "Don't treat me like a child, I share decisions and responsibilities equally with you," while Bill was expressing, "Work and be more independent, but continue to depend on me so I'll feel powerful and in control."

Through the continued practice of Heart Talks, what began as serious, often tense sharing, evolved into a healthy exchange of perspectives. Revelations of an extremely sensitive nature were discussed with care and resolved. As Julia described, "It felt so good not to have to censor myself or just say what I should to keep the peace. I felt a new freedom; like I could say anything to Bill and he would still be my best friend." A few times Bill wept deeply as well as laughed: "I never felt so exposed and yet unjudged by Julia, or anyone for that matter. I've stopped being so self-critical. Julia and I have really gotten to know and love each other in a way I never dreamed was possible."

Heart Talks didn't by themselves generate answers to all the questions in Bill and Julia's relationship. Bill and Julia still had important decisions to make about how to accommodate each other's needs, but resolving conflict and making choices became much easier than ever before. Since Julia and Bill no longer had to be so careful with each other, they learned to speak from their hearts more spontaneously. Heart Talks allowed them to exchange and explore each other's inner lives, as well as experience deeper levels of love.

Renewing Your Love

An intimate relationship must be continually nour-ished to endure. What ruins relationships? There are certainly many factors. One may be that you no longer remember, and fail to regularly bring to your attention the qualities that attracted you to your lover in the first place. The following is a special practice for "Re-newing Your Love" with a lifemate. Allow twenty minutes of uninterrupted time.

Sit facing each other as closely as possible. Be silent. Close your eyes, breathe slowly and deeply, and relax each part of your body. Tune into yourself, let go of concerns and cares of the day. Take the time to get centered, peaceful, and loving. When you and your lifemate have both opened your eyes, again with-out speaking, take each other's hands. Look into your lifemate's eyes openly and lovingly. Keep gazing into each other's eyes as you gently breathe love back and forth. You might also visualize a beam of light pouring down on both of you. With each breath the light grows brighter, especially connecting your hearts.

Now, bring to mind a specific time when you felt powerfully attracted to your lover, and most deeply and passionately in love. Reach down into your mem-ory and bask in these beautiful feelings. Continue to breathe fully and radiate love through your eyes and breath. Most important, feel how all this is happening right now; it isn't just a memory. This connection, intimacy, and passion has been there all along, cov-ered by superficial daily activities. So go ahead and feel your attraction to this wondrous being in front of you. Continue to breathe away all fear and concerns. Keep opening your heart and entire body to these exciting feelings of yearning, passion, and surrender. If sexual feelings arise, allow these to also flow through your entire body. Look deeply into the eyes of your beloved; merge every part of your being with each other. When you have completed the nonverbal aspect of this practice, take another ten minutes to have a Heart Talk, sharing with one another your experience.

The more often you practice Renewing Your Love, the more likely you are to sustain a long-lasting intimate relationship. Each time you look at each other's faces, all those powerful, loving, happy moments will be triggered. During the day all you'll have to do is to make significant eye contact to tap into your joy and love. We highly recommend Renewing Your Love before lovemaking and before you do your Heart Talk exercises. This is among the most powerful exercises that lifemates can practice. Take the time!

Family Heart Talks

The following case demonstrates how Heart Talks can help families. Ron, an engineer, was thirty-six years old when he married Alexis, whom he had met through her work as an interior designer. After the honeymoon, Ron and Alexis moved in together along with Alexis's ten- and sixteen-year-old sons from a previous marriage. Yet within six months after the wedding, their "happy family" was in serious trouble.

Ron described the problem:

"I wanted to marry Alexis. That part was easy. Unfortunately, the kids came with the package. From the beginning they did everything in their power to make life difficult for me. It may have been competition for Alexis's attention, or a way to stay loyal to their father, or perhaps they just didn't like me. In any case, after working five, sometimes six days a week, I wanted to relax quietly at home. I like to watch football on Sundays, but when her sons had their friends over, it was so noisy I could barely hear the TV. To make matters worse, when I laid down the law, those brats would run crying to their mother. No matter whether they were right or wrong, she defended them. She said I was a bigger baby than the kids and accused me of harboring bad feelings toward them. Damn right I did. Those little monsters were driving me crazy, and they knew exactly what they were up to." Ron further lamented, "For years I avoided marriage and starting a family because I couldn't imagine being a parent. When I wound up with the role of 'Dad' for Alexis's kids, it was worse than I had ever imagined it could be."

Ron was a self-critical, highly disciplined individual. He believed that "when you say something once and kids don't listen, start yelling." So, when he didn't gain immediate cooperation from his stepsons, Ron got angry and hostile to "show them who's boss."

We explained to Ron that running a family is somewhat like running a business. If the principals don't meet regularly, chaos will ensue. Too often when they do meet, it's due to an "emergency" or conflict resulting from this lack of communication. To avoid such management by crisis, regular meetings are needed to focus on what the principals are doing right, review each person's and the family's needs, and prevent unnecessary problems.

At our suggestion, Ron began the first family meeting by describing the purpose of getting together. Addressing both children, Ron stated with affection, "We didn't ask to be thrown together. But because I loved your mother and you were her children, nature put us in the same lifeboat. It would have been smarter if we'd acknowledged that to each other in the beginning and then started to work together as a family. I'd like to hear your feelings about us having been thrown together." With support from Alexis and Ron saying "tell me more," the kids talked of their lingering pain after Alexis's divorce. They vented some of their anger at suddenly being "roommates" with Ron, and they expressed rage toward Ron's critical, perfectionist attitude—not one of kindness and permissiveness like their "real father."

To Ron's credit, he stayed open and receptive throughout. He told them he was committed to learning to love and accept them. Ron concluded the meeting by affirming, "Instead of making life miserable for one another, let's see how each of us can begin to make our family life more satisfying," and gave each child and Alexis a big hug.

To improve cooperation in subsequent family Heart Talks, we suggested an additional exercise. Everyone has preferences about how others should request cooperation. In this exercise, each family member is asked to describe the words and actions that make him or her want to cooperate and those that make him or her more likely to rebel. For instance, Ron began by saying, "I feel like cooperating when Alexis or either of the boys asks me in a pleasant voice and waits to hear if I have any objections. I feel like rebelling when anyone starts by blaming me for something and makes me feel like I've done something wrong."

Alexis's older son shared the following: "Ron, I feel exactly the same as you do—I'll be cooperative if I don't think you're laying a power trip on me. I rebel when you act bossy and growl at me; I get scared and think you just hate me."

At that family Heart Talk, Ron declared that he was going to work on being more affectionate and less quick-tempered with the boys. He also requested that they tell him directly whenever they were upset with his actions, rather than complaining behind his back to Alexis. The meeting ended on a positive note, with an exchange of hugs.

Ron saw that when he gently but firmly explained his needs and preferences, the boys understood and cooperated. He discovered it actually took less effort than yelling! Ron described the change in his behavior as a result: "I don't need to blow up and cause the kids to be rebellious and defiant. Instead of playing the tough guy all the time, I'm starting to connect with them in a way that Alexis can support."

At the next meeting, Ron, Alexis, and their two sons made a list of chores and responsibilities each was willing to undertake. From then on, each weekly family Heart Talk included discussion of "The agreements I kept this week are . . ."; "The agreements I broke this week are . . ."; and "The changes I'm making so that I can keep all my agreements next week are. . . ."

At the beginning of each family Heart Talk, they went around the circle sharing two things they had appreciated about each family member during the past week. This helped maintain an atmosphere of love and support. Though conflicts arose occasionally, the level of trust and affection grew. Ron became skillful at catching the kids doing something—even approximately —right, and praising them for it.

It's easy for a parent to blame an adolescent for breakdowns in communication. A teenager's increasing demands and defiant attitudes can disrupt family life. They present a challenge to any adult, especially a stepparent, to listen openly, without judgment, and say, "Tell me more."

Weekly family Heart Talks are a way in which parents and children (as young as five years old) can share feelings on equal footing. These meetings generate a profound and heartfelt experience of family.

"I Love You, And . . ."

One final principle regarding Heart Talks is essential. Certain words and phrases inadvertently cause negative results. When you say to your loved one, "I love you, but . . . ," you actually make a coercive statement which implies, "I won't love you unless you agree to do what I say." On the other hand, if you say, "I love you, *and* I'd prefer if you would . . . ," you communicate your unconditional love, along with a request for him or her to acknowledge your needs and preferences.

Let us consider in more depth the ever-present three-letter word "but." Used automatically, particularly in intimate relationships, this little word "but" can be deceptively destructive. When you are communicating "I love you, but . . . ," you are invalidating your love. Similarly, if you say to your lifemate, "That is true, but . . . ," what you are really implying is that his or her experience or feelings are not true, or else irrelevant. The word "but" has negated everything your lover has said.

Just think how you feel if your lover says to you that he or she "agrees with you, but" or that he or she "loves you, but." When you simply substitute the word "and" instead, it creates a whole different experience of heart-to-heart communication. For example, if you say, "That is true *and* let me share with you my experience of what took place," or, "That is valuable feedback, *and* here is how I experience the same situation." The word "but" creates disagreement and resistance, the word "and" introduces agreement and creates intimate communication.

Of course, it is not just what you say, but how you say it. You can set limits with your lifemate when you maintain an attitude of love and sensitivity to his or her needs. When you are defensive, critical, or judgmental, no amount of discussion, no amount of "and" versus "but" will result in a solution both you and your lover can enjoy. In other words, our recommendations here are not just a matter of form: You must take to heart the fundamental difference in telling your lover, "I love you, *and* . . ." as opposed to "I love you, *but* . . . !"

Just as "I love you, but" causes negative results, so does "but, I love you." The commonly heard protest, "but, I love you" signals that you might feel great love and express it vehemently and yet to your great frustration you are not believed. Most of us tend to love another the way we wish to be loved ourselves. A key to becoming lifemates is to stop insisting "but, I love you" and start discovering how your love partner experiences being loved.

For many of us, it is not just the words "I love you," but specific actions that communicate love. For example, a husband may say, "I love you, sweetheart" and she responds, "No, you don't! If you did you would still look at me and touch me lovingly the way you did when we were dating. You don't bring me little surprises or take me on romantic trips anymore." For the husband to feel hurt and protest "but, I do love you" is to miss the communication. In his preoccupation with business, he has forgotten to touch his wife in the special ways that make her feel most loved. Instead of protesting, the husband would benefit much more by every few months creating a special "I love you day" for his wife. That could include her favorite flowers, a love poem, a romantic dinner, an overnight stay at a bed-and-breakfast inn, a full body massage and, once again, looking into her eyes in that special way. Such intimacy is what his wife needs to reexperience his love and what he needs to feel acknowledged.

Knowing how to make your lifemate feel completely loved is a crucial Love Fitness skill. Sit down and have a Heart Talk: "How do you experience being loved? How do you like to be touched, spoken to, looked at, and shown that your lifemate loves you?" Be very specific. This Heart Talk is a powerful means to rediscover the similarities and differences between how each of you needs to be loved.

Particularly in your Heart Talks, if you can learn to use the following four phrases, you may well experience improvement in your relationship as powerful as that which follows from "Tell Me More." Here are the four phrases:

- I love you, and . . .
- I appreciate you, and . . .
- I agree with you, and . . .
- I respect your point of view, and . . .

When you use the above four phrases, you are first of all building love, appreciation, respect, and agreement with your love partner. You are validating his or her point of view. You are building rapport and acknowledging communication rather than ignoring and denigrating what he or she has to say. Further, you are creating a bond by which you and your lifemate can accept difficult situations and acknowledge that you may have differing points of view. These four phrases will help you avoid unnecessary conflict, communicate clearly, and enjoy greater intimacy.

Chapter 4

Heart-to-Heart, Passionate Sex

KEVIN: I've been fantasizing about making love with you all day. [*But I'm not aroused now . . . in fact, I hope I can perform.*]

ANNA: Me too. I want you so much. [*Not really; I had a stressful, exhausting day at work.*]

KEVIN: Let's get under the covers. [*If I'm standing nude she'll see how flabby I'm getting.*]

ANNA: Okay. [*Why doesn't he ever undress me slowly?*]

KEVIN: I'll turn the lights down. [*Oh, oh. I should have created a more romantic, intimate setting, candles, soft music, massage oils; but it's too late and I'm tired.*]

ANNA: Great. [*I'd better look eager or he'll feel crushed. Why does he always have to be in such a rush? He hasn't even kissed or hugged me.*]

KEVIN: I'd really like you to give me oral sex. [*It's okay to be selfish about your needs; that's what all the sex books say.*]

ANNA: Sure. [*I'll just get this over with and go to sleep—he'll never change. I'll fantasize about someone who would make love to me seductively.*]

KEVIN: M-mm. That's good. [*I should have just gone to sleep. If this doesn't give me an erection nothing will.*] You really turn me on. [*Thank goodness I'm hard. I suppose I should pleasure her too, but I really don't feel like it.*]

ANNA: [*This is getting tedious. Am I erotic and wild enough? I'd like a little attention myself, but it feels like he's about to come already.*]

KEVIN: C'mon up and let's make love. [*I better screw her before I come.*]

ANNA: [*I hope I get excited quickly. I wonder if those Kegel vaginal tightening exercises have made a difference—he probably won't notice —he didn't even mention it when I colored my hair.*]

KEVIN: You're outrageous. [*I should count sheep and focus on my checking account. It's too early to come now.*]

ANNA: So are you. [*What's happened to his hard-on? Damn. I better pretend nothing's wrong.*]

KEVIN: Sweetheart, you're the best. [*I hope she doesn't think I'm a premature ejaculator. My penis is already shrinking, I've got to make her come right now.*]

ANNA: [*Sighs, moans, shudders.] [I'll fake it and not hurt his feelings.*]

KEVIN: Did you?

ANNA: Oh God, yes. That was incredible. Couldn't you feel it? [*He never knows how to satisfy me . . . but I don't want him to think I'm inorgasmic.*]

KEVIN: Oh yes. Was that a multiple?

ANNA: I was so gone, I couldn't really count.

KEVIN: Next time it'll be even wilder; I've got these great positions . . . how come you're so quiet?

ANNA: I just feel so intimate and close to you. [*What a fiasco.*]

KEVIN: Me too. [*He falls asleep.*]

There has been so much written about sex over the past two decades that most couples, like our fictional Kevin and Anna, are familiar with a myriad of ways to pleasure one another and genuinely want to create mutually satisfying sexual experiences. Unfortunately, the liberal attitudes toward sexual practices can be terribly misleading. The key to lasting, passionate sex lies not in mastering a variety of techniques or straining to satisfy your partner but rather in discovering the intensity of emotional contact without pretense, fear, or limitations.

If sex remains superficial or loses intensity, the problem for most couples is fear of letting themselves be known deeply and without reservation as loving, sexual beings. Sex is associated with primordial feelings of self-worth, potency, creativity, and self-confidence as well as shame and guilt. Sexual desire stems from deep within the psyche and tends to ebb and flow for reasons and at times beyond personal control. No wonder that sex is the cause for so much anxiety and joy. On the one hand, to lack sexual desire when your lover seems to want sex is frustrating and, for many, deeply humiliating. On the other hand, there are few human experiences more magical and more fulfilling than being in perfect tune sexually with your lover. At the outset of most love relationships, sex is usually terrific. The natural, initial sexual attunement makes it all the more disappointing to fall out of sexual balance without knowing why and with no guidance on how to recover that state of sexual grace.

In this chapter, we explain how applying certain Love Fitness principles can help you create a more fulfilling sexual relationship than ever before. We also discuss how to revitalize a sexual relationship that has gone stale. Our focus is not on techniques (there are enough sex manuals for that) but on imbuing sex with the magic of heart-to-heart communication. While we present specific Love Fitness workouts to facilitate intense communication of feeling before, during, and after sex, these exercises must be understood in the context of the Love Fitness program. Sexual malaise in a relationship is often a symptom of other problems such as unexpressed anger, accumulated resentments, or merely taking one another for granted. Working through insecurities and vulnerabilities with heart-to-heart communication is the only means to create a lasting, passionate sexual relationship.

Beyond Sexual Boredom and Fear

First and foremost, sex establishes a bonding that helps to ensure the biological survival of the species. Nature has assured that sex between new lovers almost always has a quality of urgency and excitement. Of course, there is an indefinable element of sexual chemistry that can make sex fantastic or, if it is missing, leave sex disappointing no matter how hard a couple may try. Given the chemistry, simple biology causes new lovers to be almost always in the mood. Mutual attraction stirs such intense sexual desire automatically that new lovers tend to believe they have discovered an inexhaustible wellspring of sexual passion.

For most couples, however, the bloom eventually fades from the rose. Whether over a period of months or years, sexual passion diminishes and a strong tendency toward sexual boredom develops. This ebbing of sexual passion can be particularly disturbing because almost every new couple is prone to believe their passion is so strong that it will always last. Young couples will often assert, "It will never happen to us." Only after they begin to face the stresses of work, children, the ever ringing telephone, financial concerns, and the many pressures of family life does a rude awakening occur. Sex gets postponed; sexual desire diminishes under stress; and sexual performance anxiety is prone to rise.

The loss of sexual passion in a relationship causes particular anxiety today because so many people have been sexually active before settling down in a committed relationship. With women and men free to experiment with multiple partners, the highs of premarital sex can be easily savored and the lows just as easily rationalized. Equally important, sex outside a committed relationship carries with it an aura of suspense and titillation. Discovering a new person is almost always exciting and a little "naughty." This dependency on variety to stimulate passion can become an addiction, particularly for men. Correspondingly, the limitations of a monogamous relationship can generate "withdrawal symptoms" of anxiety and depression.

A committed sexual relationship presents every couple with a challenge and an opportunity. On the one hand, there are daily responsibilities and psychological forces at work to diminish sexual passion and encourage boredom. On the other hand, the security of mutual commitment makes possible the discovery of a limitless new dimension of personal self-disclosure to stimulate sexual passion. In the beginning of a relationship, couples excite one another primarily by revealing and sharing their bodies. In a maturing sexual relationship between lifemates, couples can discover an even greater source of sexual excitement by revealing their emotional selves and communicating heart-to-heart in sexual play.

Once again, the problem is that most people grew up internalizing emotional barriers to such heart-to-heart communication. Boys are encouraged to be strong ("take it like a man"), unemotional ("don't cry"), and tough ("don't let anyone push you around"). Girls are caught in a double standard—they should be charming and attractive (virginal), but not overtly manipulative or seductive (a tease). As children grow older, these biased and unrealistic standards result in the inability to acknowledge the wide range of feelings associated with sex and to communicate deep sexual needs and desires.

This behavioral patterning in childhood results in a multiplicity of fears associated with sexual self-disclosure. Men fear that exposing their sensitive, vulnerable sides will render them powerless to women who might perceive them as weak-willed wimps. Women who are in a position of physical and emotional surrender contend with fears of being used and abandoned or, at the very least, feeling rushed through sex and left unsatisfied. Men struggle with performance anxieties and, in some cases, fear of impotence, as natural hormonal responses slow and it takes longer to become aroused. Women face an equally anxiety-laden sexual concern—asking for what they need. Having been taught to attract men without going too far, women are trained to stifle their deepest sexual needs.

These fears explain in large measure why so many people feel empty and frustrated after a sexual encounter, even with a spouse. Under extreme personal or job-related stress, many men create additional pressure upon themselves by maintaining a profile of invincibility to their lovers. Hence, a wife or girlfriend may be innocently enjoying this show of passion, which the man actually perceives as a superhuman effort to "service" her out of duty. For women, some emotional bonding is necessary for arousal. When a man looks upon sex as nothing more than a physically stimulating workout, a woman who expects an exchange of intimacy or assurance of commitment is left feeling used and abandoned.

Performance anxiety is a major source of resentment for men and women in committed relationships. Men want to validate their sexuality by creating a positive sexual experience for their lovers. They tend to resent the fact that they have no way to fake arousal or avoid the obligation to perform. Women, in contrast, tend to resent the fact that most men can have an orgasm so early—in some cases, too early. Men resent women who don't take the initiative, or expect a man to be a mind reader, instead of asking for what they need. Women resent men who rush intercourse without long seduction. Women resent lovers who appear to be emotionally uninvolved before, during, and after sex.

Another reason for sexual dissatisfaction among women is the inability to express secret fantasies and erotic desires. This problem is the result of two conflicting factors: parental and religious upbringing to be sweet and innocent, and encouragement from peers and fashion to appear seductive and be sexually free. Thus, a woman may be in conflict about expressing normal healthy sexual desires for fear of being branded as uptight or a slut.

In a fit-for-love relationship, sexual excitement and pleasure are not based upon any standard of performance but develop from emotional intensity and the ability to recreate passion. Skillful couples create great freedom by establishing a bond of trust that alleviates the pressure and fear of judgment, rejection, imperfection, and performance. Being together in a fully present, intimate way opens the channel of communication to allow for full disclosure of emotions, desires, fears, and fantasies.

Sex can be a routine act of fulfilling desire, in which case boredom is inevitable, or it can be a window of discovery to yourself and your lover with a depth of passion to last a lifetime. It is only by trusting your lover with your most intimate feelings and slowing down to savor your natural rhythm that sex will remain an adventure.

How Satisfied Are You with Your Sexual Intimacy?

Here is an exercise that can help you assess your own concerns about self-disclosure during sex and help you begin talking about these issues with your lifemate. Answer each question with a yes or a no. There are no right answers, only feelings that serve you most through honest expression.

1. I worry about sexually pleasing my lover.   Yes__No__
2. I sometimes wonder if my love partner is really that sexually turned on to me.   Yes__No__
3. I have difficulty "letting go" and experiencing intimate sexual pleasure.   Yes__No__

4. I feel blamed by my lover for any sexual problem that we have. Yes__No__

5. I am likely to blame my lover for our sexual difficulties. Yes__No__

6. I am irritated when my lover is reluctant to have sex with me. Yes__No__

7. I get frustrated trying to seduce or turn my lover on. Yes__No__

8. When it comes to sex, I sometimes feel my lover just wants to "get right to it" and doesn't enjoy cuddling or getting me aroused. Yes__No__

9. I am afraid of losing my desire and passion in the midst of our sexual play. Yes__No__

10. It seems as if we find many distractions to avoid enjoying each other sexually. Yes__No__

11. I am afraid of my lover's reaction when I refuse to have sex. Yes__No__

12. Sometimes, "out of duty," I submit to sex and then later resent my lover for it. Yes__No__

13. I don't like to respond sexually when my spouse pressures me; the more the demands, the more I turn off. Yes__No__

14. I sometimes feel my mate withholds sex to control, manipulate, or punish me. Yes__No__

15. I sometimes feel so angry that I don't want to be sexually intimate. Yes__No__

16. I turn off sexually when my love partner doesn't show enough sensitivity, care, and tenderness. Yes__No__

17. I sometimes feel depressed, angry, or alone following sex. Yes__No__

18. Although I would like to experiment with new and different techniques for sexual play, my love partner is unwilling to try them. Yes__No__

19. I feel that we do not set aside enough quality time for intimacy and spontaneous sex.   Yes__No__

20. It seems the only time we intimately touch is when we have sex.   Yes__No__

21. I am not comfortable touching my genitals and pleasuring myself when I am having sex with you.   Yes__No__

22. We tend to repeat a sexual routine with regard to foreplay, positions, and time of day.   Yes__No__

23. During sex my mind strays from you into private thoughts and fantasies.   Yes__No__

24. Sex has become more of a pleasant pastime as opposed to something passionate and exciting.   Yes__No__

25. I am sometimes troubled by the memory of a negative or painful sexual experience.   Yes__No__

26. Sex seems like a victory for my mate, but a yielding, submitting, or surrendering experience for me.   Yes__No__

27. I have sexual fantasies that I'm too embarrassed to share.   Yes__No__

28. I am unsure about the effectiveness of our method of birth control and often worry about getting pregnant.   Yes__No__

Tally the checks in both the yes and the no columns. A greater number of yes responses indicates increasing dissatisfaction with your sexual intimacy. The issue here is not achieving a specific score to measure a particular level of sexual love fitness; rather, this quiz is intended to help you and your lover explore those beliefs, attitudes, and habits you "bring to bed with you" that limit sexual intimacy.

When reviewing answers with your lover, remember each of you is 100 percent responsible for your own sexual satisfaction. The more open, honest, and specific you are, the more receptive you will be to learning about each other's sexuality while discovering greater intimacy. Now review each response while considering the following:

1. What I need to let you know about my sexual needs is:
2. You could excite me sexually by:
3. I would feel less pressured if:
4. You could assist me by:
5. I could assist you by:
6. Some things I specifically want to do to expand our sexual intimacy are:

Remember, when it comes to feelings, no one is wrong. This Love Fitness principle is especially important when it comes to sex.

Issues in Your Sexual Relationship

Here is another quiz that can help you learn more about your own sexual concerns and desires, as well as those of your lifemate. You may find that more than one choice applies to each question. Remember, the issue is not a "right answer" but rather taking the time to speak intimately and openly about your mutual sexual needs and preferences.

1. What you could do to add intimacy to our sexual relations is
    a. Be more spontaneous, playful, and creative instead of practical, unemotional, and realistic.
    b. Ask what would give me great sexual pleasure.
    c. Express your deepest fantasies and turn-ons.
2. Some of the ways we could be more physically intimate without intercourse are
    a. Gentle stroking—hair, forehead, thighs, etc.

  b. Deep massages—back, legs, feet, etc.
  c. Kisses everywhere and anywhere.
3. Communicating how much I love you during sex with words, eye contact, and genuine feeling is
  a. Difficult, uncomfortable.
  b. Something I want to work on.
  c. Quite easy and enjoyable.
4. Troubles I sometimes have with my sexual self-confidence include a feeling that
  a. I can't believe I am really that special to you.
  b. I am afraid you'll abandon or reject me if I expect too much from you sexually or romantically.
  c. I need you to take the risk and be intimate first; I prefer to respond rather than initiate.
5. If I am not affectionate or giving in our sexual relationship it is because
  a. I am angry, blocked.
  b. I am preoccupied with thoughts from the day.
  c. I am tired, exhausted, not "present."
6. When I undress in front of you I
  a. Frown and feel upset with the way I look and get under the covers as fast as I can.
  b. Look with scorn at my profile and make sarcastic comments about my inadequacies.
  c. Enjoy being nude.
7. Some ways I prefer to make love are
  a. In the dark, where we always do.
  b. In unique places, indoors and outdoors.
  c. At certain periods of the day—morning, afternoon, or evening.
8. Sharing my most intimate desires and fantasies with you is
  a. Difficult, uncomfortable, impossible.
  b. Okay, except for my most secret erotic fantasies.
  c. Easy and enjoyable.

9. Your sharing secret sexual fantasies with me is
    a. Highly pleasurable, erotic.
    b. Okay, except for fantasies that are threatening to me.
    c. Unacceptable, difficult.

10. The way I sometimes take sexual responsibility for you is by
    a. Faking an orgasm.
    b. Trying to give you an orgasm.
    c. Worrying about how satisfied you are with my performance.

11. When it comes to romance in our intimate sex lives
    a. It seems we have more important things to do than think about romance.
    b. We have a romantic side that we turn on when we "get away."
    c. Who needs romance?

12. When I feel your discomfort at being sexually intimate with me you
    a. Tune me out and engage in sex mechanically.
    b. Create an argument.
    c. Complain of fatigue and exhaustion.

13. Intercourse with you is
    a. Passionate, romantic, and loving.
    b. Spontaneous, creative.
    c. Boring, routine.

14. Having you stimulate me orally to orgasm is
    a. Uncomfortable, difficult.
    b. A turn-off, repulsive.
    c. Exciting and highly pleasurable.

15. Orally stimulating you to orgasm is
    a. A turn-off, repulsive.
    b. Acceptable only as foreplay.
    c. Erotic and highly exciting.

16. When we're making love and you say, "A little slower, please," or "Ouch, please be careful there," I feel
    a. Criticized as a lover—"I can't win with you, can I?"

    b. That I must instantly stop and apologize.

    c. Glad that you trust me enough to be outspoken.

17. Using a vibrator as part of sex play and to achieve orgasm is
    a. Erotic and exciting.
    b. A crutch and wrong.
    c. Unnatural, repulsive.

18. For you or me to have fantasies while making love
    a. Is erotic and exciting.
    b. Is okay on occasion.
    c. Indicates something is wrong.

19. Your being open enough to masturbate in front of me
    a. Is enjoyable, erotic.
    b. Is okay only as part of lovemaking.
    c. Is a turn-off, disgusting.

20. The thought of masturbating in front of you is
    a. Exciting, erotic.
    b. Unacceptable except as part of lovemaking.
    c. Very difficult, a turn-off.

21. During intercourse you and I
    a. Intimately flow back and forth between each other's feelings.
    b. Are each in our own feelings and thoughts.
    c. Are automatic and engaged in a routine.

22. When we make love, I have an orgasm
    a. Often and easily.
    b. Sometimes, with difficulty.
    c. Orgasm, what's that?

23. When it comes to orgasm
    a. Simultaneous orgasm is to be strived for.
    b. Multiple orgasm is to be strived for.
    c. I am not goal oriented and can simply enjoy whatever is happening.

24. I think you would be disapproving of me or disappointed if I
    a. Didn't have an erection or get aroused.
    b. Didn't reach orgasm.

    c. Didn't say yes to all your sexual advances and desires.

25. Sometimes when we are sexually intimate for "too long" I feel an urge to
    a. Pull back from you by making jokes or changing the subject.
    b. Escape by turning the TV on or making something to eat.
    c. Withdraw into fantasies and private thoughts.

26. When you have an orgasm
    a. I always know it.
    b. I want my partner to verbalize what is happening.
    c. I never know it.

27. For men only: Having and maintaining an erection
    a. Sometimes causes me anxiety.
    b. Is easy, relaxed, something I don't think about.
    c. Is a constant fear in the back of my mind.

28. For women only: When you have difficulty achieving or maintaining an erection
    a. I pretend that it's all right, while wondering what I've done wrong.
    b. I get angry and feel cheated.
    c. I don't feel responsible, but I am supportive.

Just as in the first quiz, take time to share with your lover what you learned about your sexual experience. Were certain issues difficult for you? Which fears, expectations, and difficulties regarding sexual intimacy were more pronounced? What in your lover's responses surprised you? What in your own responses were a surprise to your lover? Use this questionnaire as a tool for further discussion about your sexual intimacy.

Sexual Heart Talks

Sustained passion in a sexual relationship depends on discovering the excitement of vulnerability. When

John came for a consultation he was troubled by sexual guilt; so much so that sex with his wife had become a source of major anxiety. "I love Karen dearly," John explained in our office. "She's intelligent, support-ive, and beautiful. We don't fight very often but when we do, we make up without holding grudges. All that's great, except there's this major problem. I can't be passionate with her. When I am, I feel terrible, really rotten; I can't explain it."

The source of John's guilt became evident when he re-vealed numerous sexual encounters in his past. "I dated a lot of girls who were fun to take out but not the marry-ing kind," he admitted. Now, due to rigid sexual up-bringing, John was subconsciously acting out the belief that you can't have wild, erotic sex with a woman without losing respect for her. John viewed Karen as the mother of their child, and felt enormous guilt over sexual fan-tasies that he had fulfilled with other women in the past.

During their courtship they had been much more intimate with one another, and had had a genuinely fun and exciting sex life. After six years of marriage, however, each had become disenchanted with their lack of sexual desire. When Karen relaxed enough to open up, she revealed, "I can't act out my sexual fantasies. I've become afraid of my own passion. Every evening is the same. We eat, clean up the house, play with our daughter, and put her to bed. When we finally get to bed, we're exhausted. I'm bored and in a rut."

Sex can be a barometer of intimacy in a long-term relationship. When sex goes flat and remains boring, often the relationship is on its way to trouble. For-tunately, it was not too late for John and Karen. Rather than blaming one another or their upbringing, we asked them to practice sexual Heart Talks (see Chapter 3 for guidelines and instructions).

With some anxiety but a lot of enthusiasm, they took turns nightly with one or two of the following sexual Heart Talks. They were careful to not interrupt, to give their undivided attention, and to be specific, open and honest.

1. When I fear that I will not perform sexually to your satisfaction, I . . .
2. The best thing about our sex life is . . .
3. My father gave me the impression that sex was . . .
4. My mother gave me the impression that sex was . . .
5. Sexual thoughts I feel guilty about are . . .
6. What I find sexually attractive about you is . . .
7. What I would like to add to our sexual and physical intimacy is . . .
8. When I would like to be sexually romantic and you don't respond I . . .
9. I feel like withdrawing from sex when . . .
10. I turn on to you most when . . .
11. Three sexual fears I have are . . .
12. I feel sexually frustrated when . . .
13. It would be easier to express my sexual desires if . . .
14. If I told you what I sexually desire and would enjoy most, the way I think you would respond is . . .
15. A sexual secret I am afraid to share with you is . . .
16. I think our experience of sexual pleasure is . . .
17. A sexual delight I would like to indulge with you is . . .
18. A sexual fantasy I would like to act out with you is . . .
19. We would improve our experience of oral sex by . . .
20. The way I would like to be touched is . . .

As we suggested to John and Karen, you and your lifemate could also consider the following additional questions:

1. What underlies the fear of expressing your thoughts? What are you afraid might result?
2. How do these secrets and hidden feelings reduce your ability to love yourself?

3. What do you hope to gain by hiding or withholding this fear?
4. What is the cost to the relationship of not communicating whatever it is you are afraid to share?
5. How does it affect your self-image?
6. What is the worst that you imagine your partner might think, feel, or do if you revealed yourself?
7. What is the best that you imagine your partner might think, feel, or do if you revealed yourself?

Like many couples, John and Karen had become so centered on sexual lovemaking that they neglected other aspects of physical intimacy. We reminded them of another Heart Talk that, though nonverbal, is crucial to well-being. We each need two hugs a day to survive, four hugs a day for proper maintenance, and six to really thrive. In addition to emotional sharing, Love Fitness entails regular physical embracing with your intimate partner. This heart-to-heart contact is often more intimate and fulfilling than trying to rush to a quick orgasm.

Sharing X-Rated Fantasies: Overcoming Guilt

Another valuable exercise for enhancing sexual communication is to explore fantasies with your lover. We suggested that John and Karen write in detail one sexual fantasy that each had been afraid to share. The fantasy didn't have to involve each other, but after writing it down, we instructed them to insert each other's names as participants. This was crucial for John because he felt too much guilt to fantasize about Karen. Each came up with exciting scenes. Here is John's:

I imagine taking Karen out to the woods on a picnic with our favorite wine and foods. After a great meal, we lie in the sun and slowly take off one another's clothes. We kiss and caress for a long while, each growing aroused. Karen begins kissing my belly, then works her way down to my erect organ. She tongues and blows gently, before taking me fully into her mouth. Sensing I am on the edge of intense release, Karen quickens the pace—licking and massaging until I lose control and surrender completely to her command.

Karen's fantasy was more elaborate:

One afternoon while I'm at the office, John calls to ask me out on a date. After assuring me of the seriousness of his offer, I accept and agree to meet him later at the French bistro where he proposed to me. Intrigued, I leave for home early, giving myself time for a long soak in the tub. After slipping into the blue silk dress he loves, I spritz on some perfume, don my highest heels, and drive out to the restaurant.

John is waiting for me at "our table" decorated with candles and, surprise! A vase of gardenias that he'd ordered. When I ask him what the occasion is, he just smiles and says mysteriously, "We're celebrating you!"

After champagne and dinner, we return home and John leads me upstairs to our bedroom. John says to me, "You look so beautiful tonight, Karen. I want to spend the rest of this evening showing you just how much I love you." Taking me in his arms, we exchange slow, deliberate kisses; flushed with the heat of passion. Then John pulls away the silken sheath to fully reveal my naked body. I lay upon the bed while he undresses, telling him how much I desire his touch. John asks me to close my eyes and soon I again smell the fragrance of flowers. My body is taut with anticipation, and suddenly I experience the delight of gardenia blossoms being drawn playfully across my breasts. I laugh with happiness and reach up to embrace John, filled with an intensity of longing that demands release.

Feeling the full contact of our bodies, John kisses me tenderly as he slowly penetrates my being. I wrap my arms around his waist and whisper words of desire, as we fall into a natural rhythm of thrusting and retreating.

We are in absolute harmony, sharing deep, loving kisses as the passion rises within us. Suddenly, John's fingers slip through mine, and we allow the overwhelming pleasure to bring us to ultimate unity. Our bodies still pulse with energy as we surrender to the sweetness of the moment—needing no words, no promises, only the knowing that our love has forged a bond even stronger than we had before.

At first, the thought of reading each other's sexual fantasies generated some anxiety. Karen, however, convinced John she was excited to learn how to please him. She also volunteered to read her fantasy first. "Why didn't you tell me this before?" John asked, flushed with passion and excitement, which surprised her.

They chose a Friday evening to "experiment." John played some light jazz on the stereo, while they prepared and enjoyed a gourmet meal. Afterward, they climbed the stairs to their bedroom. As John lay on the bed watching her, Karen indulged in another fantasy. She danced erotically and uninhibitedly—John was amazed at seeing this new side of her. Then she undressed seductively, caressing her breasts, teasing herself and John into a state of high sexual excitement. "When I saw him getting aroused," she says, "I felt a release inside, and lay down on the floor. His hands traced the outline of my body as he probed my clitoris with his tongue. John started fondling himself too, and that got me doubly excited. He finally moaned with pleasure and that pushed me over the edge. I screamed, 'I'm coming!' And I had the wildest orgasm of my life."

John later explained, "The next afternoon while our daughter was out playing with neighbors, we shared some more intimate Heart Talks and then made love for hours."

The experience of sharing sexual fantasies with each other had a profoundly liberating effect on John and Karen. They began to explore other fantasies, one where Karen was the innocent virgin turned into a sex slave, another where she was his master. Soon John and Karen were enjoying a new freedom and desire in their sex life. No matter how committed one is to a lifemate, monogamy of the mind is not only difficult, it is probably impossible. Fantasy is a powerful stimulus to sensual pleasure.

Sexual fantasy can also be very helpful in reducing anxiety and nurturing arousal. It can also help dispel boredom and monotony. You and your mate can use it as a stepping-stone to exploring sexual adventures that can enhance your love life. Finally, sexual fantasy can be used to develop communication and trust. By sharing your fantasies with your lover, you can mutually disinhibit each other. You can create a warm, safe environment where any anxieties that may surface dissolve in love and pleasure.

Many people are troubled by guilt feelings caused by sexual fantasies. It is quite natural, however, for men and women to have fantasies, and often outrageous ones at that. By any criteria or classification, quite normal people have reported fantasies of group sex, homosexuality, lesbianism, extramarital affairs with known or unknown people, fetishes, incest, sadomasochism, etc. In all of these examples, the fantasies may have been recurring but not exclusive or constant. The only harm was needless guilt, fear, or worry. Sexual fantasies are just that; they require neither action nor guilt.

One caution: It is important to create an intimate and trusting atmosphere for sharing sexual fantasies. Disclosing your fantasies without warning, to arouse jealousy or hostility, can bring devastating results. So, keep in mind that sexual fantasies are normal, but you must agree to follow the Heart Talk guidelines while sharing them. Also, remember that when experimenting with erotic fantasy, no matter what its twists (for example, making love to a stranger or movie star), the exquisite joy lies in discovering your own and your lover's passion. Let your fantasy life bring you closer to your lover.

Can Love and Passion Last?

Kirk is a thirty-one-year-old engineer and Vicky is a twenty-eight-year-old schoolteacher. They were married seven years ago and have two children. Now that the children are in nursery school and kindergarten, Vicky has gone back to work part-time. From the outside it appears they have an ideal relationship, with jobs they enjoy, children they love, and a bright future. They don't talk their problems over with friends, but in the bedroom, arguments prevail. "When I come on to her at night, she isn't interested," Kirk complains. "I don't know what the problem is or what she expects, but holding back isn't going to solve anything. I'm at the point where it's not worth it anymore. I'd just as soon forget the whole thing. It seems we're arguing constantly."

Vicky says, "If only Kirk could see himself! It's always the same routine. He kisses me and caresses my breasts. Then he kisses my nipples awhile, and a little oral sex. Before he gets too excited he penetrates me. He usually comes in five minutes or so; sometimes I climax, mostly I don't. It's boring, the passion is gone. It's like watching the same movie over and over."

Boredom is the principal problem in long-term sexual relationships. "There's no adventure in our lives," Kirk laments. "Every evening is the same. I come home from work exhausted. While Vicky puts the dinner on the table, I have a few minutes with the kids. We eat, I help clean up, and we put the kids to bed. Then I may have two or three hours of work to finish. When I come to bed, Vicky is usually asleep. If I wake her, she's irritated with me, and very rarely responds to sexual overtures. We're in a rut, but I don't know how to get out of it. I wonder if our sex life will ever be passionate again."

Vicky has her own complaints. "Kirk comes to bed at 1:00 A.M. and expects me to be ready and waiting for him. He hasn't paid any attention to me all day, isn't sensitive to the fact that I have to get up before he does to serve breakfast before we all leave the house. He doesn't spend time with me on weekends, either. If he doesn't have chores around the house, he has work he's brought home or there's some damn sports event he has to watch. Tell me why I'm supposed to be waiting for him, all steamy and wet like some whore in a movie? That's what it's like. Sex with hardly a word between us. I think he has lost all real interest in me."

Kirk and Vicky are not alone. Millions of young couples are faced with a similar problem. Sociologists have cataloged ad infinitum the cultural forces (such as the corporation, the growth of suburbia, the isolation of the nuclear family) that put pressure on marriage. The solution to Kirk and Vicky's problem lies in discovering how they are asphyxiating the magic in their relationship and how they can revitalize their sex lives.

When Kirk and Vicky came in for therapy, we said, "You both realize that you're still in love. The question is whether you are motivated to break your patterns now or go your separate ways." Fortunately, they came in early enough and were still optimistic about becoming lovers again. To help them regain the sexual pleasure and romance they enjoyed when they first met, we suggested the following exercises.

Sharing Acknowledgments Like most couples in conflict, Kirk and Vicky became tense, defensive, and emotionally withdrawn whenever they were together. They had trouble making eye contact. When they argued, neither listened. Both felt unappreciated. To help remind them of why they were together, we asked them to sit face to face, making eye contact as they exchanged acknowledgments with each other. This simple exercise has very few rules: The person speaking describes in one or two specific sentences what he or she appreciates about the person listening. The listener must accept the acknowledgments, say either "Thank you" or "I got it" after each statement, and repeat the communication as close to the original as possible without adding anything, dodging the compliment, or arguing the point.

This exercise was a radical departure from Kirk and Vicky's usual mode of communication, consisting of accusations, demands, threats, and counterthreats. While at first the tension between them seemed to build, it quickly peaked and then slowly melted away. A few minutes after Kirk began listing the things he appreciated about Vicky, her eyes filled with tears. Immediately Kirk also began to cry. Neither could deny the love that was underneath the struggle in their relationship.

Releasing the Flow of Love Another beneficial exercise was to make a list beginning with the statement, "The ways I've been blocking love in my life is . . ." This technique helps you stop blaming your partner and start seeing how you contribute to the relationship's failure or success. Since both partners were defensive and hostile, Kirk and Vicky each needed to learn how they had fallen into those patterns and how to break out of them. Revealing how you inhibit your pleasure, keep up your defenses, and prevent feelings of trust and intimacy can help you free yourself. By admitting honestly how you stand in the way of giving or receiving love, you no longer need to attack or blame your partner.

On her list, Vicky described, "The ways I've been blocking love in my life is"

- By blaming Kirk for the problems in our relationship
- By shutting off my feelings and withholding sex to punish him and gain power
- By making Kirk feel insecure, isolated, and angry

On his list, Kirk included:

- By getting angry and demanding sex
- By working too hard and then using sex to alleviate the stress more than to express my love

- By trying so hard to make Vicky have an orgasm that I stop feeling tender or listening to her feelings

Having an "A.F.F.A.I.R."
with Your Spouse

By acknowledging how each had been stifling their love, Kirk and Vicky created a small breakthrough. They felt a great release when recognizing that their sexual problems were not causes, but symptoms of other difficulties in their relationship. This expanded perspective helped them explore other aspects of the Love Fitness program to regain the spontaneous affection that first characterized their relationship. In order to help Vicky and Kirk overcome their sexual conflicts and renew enjoyment and sexual satisfaction, we suggested they have an A.F.F.A.I.R.:

A—Adventure
F—Fun
F—Fantasy
A—Affection
I—Intimacy
R—Romance

A: Adventure Kirk and Vicky realized that their relationship was filled with shoulds, oughts, and have tos, in which each took the other for granted. They decided to do everything they could to avoid getting locked in boring routines. As a result, they set up creative adventure days. At least once a month, Kirk or Vicky took turns being responsible for a day trip or weekend outing that proved to be a memorable adventure. One day, Kirk took Vicky on all of her favorite rides at a nearby amusement park. Another weekend Vicky took Kirk on an art tour to the museums and galleries he "never had time for." One Sunday Kirk encouraged Vicky to spend the morning lounging in bed while he brought her breakfast in bed and catered to her sexual desires.

1. Draw a *pleasure map* of your body and describe an adventure you would like to go to explore your lover. Indicate the spots where you will be exquisitely pleasured by long, slow loving strokes. There may be areas that you would like kissed or massaged with oil. Use your imagination and think of how delicious it would feel to have your body erotically pleasured in just the way you've dreamed.

2. You are driving along in the car and you suddenly get the urge to pull over onto a country road and make love. Tell your partner you have a surprise in store for him or her, and take the risk.

F: Fun Couples who play together, stay together. Marriage doesn't always have to be "grown-up." All work and no play makes any love relationship dull. You can often increase your energy for problem-solving, challenges, and responsibilities by taking time out for fun and play. The critical principle here is to do less and accomplish more. The couple who finds time to relax and play will also find the time to meet larger responsibilities with energy and vitality. Here are some fun suggestions:

1. Have a party in your bedroom. Cover the bed with rose petals or tie balloons on the bedpost. Wear something sexy, turn on the stereo, pour a glass of champagne to share before slipping into a bubble bath.

2. Create a theme for dinner: Make a Japanese setting on the living-room floor with two pillows facing each other, some incense, candles, chopsticks (cups of hot sake or tea, along with take-out sushi you picked up on the way home), and whatever else creates the mood. Slip into your favorite kimono and have one ready for your lover.

3. Have your love partner treat you like a young ingenue, innocent and uncertain of what to do. Say you've never done anything like this before, and that you feel nervous. Make it brand new. State the

rules, no intercourse, petting okay, etc. Dress for the part.

F: Fantasy Allow yourselves the freedom to act out a safe fantasy, giving your imagination and creativity free rein. Take turns or else create the fantasy together. Consider the following questions:

1. What kind of person would you/your lover be?
2. Describe the place, time, and situation you would find yourselves in.
3. What kind of life would you lead?
4. What would your character's sexual fantasy be?

This exercise is not only fun but very revealing. It allows lovers to explore their daydreams and fantasies while learning more about themselves and one another. You might consider indulging your fantasies for a few hours or the entire day, using costumes and props. You might choose to stay in role as fantasy lovers. Here is how some couples have used their imagination:

1. The two of you go back to the time you met and the first time(s) you made love.
2. You imagine playing the courtesan and the conqueror.
3. You have entered a palace of sexual pleasure with a personal slave at your beck and call.
4. You switch sex roles completely—role reversal dating and lovemaking.
5. You write down your most erotic fantasy and read it to your partner, or write out five fantasies, put them in a hat, and have your partner pick one to enact.

A: Affection The word "affection" comes from "affect." There is nothing more welcome when you're feeling down than a big hug from your lover. In every relationship there will be occasions when one lover needs more from the other and vice versa. Be sensitive to those times while responding with considerate, loving gestures. Love blossoms when deep feelings of affection are communicated. For example, write your partner a poem, give foot rubs, or wash and comb each other's hair.

Try the following Heart-to-Heart exercise without speaking. Close your eyes, take a deep breath, and release the day's tension as you exhale and relax your entire body. Continue breathing in this way until you feel quite relaxed. Rest your hands on your lover's heart, feel it pulsating with life and energy. Be receptive to everything the heart is conveying and remain open and silent, simply receiving. Then have your lifemate do the same for you, holding his or her hands over your heart while you relate your feelings through nonverbal communication.

After about ten minutes of intimate silence take turns sharing what you were nonverbally saying and feeling with your partner. Gentle, appreciative touch can relax a tired mind, soothe the soul, and comfort the body. Heart-to-Heart touching must be practiced on a regular basis until it becomes a normal part of relating sensually as well as sexually to each other.

Allow your heart to speak to your lover through gentle massage. A slow, sensual touch gratifies all the senses. Glide your hands over each other, caressing and communicating with all parts of the body, mind, and spirit that are being explored. With slow, deliberate strokes, caress and fondle all of the sensitive contours of each other's bodies. Be absolutely involved in the moment, allowing yourself the experience of exquisite touching without having your lover expect or need anything from you. This inspires a new level of trust and openness that will add immeasurably to the quality of your communication. If you find this process uncontrollably leads to intercourse, that is all right, but the real focus is to unlock sensual feelings and speak to each other through touching in a relaxed, effortless manner.

I: Intimacy   Intimate sex means enjoying each other

sexually in the here and now, whether or not you reach orgasm. Sexual energy is a form of vitality. Intimate energy is another form of vitality. Discuss ways that you and your lover can find intimacy in everything you do, like going for a walk in your neighborhood, cooking a meal together, and reading to each other. Consider the following explorations:

1. Compose a list of the most intimate thoughts your lover can ask. For example: How does it feel when I reach orgasm with you? Is there a way in which you feel I could be more sensitive during lovemaking? Are you happy with how I touch you while we are sensually exploring?
2. When you make love maintain eye contact to establish a connection for channeling love while physically bonding.
3. Be willing to share your deepest feelings and fears with each other:

"I'm frightened of being too close to you, I might lose myself."

"I don't want you to become bored with me."

"I am not interested in sex right now but would like you to hold me."

"I feel like you tune me out when we are making love."

"I like it when you talk to me about your fantasies."

"Sometimes I just want to go off by myself and not worry about you."

"I feel you can't accept my imperfections."

"I like it when you are patient and don't expect or need an orgasm."

"I like to act like a naughty girl when we make love."

"I'm afraid I can never satisfy you."

"I wish you would put more energy into keeping the passion alive in our relationship."

Remember, intimacy cannot be rushed. It begins by letting your lover see into you, and assisting your lover in feeling safe enough to let you see into him or her. Take the risk of opening your innermost feelings and sex with your lifemate can become a fantastic lifelong adventure.

R: Romance If you continue to kindle romance you will continue to experience your lifemate as your *lover*. If you treat your mate as "my old man," or the "little wife at home" you will be bored. A monogamous relationship is a creative challenge. The first few months of bonding are easy. The challenge over time is to always treat each other as special and keep the magic alive. True romance is a willingness to seduce your partner into intimacy and passion—to have him or her fall in love with you again and again. Remember, the experience of passion is directly related to the state of fitness of your body. Regular exercise, good nutrition, and regular meditation allow your energy and desire to be at peak levels.

You are responsible for creating romance and recapturing it. Here are some romantic ideas:

1. Imagine a romantic evening for this week and a romantic weekend in the next two months. What would make it special, memorable, unique? What would you wear and eat? What music and sights might you fill your environment with? Now actually follow through and make it happen.

2. Romance does not have to cost you anything—only your intention (a love letter, a wildflower, a walk by the seashore). Be tourists in your own city; guests in your own home.

3. Give yourself the freedom to be apart. Absence does make the heart grow fonder. Some couples stifle romance with constant togetherness. By trusting each other to be apart, you both nurture commitment and give each other the opportunity to grow as individuals. The result will be the excitement of discovering each other anew.

Choosing Monogamy:
A Daring Adventure

In the course of our work with Kirk and Vicky, each revealed strong temptations to have an affair. Vicky in particular had a friend who extolled the benefits of an affair for a sex life caught in a routine. This concern is not unusual, given the past two decades of liberated sex. Tragically, statistics indicate that over 75% of married men and over 60% of married women have had affairs.

Our view is that extramarital affairs result not so much from being bored with the relationship, as from boredom with yourself. Affairs are a flight from the more difficult tasks of confronting inadequate communication and making changes that result in growth for you, your lover, and the relationship. Yielding to the temptation of an affair is the exact opposite of accepting the challenge of becoming true lifemates.

The once cherished dogmas of "liberated sex"—erotic pleasure without consequence, multiple partners without jealousy, recreation without creation—have proven false. We now see that "liberated sex" has bred sexual exploitation, performance fears, manipulation of "love," disease, unwanted pregnancies, boredom, and spiritual malaise. Indeed, most singles now create arm's-length relationships out of mistrust and the pain of repeated dishonesty, manipulation, and rejection. AIDS is the tip of the iceberg, the outstanding current example of the results of widespread sexual exploitation.

We encourage couples to choose monogamy openly and thoughtfully. When we discussed this issue with Kirk and Vicky, we asked them to examine their feelings about sexual exclusivity, and we encouraged their affirmation of commitment, not out of religious or legal duty, but voluntarily out of their desire to create the most rewarding relationship possible. We talked about the appeal of superficial erotic novelty and the challenge of a richer intimacy that allows a deeper eroticism to begin. We discussed how a committed monogamous relationship forces you to look at each other's needs and fears without self-deception. We talked about how sexual play between lifemates need not be a serious burden, and how a couple can help each other release fears and discover limitless energy.

Monogamy, when freely chosen, becomes a spiritual quest. There is no external place to go; you must go deep within yourself and your love partner. Beware that in letting go of old habits, your worst fears such as boredom, restlessness, and sometimes impotence, must be acknowledged and resolved. Sexual Heart Talks are a way to heal these fears and discover the higher meaning of sexual liberation. When you and your lover can share your passion without fear, and with patience, commitment, and trust, you may discover a state of sexual grace. Lovemaking takes on a fresh quality energized by the intensity of feelings. This intense emotional sharing generates a limitless flow of sexual energy. It is as if you discover an inner hotspring of passion that flows spontaneously when you and your lover go inward in sexual sharing.

Once you discover this level of intimacy with your lifemate, monogamy loses all sense of bondage and becomes a source of liberation. An affair ceases to be a temptation because neither you nor your lover would want to adulterate your sexual fulfillment with each other. If this sounds idealistic, it is only because so few people have discovered the intense satisfaction of heart-to-heart communication during sex. That discovery is among the great rewards of becoming lifemates and worth the time and effort to develop love fitness.

Exercising Sexual Passion

Kirk and Vicky launched a new and exciting A.F.-F.A.I.R. They used these additional strategies to deepen the heart-to-heart communication in their sexual relationship:

- *Slow down, take your time, and cherish your lover.* This is the single most important "sexual exercise." An orchestra does not open with a crescendo, and you can't make a symphony out of lovemaking if you rush to climax. Slowing down is important because it allows you to tune in to the rhythms of your own and your partner's feelings.

- *What do you do during pleasuring? Anything that gives you and your partner pleasure.* Don't think that pleasuring means you must immediately fondle each other. Try a feather-light stroking with your fingertips up the underside of the arm. Or light kisses on the nape of the neck, between the breasts, along the stomach and inner thighs. Use your imagination and enjoy. Open your heart to what your lover is feeling in response to your touch and let yourself relax, become warm, and just feel close.

- *Be sensitive to what your mate needs and communicate what arouses you.* You may find slow, light touching most enjoy able while your partner prefers firm stroking of muscle. Common turn-offs are a hasty jump to coitus and a demanding attitude. You must learn through clear communication what you and your mate find most erotic. Don't be afraid of simple direct statements such as: "I like it when you . . ." "It turns me on when you let me . . ." "I'd like it if you'd . . . more." Remember, however, never hurry!

- *Especially in bed it is important to communicate your feelings.* If you feel anxious during pleasuring, tell your partner "I get uncomfortable when you . . ." Expressing your feelings increases trust and lessens anxiety. Give yourself permission to take the pressure out of lovemaking and open unexpected possibilities for enjoyment. You may find that intercourse becomes just one more delightful part of your lovemaking and not its only element.

• *Enjoy erotica.* While a considerable portion of today's erotic literature and film is actually boring and downright distasteful, selective viewing and reading can be worthwhile. If you both agree to try erotica, you may find that it can enhance your capacity for arousal and heighten your sexual responsiveness. By enjoying an erotic video with your mate and talking about your feelings afterward, you can break down inhibitions and learn what turns each other on.

• *Intimate massage.* You need a warm, quiet setting, soft lighting, scented oil, a firm mattress, pillows or carpet, and lots of time. Use plenty of massage oil and rub continuously in a regular, easy rhythm. Use the full surface of your hands. Try different techniques—circling, pressing, kneading, shaking, lifting, pulling—for different parts of the body. A rolling pin on the back and legs, a vibrator (or two, one in each hand), and an alcohol rub can add delightful effects. Above all, an atmosphere of safety and trust is essential. Never criticize or tease your partner about being tense, ticklish, or guarded. The purpose of this exercise is to help tension and anxieties fade.

• *Among the most effective pleasure-enhancing aids for some women is the vibrator.* It is often effective in stimulating unresponsive women to orgasm. By increasing the frequency of your orgasms with a vibrator, you can also enhance your orgasmic potential during coitus. Don't be embarrassed or ashamed about adding a mechanical dimension to your sex life. Even fully orgasmic women report that vibrators expand their pleasure. Talk about using a vibrator with your lover. By acknowledging feelings of shame, inadequacy, fear, or "being replaced," you and your lover can share your emotional vulnerability. You may also find that a mechanical toy is a wonderful addition to your sex life.

• *Oral sex is an avenue for giving and receiving delightful pleasures.* Developing your skill in satisfying your spouse orally can be helpful in reducing anxiety about intercourse. Again, the key is to communicate freely with your lover. Once you know that you can satisfy him or her orally, pressure to perform through coitus diminishes drastically. The result is a twofold enhancement of your sexual experience. You develop a new way to give and receive pleasure, and you free yourself to enjoy coitus without anxiety. Skillful oral sex requires practice and communication. Take your time. Your partner must tell you what he or she likes just as you must tell him or her. Because some people have an initial aversion to the idea of oral sex, you should never try to force it on your partner. Go slowly, share your fantasy, practice good hygiene, and be tender, and initial barriers will disappear.

• *Two techniques have proved helpful for men to increase their orgasmic control.*

The pressure to perform remains a great burden for many men. You may be surprised at how many men fear the label "premature ejaculator." Sexual control for a man is a learned skill that develops with greater acceptance of erotic feelings. Acknowledging the fear of poor ejaculatory control and taking steps to improve can be an opportunity for you and your lover to develop greater intimacy.

One technique to help is called Seeman's maneuver. Once you achieve erection, you or your partner should squeeze your penis just below the glans (head). This will not hurt, but your erection will partially diminish. When it returns, you will have enhanced your staying power. You can also use this technique to advantage during coitus. When you feel the impending orgasm, withdraw and ask your partner to squeeze your penis until your erection partially abates. Don't worry, it will return and you will be able to resume with better control.

You may feel embarrassed to try this technique. Give yourself permission to talk about your feelings. A little tenderness and understanding can lead to a great breakthrough both in your relationship and your lovemaking.

The second technique is known as stop-start. Several seconds prior to ejaculation, the male experiences pleasurable contractions. If you stop thrusting when you feel them, you can postpone ejaculation. When you stop, you should concentrate on your feelings. Don't get lost in fantasy or you may lose control. Breathe deeply and relax. The pressure for orgasm will lessen. After a few minutes, you can slowly resume thrusting. A cooperative partner is essential for developing orgasmic control. You must be sensitive to each other's signs of impending orgasm. Describe what happens and how you feel. Initial success will build confidence and control.

• *Give yourself permission to develop your potential for "multi-orgasms."* Men, like women, can have one orgasm after another. The key is for the male to relax and get in touch with the full range of erotic feelings. By concentrating on your sensations immediately prior to orgasm, you can experience a minor orgasm. The net result is a building of pleasure until you decide to give in to the grand finale. If you make a competition of multi-orgasm by keeping score, you are bound to be disappointed. What you are striving for is a close relationship with your partner physically, emotionally, and spiritually.

Safe Sex

In this era of AIDS, herpes, chlamydia, and other sexually transmitted diseases, heart-to-heart communication about your and your lover's medical history is essential to love fitness. Here are a few of the key points.

Raising the Issue In any new relationship or in a relationship that may not be monogamous, you can't hide from the risk of sexually transmitted disease by avoiding the questions. It is quite natural to feel uncomfortable opening the discussion, for a variety of reasons. Asking your love partner if he or she may be at risk in connection with a sexually transmitted disease raises fundamental issues of trust and loyalty, as well as basic fears of rejection and shame. The irony is, however, that once you have an open, loving discussion about your sexual histories, you and your lover can allay each other's fears and create an intimate bond of trust. We suggest the following ways to open the discussion:

> "I am very turned on, but let's take a moment to talk about our health so neither of us will worry later."

> "I love you. Let's talk about commitments and practices to safeguard our health."

These questions can be difficult to pursue in a romantic setting, because they inevitably involve some clinical issues. It is best to have these discussions before you go to the bedroom, so that you can make your decisions in a nonpressured emotional environment.

Sharing Your Sexual and Medical History Once you have broached the subject of sexually transmitted diseases, there are several key questions to be discussed. Here is a short list:

1. When have each of you last had a medical checkup?
2. Do either of you have, or are you carriers of, a sexually transmitted disease?
3. Have either of you recently exhibited symptoms of a sexually transmitted disease?
4. Have you recently made love with someone who either had a sexually transmitted disease or exhibited symptoms?
5. Are either of you IV drug users or bisexual?
6. In the last seven years have you had sexual relations with a prostitute, IV drug user, bisexual, or homosexual?

Making Decisions: Acting with Integrity Once you've started this discussion, you may find yourself facing some difficult decisions. If your lover says he or she may have made love to a bisexual person or prostitute in the last seven years, what do you do? If your lover says that he or she is a herpes carrier, but not currently showing symptoms, what risks do you take? The first decision is whether to believe what you have been told. If you doubt your potential lover's sincerity, then certainly caution would be advisable; however, it may not be that your lover is insincere, but merely afraid of rejection in disclosing secrets. In that case, it may be appropriate to have a Heart Talk about your sexual pasts. It is very difficult to make responsible decisions without full disclosure, and the Heart Talk exercises described in Chapter 3 can be helpful.

Aside from abstinence, there are several steps to take to minimize risks. First, use a condom and a spermicide at the outset of any relationship; each of you should see a doctor and get tested for AIDS. Depending on your medical examination and sexual histories, and your intentions with respect to birth control, you may decide with the help of a doctor that these forms of protection are not necessary for you as a committed couple. If, however, one of you is a carrier of a sexually transmitted disease such as herpes, which can flare up from time to time, your physician can instruct you how to handle these outbreaks. Become informed. We recommend that you discuss these issues with a knowledgeable doctor so that you and your lover can safeguard one another's health.

Comeback for Courtship

One of the most often heard concerns about AIDS is the risk of infection in the heterosexual population. Recent studies have shown that the risk of contracting the disease is low as long as you restrict sexual activity to partners with a low risk of being infected with the AIDS virus. If a heterosexual begins relations with a member of a high-risk group (e.g., prostitute, intravenous drug user, homosexual), however, the risk of AIDS infection rises dramatically. For example, in a single act of vaginal intercourse with a known member of a low-risk group, the risk of contracting AIDS is one in five million. Vaginal sex with a high-risk partner raises the odds five hundred times to one in ten thousand, even with a condom.

These statistics make a strong case not just for the return of monogamy, but also the return of good old-fashioned courtship. The era of multiple partners even for young singles may have run its course. Perhaps the real value of the sexual revolution has been making it possible to talk about sex and for lovers to acknowledge all their feelings about this most intimate of personal issues. What this means is there are no substitutes for taking your time and really getting to know your partner. While condoms reduce risk, they are certainly not foolproof and must be used properly to have any value at all.

This data supports the old-fashioned idea that sex should not be enjoyed without a substantial emotional commitment. Getting to know your partner well before you have sex is perhaps the best protection against sexually transmitted diseases. When it comes to safe sex, the best medical advice may be to fall in love before you fall into bed.

Sexual Fulfillment and Love

By far the most important element for fulfilling sex is love. The more fully you and your lover are in touch with each other's feelings, the better your sexual experience will be. A compulsive search for bigger and better orgasms alone will only produce flashes of excitement followed by boredom and irritation. The key to developing your full sexual potential lies in exploring the adventure of intimacy.

Too often couples fall into the trap of taking sexual issues in their relationship too seriously. The more they try to fix the sexual symptoms through manuals, techniques, devices, etc., the worse things often get. The key to solving "sexual problems" may in some cases be simply to relax, rekindle the romance, and have more fun together.

Reinvesting in your relationship is an opportunity to rediscover each other, to fall in love anew. You remain familiar *and* fresh, instead of growing bored and tired of one another. Remember, the great adventure of intimate sex is inward, a journey of the heart and soul as well as the senses. Your spirits can leap free of boundaries and roles and experience the deep joy and renewal of letting go. Intimate sex is a spiritual journey to discovering how open, sensitive, caring, and loving you and your lifemate can be.

Chapter 5

Working Out Anger and Getting Close

An irony of love is that it guarantees some degree of anger. When two people fall in love, they expose the most sensitive parts of their personalities. At some time in every love relationship, lovers are inconsiderate, hurt each other's feelings, or let each other down. Anger is the natural result, and to keep love vibrant, the anger must be expressed. Not that love is a license to express anger indiscriminately. The closer you are to someone, the more adept you must be at venting your anger constructively. This chapter presents key Love Fitness workouts to help you transform anger in your relationship from a destructive problem into a challenging opportunity for intense communication, greater commitment, more mutual respect, and ultimately deeper love.

No one enjoys being a target of another's anger, especially from a lover. Often, anger compounds misunderstandings and hurt feelings. When resentments accumulate, emotional defenses harden and feelings of love wither. Can you recall a recent incident in which your lover got angry with you? How did you respond? Was the situation fully resolved, or were you forced to swallow your feelings?

Jim, a client, recounted a Sunday morning exchange with his girlfriend, Donna.

DONNA: Oh, Jim, you did it again! You took a shower and left the floor soaking wet.

JIM: Well, you forgot to put the cap back on the toothpaste; it oozed onto the counter.

DONNA: You left the cap off, not me.

JIM: Gimme a break. I work so hard [*puts on a hang-dog expression.*] Can't I even take a shower in peace?

DONNA: [*Gritting her teeth*] Okay, honey, just do what you want.

JIM: Geez, how come you always get to be "right"? You're always bitching at me. I can't even relax in my own home.

DONNA: You never listen to me; you keep trying to intimidate me.

JIM: Me, intimidate you?

DONNA: Yes. You never let me finish a sentence. Every time I start to say something, you jump right in and—

JIM: That's not true!

DONNA: There you go again.

JIM: Okay, go ahead, say whatever it is you need to say.

DONNA: I'm tired of cleaning up after you—why can't you be more conscious of the extra work you create for me?

JIM: Hey, I'm no pig! Can I help it if you're a compulsive nut about sterilizing the bathroom, just like your mother?

DONNA: I'm like my mother? Hah! You should talk— your mother . . .

JIM: Don't drag my mother into this.

DONNA: . . . She camps out here five weeks a year and . . .

JIM: You leave my mother out of this! I can't believe this is happening.

DONNA: Ah, forget it. You'll never change. Go ahead, flood the bathroom and ruin the tile.

JIM: C'mon Donna, this is ridiculous. We're getting ready to divorce over a toothpaste cap and some water on the floor!

Sound familiar? How many times have you and your lover found yourselves quarreling over something so minor that you later forgot why you were arguing? How much bickering, insomnia, or cold silence did it take before you finally made up?

In most relationships, anger erupts and subsides with few, if any, positive results. There is no deep exchange of feelings beyond heated words and defensive responses. No one learns what must change in the relationship to avoid future emotional explosions. There is no resolution of feelings or convergence of points of view. Instead of using the energy of anger to deepen heart-to-heart communication, most couples find that angry outbreaks leave them emotionally bruised and resentful. They rely on time to do the healing and know from experience that most anger eventually blows over. The tragedy, however, is that this approach ultimately leads to emotional distance and the erosion of passion. It slowly poisons love.

Equally damaging to a relationship is the failure to recognize and resolve anger. Women typically internalize anger while men typically have difficulty perceiving when their mates are angry. This inability of some men to "read" their spouses' anger exacerbates conflict and resentment in relationships. When a man fails to perceive his lover's anger, he appears all the more insensitive and unloving. As a result, his wife becomes even more angry. He compounds his wife's hurt by ignoring her pain. The result is resentment and barely suppressed rage.

Anger with Heart

Anger is not in itself a problem. It's what you do or fail to do with anger that can result in a breach in your love relationship. When anger is misdirected, turned inward or used as ammunition, it can initiate a destructive, hostile interchange. When anger is accepted—that is, experienced, identified, and expressed in an intimate way—it can provide the impetus to solve the inevitable conflicts and problems that arise in love relationships.

Elise and Hunter sought our help near the end of their first year of marriage. "Before we were married," Elise lamented, "Hunter was so thoughtful. We compromised a lot. He really listened to me. Now it's all changed. Everything has to go his way all the time!" Hunter's point of view was quite different. "I don't know what she's so upset about. Our relationship is great. There's no reason for us to be here except that she's become so damn cold. I can't understand it." Elise and Hunter had a common problem. Once they got married, Hunter became more absorbed in the pressures of his career and less attentive to Elise's feelings. Elise, however, had never before experienced Hunter's insensitivity. Now she was shocked, disappointed and confused about how to break through to him.

Elise was clearly hurt but unable to express her anger. We explained that to accept and express her angry feelings effectively, she had to first understand its multiple, positive purposes. Anger serves to get attention. Quite often, couples hurt one another without intention or knowledge. That is why Hunter responded to Elise's cold silence with the question, "Why are you so upset?" When you get angry, your body and mind are giving you a signal that you have been hurt by your lover and you should stop and pay attention to the hurt. By accepting your angry feelings, you gain the ability to get your lover's attention.

It was important for Elise to understand the relation between hurt and anger. Whether you feel ignored, unappreciated, manipulated, wronged, put down, controlled, or used by your lover, a common denominator of all such feelings is pain, and anger is the inevitable mental, emotional, and physical response. Anger is as much a natural response to being hurt by a lover as fire is a natural response to applying intense heat to wood. Once Elise realized that underneath her anger was hurt, underneath her hurt was sadness, and underneath her sadness was love, she also recognized why expressing her anger was so important. Healthy anger releases the hurt, exposes the sadness, and unblocks the underlying love!

We also helped Elise understand how anger empowers her to communicate to Hunter and break through his insensitivity. When you get angry with your lover, you are saying, "Stop! You are hurting me. This relationship has to change." Elise felt the intense need to express just these simple feelings to Hunter, but denied herself the freedom of such intense, direct communication because she had a habit of internalizing anger. By helping Elise learn to accept and express her anger constructively, we showed her how to break through to Hunter.

Becoming comfortable with anger, Elise also learned how anger allowed her to affirm herself. When you are hurt by your lover, the initial response is often shock. Elise initially felt both shaken and powerless in the face of Hunter's insensitivity. Repeated hurts can make you feel quite small and powerless. The emotional energy of anger surging through your body is empowering. Anger is nature's way of giving you back your strength when your lover may have intentionally or unintentionally knocked you for an emotional loop.

We recommended that Elise and Hunter work with several of the Love Fitness workouts described in this chapter to become more comfortable with anger. In particular, we encouraged them to talk about each other's anger styles. Hunter learned that Elise's cold withdrawal was not a rejection of him, but her response to hurt. He learned to "read" her anger and even encouraged her to express her feelings so that they both knew what needed to change in the relationship. Once they each understood that anger is to be welcomed as an emergency form of heart-to-heart communication, they unlocked a new passion in their relationship. They also discovered a new freedom to talk about other feelings.

Even though Elise and Hunter made significant progress, Elise's habit of internalizing anger remained a problem. To solve this problem, we recommended that they try a special Heart Talk agreement that we call the Anger with Heart exercise. We asked Elise to describe as simply as possible what she needed in order to express her anger. She decided that she needed Hunter to ask, "Would you please trust me with your anger?" We also asked Hunter to list those signs of Elise becoming upset but withholding anger. They agreed that when Hunter noticed signs of Elise's distress, Hunter would use this phrase as the key to help Elise unlock her hurt feelings. After having become very conversant with the role of healthy anger in a love relationship, Elise and Hunter found this simple Heart Talk agreement to be a final cure to Elise's habit of withholding anger.

Making anger work is among the greatest challenges to becoming lifemates. The more you care for someone, the harder it may be to accept his or her anger. When your lover hurls vicious accusations, perhaps even threatening to strike you, it becomes almost impossible to keep in mind that those outbursts belie feelings of love, not hate. On the other hand, if you are angry with your lover but unable to express your feelings, then your love for that person can also die. Remember, repressed anger can cause love to wither just as quickly as badly expressed anger.

As you become skillful at using anger to communicate hurt and your need to make specific changes in the relationship, your capacity for intimacy will also grow. Healthy anger requires skill, courage, and a proactive stance; you must be committed to "work out" feelings with your lover, rather than surrender to negative emotional habits. Essential to the Love Fitness program is using each argument as an opportunity to create more mutual respect and greater intimacy. The key is learning how to use anger for clear communication.

Quiz: How Do You Handle Anger?

Most people did not grow up in households where they watched their parents expressing anger in ways that strengthen love. On the contrary, anger is such a difficult emotion that few adults have learned to handle it well. Instead, most people develop styles of coping with anger. None serve clear communication, but understanding your own style is a helpful step toward eventual mastery of anger.

Below is a list of various anger styles. First identify which style(s) is/are most characteristic of you, and then identify those of your lover.

The way that I/you deal with anger most characteristically is as follows:

1. *Snake: Venomous Anger.* The snake can be silently hostile but deadly. When angry, you avoid sex or intimacy with your partner. You don't seem to have the time or be in the right mood. But, in fantasies or in actuality you lust for those other than your lover. You act out anger by attracting others with the intent of making your lover jealous. When you feel provoked or attacked by your lover, you hiss and recoil, and may venomously release your poisonous accusations. The snake demonstrates passive aggressive anger.

2. *Lion: Roar and Rage.* The lion strikes with claws bared and a terrifying roar, aiming to chew the head off its victim. Lion-style anger utilizes intimidation and control, the King of the Jungle: "You should," "You must," "Obey." The lion establishes power by an ever-present threat of violence. If you disagree with the lion or fail to meet its needs, it will literally tear you apart. The lion's style of anger leaves no other animal wanting to speak for fear of being destroyed. The lion's message is, "Worship and fear me from afar but don't come too close."

3. *Turtle: Cold Anger.* The turtle responds to the first sign of disagreement by tucking its head and waiting until all the criticism and hostility blow over.

The turtle withdraws into its shell and deals with anger by avoidance or pretending not to understand, playing weak and helpless. When confronted, it utters, "I can't help it. I didn't hear you." The turtle's style is defensive and protective, to put a shell around its feelings. A turtle appears hard and impenetrable, but is actually soft and vulnerable within.

4. *Chicken: Fear of Anger*. The chicken is frightened, nervous, and tense about anger, because it feels helpless and in desperate need of protection. The chicken is easily victimized and commands no respect from others. It can easily wind up carved and served on almost anyone's plate. The chicken, therefore, tends to remain fenced in or cling to anyone who appears protective. At the first sign of anger it panics, looking frantically for someone to help the "poor me" chicken.

5. *Skunk: Stinking, Intimidating Anger*. The skunk raises a terrible stink but has no bite. The skunk speaks critically and condescendingly to his or her love partner. Its stench can be so intense—"You're stupid"; "It's always your fault"; "I hate you"; "I want a divorce"—that it can easily bring a loved one to tears. The skunk's smell, in the form of blaming and complaining, sometimes induces change in others through intimidation but inevitably leads to resentment. The skunk is fiercely protective of its territory but may cause such a stink that the other animals turn on it and force the skunk to flee.

6. *Puppy: Denying Anger*. The puppy deals with anger by trying to make everything wonderful, happy, and nice. The puppy is like a little kid trying to smile and smooth over differences. "Oh, it's not so bad, really." "We basically agree." "We never fight." The puppy, however, remains stuck in this childlike state of innocence and, even when tread upon, fails to bark loudly, much less bite. The puppy tries to lick and please in the face of anger, or scurry under the bed. Despite attempts to gain approval, it eventually gets kicked around.

7. *Bull: Stubborn Anger.* When the bull gets angry, he forgets about everyone and everything except getting done what he wants to accomplish. He doesn't want to hear any answer but his own. He becomes so stubborn and self-righteous that he has no concern for victims of his painful attacks. "What do you mean, I hurt you? That's ridiculous." To this animal, any disagreement is bullshit, but he can't understand why people complain that he is insensitive. The bull is so fixated when he gets angry that he may be unaware of his fury. "I'm not angry," he says, "I'm just intense!"

Take turns explaining your views of anger style(s). If your selections differ, discuss them until you can see more clearly each other's point of view. You do not need to agree, just learn about how you perceive each other's style(s).

Here is a second quiz that will help further identify how you and your partner express and receive anger. Mark each statement that applies to you with an (M) for "me." Then review the list again and mark each statement that you feel applies to your lover with an (H) for "him" or "her":

The way that I/you deal with anger is as follows:

1. Bottle up frustrations until there's a volcanic explosion.
2. Withdraw from anger and cry.
3. Stonewall or deny it, "Angry, who me?"
4. Smile on the outside, covering up inner rage.
5. Displace or redirect anger at a child, other people, or a pet.
6. Swallow the anger and release it through physical symptoms such as headache, ulcers, or fatigue.
7. Release energy by going for a run or some other physical outlet.
8. Pray or try to meditate it away.
9. Threaten to pack up and leave.
10. Become emotionally distant and bitter.

11. Discuss the upset and see how better to deal with the situation now and in the future.
12. Try to make you feel guilty, wrong, or bad for being angry with me.
13. Give in for fear of your rage.
14. Listen receptively until a solution can be found.
15. Become sad and depressed and allow it to affect me through a lack of motivation, boredom, or apathy.
16. Become tense and nervous.
17. Argue vehemently to badger you into agreeing with me.
18. Attack your position as stupid, misinformed, or obviously incompetent.
19. Withdraw, sigh, or sulk until you apologize to me.
20. Avoid any controversy or upset to try to keep the peace in our relationship.
21. Try to cheer you up as soon as you get angry.
22. Let you know it's okay to be angry; listen empathetically to what you have to say.
23. Tell you in detail about a similar problem I once had, saying, "It's nothing to be angry about"; "Don't feel bad."
24. Say, "It's your problem so don't bother me."
25. Overeat, drink alcohol, or use drugs.
26. Say, "You're crazy; you should see a therapist."
27. Try to win the argument at all costs, to be "victorious."
28. Threaten to expose your behavior to family and friends.

For each item you marked with an (M) or (H), explain your choices to your lover. Don't analyze whether a response is right or wrong, good or bad. The purpose of this quiz is to help you understand how you deal with anger. This exercise will allow you and your lover to hold up mirrors for each other and gain valuable feedback about your individual anger styles.

Intimate versus Destructive Anger

Now that you have an understanding of how you and your lover cope with anger, you can begin making changes for the better. The five questions below provide a guide for evaluating whether you and your lover are expressing anger effectively. Consider these questions as tools for evaluating the anger styles you have identified in yourself and your lover:

1. Does this response call immediate attention to a problem?
2. Does this response release hurt and unblock underlying feelings of sadness and love?
3. Does this response communicate my/our need for a specific behavior change?
4. Does this response affirm my self-worth?
5. Does this response energize my/our love?

Healthy expressions of anger serve all of these purposes. Don't be discouraged if you find that few, if any, of your anger styles meet these goals. You are not alone. Anger is an extremely difficult emotion to master, all the more so in love relationships because most children are brought up to believe that anger and love are essentially incompatible.

Because anger is of necessity a forceful emotion, it can very easily be destructive to a love relationship. Review the purposes of healthy anger and you may be tempted to believe that healthy anger is only possible for saints. Take heart. Our clients have learned to transform anger into a positive force in their love relationships, and so can you.

Let's begin by simplifying the analysis of anger. Basically, anger can take two directions: intimate and destructive. Whether anger is intimate or destructive depends on how you develop your intention when you first start to feel angry. Intention is subtle and can be easily overlooked amidst the surging adrenaline that accompanies anger, but how you formulate your intention at the earliest moments of feeling angry is absolutely critical.

If your intention is merely to strike back, then your anger is almost inevitably destructive. You wind up trying to put down, punish, or manipulate your lover while the positive goals of communicating needs and changing the relationship go unmet. Your anger spurs hostility and bitterness and freezes the relationship in an event of the past. You explode in rage to punish your love partner for the hurt he or she caused you. Whether you scream at the top of your lungs or sulk in cold silence, the goal remains the same—vengeance and retaliation.

In contrast, if your intention is to communicate your pain and your need to change the relationship in specific ways, your anger will be constructive. This intention makes anger supportive and imbues your expressions of anger with a commitment to a positive outcome. You assertively communicate your hurt feelings and explain what specific changes you need. Your anger releases tension and facilitates an emotional breakthrough that helps your relationship evolve to a new level of mutual understanding. Consider for a moment the following characteristics of destructive versus intimate anger.

Destructive Anger

Destructive anger is often a self-fulfilling prophecy in which anger begets anger. Destructive anger usually involves the following elements:

1. Manipulative comments to coerce your lover ("If you loved me, you would . . ." "If you don't like it, leave." "Do what you want, but don't come crying to me.").
2. A lengthy monologue to control and dominate ("Let me finish; I've got more to get off my chest." "I don't want to hear your excuses." "You'll just have to wait.").

3. Global, all-encompassing accusations that use words such as "never," "always," "should," and "ought" ("You *never* listen." "You *always* do this to me." "You *should* be more considerate." "You *ought* to know better.")

4. An attempt to make your lover wrong and guilty ("You know how much I count on you." "This shows you don't really care." "You're a fool; after all that I've done for you.").

5. An uncontrolled outburst of anger, impatience, and yelling to intimidate your love partner ("Look at what you've done now." "This is the last straw." "I hate you.").

6. The use of old resentments as ammunition ("This is just like the time you . . ." "You're just like your mother." "You've always been that way.").

7. The use of emotional blackmail, playing the martyr ("Telling you this hurts me more than it hurts you." "I'm wasting my breath talking to you." Sighs and moans signaling "Poor me.").

Caution: Alcohol is the number one precipitant of family violence and destructive anger. Even "a couple of drinks" can increase feelings of irritability and suspicion, as well as loss of impulse control. If destructive arguments and hostility in your love relationship can be attributed in part to alcohol (or drug) abuse, contact your physician, Alanon, or Alcoholics Anonymous.

Intimate Anger

Intimate anger is committed to a positive outcome and is shaped by the following characteristics:

1. Gets immediate attention through assertive but warm statements ("We've got to talk now, I'm angry . . ." "I'm upset and need to explain why . . ." "I'm hurting, please give me your attention.").

2. Communicates your hurt using "I" statements to express your feelings ("I feel let down, disap-

pointed, hurt." "I have trouble when you . . . so I'd prefer it if you would . . .").

3. Communicates specific requests for change ("I am hurt when you don't call me if you are going to be late. I am busy too . . ." "I am hurt when you ignore me at a party; I'd like to be introduced to your friends.").

4. Leaves you open to your lover's feelings and point of view ("I can see how you feel." "I understand now the miscommunication, so what can we do to avoid this problem in the future.").

5. Empowers both partners to change a destructive pattern through mutual cooperation ("Since we both want . . . we'll need to watch out for . . ." "What could we have done differently?" "If we remember to each say, 'Tell me more,' we'll do fine.").

6. Expresses patience while expecting your lover to make a determined effort to change ("I want you to stop hurting me, but I know it's going to take some time." "It's normal to have some ups and downs, but we have to change . . ." "I know you're trying and I appreciate it; what more can we do to solve this problem?).

7. Prepares the emotional ground for forgiveness once the relationship begins to shift to a new footing ("I still think you're terrific and I love you, and what we need to work on is . . ." "I value you greatly as a lover, and that includes your ability to discuss these difficult matters.").

We understand that shaping your angry feelings with constructive characteristics isn't easy. Your effort to make anger constructive must not leave you feeling that your anger remains bottled up. The heat and hurt must be released. Practice is crucial. Anger becomes intimate when you express it with the following elements:

1. *Warmth.* You communicate intensely but with care how you have been hurt.

2. *Specificity*. You communicate clearly and you request a specific change in the relationship to avoid future misunderstandings.

3. *Release*. You effectively and safely release the tension that accompanies your anger so you can feel healed and able to forgive.

4. *Brevity*. You release your anger in five or ten minutes, avoiding lengthy monologues. Although many issues may need examination, you express your feelings succinctly.

5. *Fairness*. You avoid global, all-encompassing accusations and strive to recognize that your lover may also have legitimate disagreements and grievances. At all times, you remember that when it comes to feelings, no one is wrong.

6. *Receptivity*. You avoid blaming, attacking, or otherwise trying to control your lover's responses. This means listening receptively and empathetically to your lover's anger without becoming defensive.

7. *Creativity*. You seek to resolve the issues that are confronting you so that you both win. Constructive anger mobilizes you to find mutually satisfying solutions, multiple options and creative choices.

8. *Acceptance*. You accept your need to change the relationship without having to prove your lover wrong. You avoid assuming your lover has intent to hurt you because such assumptions will only make your lover defensive and cause the argument to escalate.

9. *Love*. You remain committed to creating a better relationship. You speak from your heart in a way that reflects the full intensity of your pain, as well as the strength of your underlying love.

The Repetition Exercise:
Dissolving Anger

In the heat of anger, it is obviously difficult to remember all the characteristics of constructive, intimate anger. The "Repetition Exercise" is a tool to resolve hurt feelings and ease tension between you and your love partner.

Jean and Daniel were married for three years. Both were in their mid-thirties. Daniel was an architect, and Jean trained show horses. Both were so involved in their careers that they sometimes went for days without intimate sharing. Bouts of destructive anger threatened their marriage. When their sex life began to suffer, Jean insisted they seek help. The crisis involved conflicting visions of their future. Daniel wanted children and a wife who would be a full-time homemaker. Jean was ambivalent about having children and was committed to her career.

When Daniel tried to explain why he wanted Jean to stay home, she was too preoccupied preparing counterarguments to listen because she felt so threatened. It was the same with Daniel when Jean spoke. They resorted to below-the-belt personal attacks because neither felt the other was willing to listen. This strategy was particularly destructive because the intimacy of their love armed them both with enough knowledge to hurt each other deeply. They were entrenched in bitter arguments that led to feelings of betrayal and abuse. These yelling matches soon carried threats of divorce.

The first question for a couple faced with a major crisis is the degree of commitment to stay together and "stick it out." Despite the festering hostility, Daniel and Jean said they still loved each other and wanted to make the relationship work. The fact that they came for help together was a sign of their commitment. What they needed more than anything else was to learn a specific exercise to practice constructive anger.

Here is the Repetition Exercise we taught them:

1. Each person begins by affirming his or her commitment to love and to reach a positive outcome by stating, "Out of the love I have for you and out of the love I know you have for me, there are some difficult feelings we need to share."

2. One person speaks at a time and is never interrupted. You face each other in an open body position, giving each other undivided attention.

3. Each feeling or point must be delivered briefly; *no* more than two sentences are permitted at a time; no monologues are allowed.

4. Communication is specific, empathic, and nonjudgmental. Words like "always," "never," "should," and "ought" are to be avoided.

5. Both partners maintain eye contact and do their best to stay relaxed. You are *each* creating an atmosphere of safety and trust.

6. After your partner speaks, you must accurately restate what was said without judging, defending, or adding your own interpretation. This requires active, attentive listening. Repetition dissolves tension, creates connection, and produces empathy. If you misunderstand, you can ask your lover to "Please repeat."

7. You don't have to agree with what your lover says in order to repeat the communication. Imagine you have become your love partner. You may find yourself not only repeating the words, but also temporarily experiencing his or her viewpoint.

8. When you have finished restating your lover's feelings, switch roles. You now have a chance to be the speaker. Remember, you can speak in only two sentences at a time. Your love partner now repeats your lines until your anger has also been fully expressed, heard and dissolved.

9. Especially for couples, it is helpful at the end of this exercise to share a hug and say, "I love you." Remember that one of the greatest gifts you can give someone you love is to hear his or her anger and frustration without judging, getting defensive, or contradicting.

10. The Repetition Exercise should be practiced as long as necessary to reach a resolution. No appeals to responsibilities at work or in the home are permitted as excuses for leaving, therefore set aside at least half an hour free of interruptions.

After reviewing the intimate anger guidelines described earlier, Daniel began by telling Jean that he strongly desired children, and reminded her of an agreement to start a family after they got married. Daniel explained how upset he was, and Jean repeated each statement back to him. At first, Jean felt uncomfortable repeating Daniel's lines, since it was his anger that she had been resisting. She strove to listen without interruption, to repeat without adding her interpretation, and to avoid any wisecracks or snide comments, knowing she would have her turn later.

Here is a summary of Daniel and Jean's initial Repetition Exercise:

DANIEL: Out of the love I have for you and out of the love I know you have for me, there are some difficult feelings we need to share.

JEAN: [*Repeats his sentence*] Out of the love you have for me and out of the love you know I have for you, there are some difficult feelings we need to share.

DANIEL: I am furious you keep refusing to have a child. Your, and therefore our, biological clock is ticking away.

JEAN: You are furious I keep refusing to have a child. My, and therefore our, biological clock is ticking away.

DANIEL: I feel betrayed—you and I had an agreement to start a family when we got married.

JEAN: You feel betrayed—you and I had an agreement to start a family when we got married.

DANIEL: I hate your show horses; I can't believe they mean more to you than having a child.

JEAN: You hate [*pauses*] my show horses. You think they mean much more to me than having a child.

DANIEL: I am frustrated and turned off that in the last few months you've been more into showing off your horses than having sex with me.

JEAN: You are frustrated that . . . Please repeat. [*Daniel repeats his statement.*]

JEAN: You are frustrated and turned off that in the last few months I've been more into showing off my horses than having sex with you.

DANIEL: And I feel angry that you don't understand my desire for a family and how terribly hurt I am.

JEAN: [*Repeats*]

DANIEL: I am scared when you're finally "ready" it'll be much too late and we'll fail.

JEAN: [*Repeats*]

DANIEL: I feel like we've both been exploding; I'm scared we're going to break up.

JEAN: [*Repeats*]

DANIEL: I want you to trust me to start a family.

JEAN: [*Repeats*]

DANIEL: It hurts me to see you so upset.

JEAN: [*Repeats*]

DANIEL: I want you to feel safe and happy with me—to have a child because you want to.

JEAN: [*Repeats*]

DANIEL: I've been bullying and pushing you; I'm sorry.

JEAN: [*Repeats*]

DANIEL: I feel better, released.

JEAN: [*Repeats*]

DANIEL: I want a child with you—but only if you want to.

JEAN: [*Repeats*]

DANIEL: I love you very much. I hope we can work this out. I appreciate your listening; I feel great relief.

JEAN: [*Repeats*]

SWITCHING: Daniel and Jean now switch roles.

JEAN: Out of the love I have for you and out of the love you have for me, there are some difficult feelings we need to share.

DANIEL: [*Repeats*]

JEAN: I am fed up with how you've been bullying and coercing me.

DANIEL: I've been coercing . . . Please repeat. [*Jean repeats her previous statement.*]

DANIEL: You are fed up with how I've been bullying and coercing you.

JEAN: I hate you when you start pushing and panicking and won't let up.

DANIEL: You hate me when I start pushing and panicking and won't let up.

JEAN: I feel constantly attacked by you.

DANIEL: You feel constantly attacked by me.

JEAN: I hate when you don't listen to my fears and concerns.

DANIEL: [*Repeats*]

JEAN: When you panic and yell, I don't feel safe to even talk about having a child.

DANIEL: [*Repeats*]

JEAN: I'm the one who would be pregnant and be the primary caregiver, not you.

DANIEL: [*Repeats*]

JEAN: Don't bull-crap me with "I'll raise our child." You can't even fix your own meal.

DANIEL: [*Repeats*]

JEAN: I want us to be very realistic; I'm terrified I'll have all the headaches and responsibilities while you run free.

DANIEL: [*Repeats*]

JEAN: I'm angry you resent my show horses.

DANIEL: [*Repeats*]

JEAN: I want us to be able to talk like this, not panic.

DANIEL: [*Repeats*]

JEAN: I want you to gently listen to all of my feelings and concerns, not dismiss them automatically.

DANIEL: [*Repeats*]

JEAN: I've been terribly hurt and jealous that you care more about having a child than just being with me.

DANIEL: [*Repeats*]

JEAN: I am terrified you've resisted my concerns; that's not the way to start a family.

DANIEL: [*Repeats*]

JEAN: I'm sad I won't be able to ride my show horses while pregnant.

DANIEL: [*Repeats*]

JEAN: I'm scared that if we have a child, you won't honor and support me in my horse business.

DANIEL: [*Repeats*]

JEAN: I've been so worried, I don't want to lose you either.

DANIEL: [*Repeats*]

JEAN: I want you to care about my feelings—like you are right now. [*Jean starts weeping.*]

DANIEL: [*Repeats*]

JEAN: I love you so much. I do want to have your baby.

DANIEL: [*Repeats, and begins weeping.*]

JEAN: We've been so stubborn, so silly.

DANIEL: I'm sorry, sweetheart; I've been a fool.

Daniel and Jean completed the Repetition Exercise with an embrace and deep, committed "I love yous." They decided that their needs could both be met within the relationship. Jean agreed to have a child; Daniel was deeply touched and agreed that she ought to also have her career. They recognized the need for careful planning and closer communication to make their decisions work. Once the conflict was moved from the arena of antagonism and misunderstanding to empathy and planning, it stopped being a source of hostility and became an opportunity for Daniel and Jean to grow. Learning to express intimate anger through the Repetition Exercise empowered Daniel and Jean to solve problems that had seemed insoluble. Since then they have had not only one child but two. They have their challenges, but a four-year follow-up revealed they are closer and happier than ever.

The Repetition Exercise is an opportunity for each

lifemate to make certain that the other understands exactly what he or she is feeling and why he or she is angry. When you practice this Love Fitness exercise, you and your lifemate step into each other's shoes. The relief can be tremendous as you experience that your lover understands exactly how you are feeling. This intense heart-to-heart communication literally transforms destructive anger into an expression of love.

Becoming an Emotional A. C. E.

For some people, acronyms are helpful devices to remember specific skills under pressure. We have found a simple acronym particularly useful for helping clients recall their constructive anger skills in the heat of fury. When you get furious with your lover, stop for a moment and remember the following acronym:

> A—Assess Appropriately.
> C—Choose Constructively.
> E—Express Effectively.

For example:

A: Assess Appropriately. Particularly with a lover, it is easy to assume inaccurately that he or she is angry. Your lover may be rushed and tense due to the pressures of work. He or she may be anxious or short-tempered. It's important to learn to distinguish this work related pressure, and to avoid assuming that your lover intends to ignore you or is angry with you. Unfortunately, if you assess this situation improperly and keep pressing your love partner for what he or she simply cannot give at that time, your pressure itself can be hurtful and your lover may respond in anger.

C: Choose Constructively. We have contrasted destructive versus intimate responses at length. Don't say, "You are stupid." Rather say, "You are very bright, but that wasn't the smartest thing you could have done." Don't say, "That is the ugliest suit I've ever seen," rather try something like, "You are a handsome guy, but that particular suit looks unattractive on you." Don't say "I hate your guts," rather try, "Right now I am really angry at you."

E: Express Effectively. Stop for a moment when you become angry and ask yourself, "Why am I angry, and what do I specifically want to change?" Rather than being "right," you must be committed to being effective. Ask yourself, "How can I best express my anger to get the results I want?" Remember, specificity is critical. For example, one client said to her husband, "You keep promising to come home for dinner at seven, but you've been a half hour late or more eight nights in the past two weeks. Not once did you call to let me know you'd be late. It makes me feel like you don't care, and that hurts; I'm angry." It would have done no good to say, "You make me furious because you're always late. You don't love me, and you're a selfish, inconsiderate brute." Effective anger asks for an acknowledgment of your hurt but moves on to a commitment to avoid the same mistakes in the future.

Becoming an "Emotional A.C.E." is not a competition. The goal is to make anger an opportunity for you and your lover to learn about one another, to meet each other's needs, and to affirm your love by working out conflicts together. You should both wind up feeling good about the outcomes of your arguments. This requires not only skill in expressing your anger, but also acceptance of your lover's anger as well. Whenever you have resolved a difficult argument, remember to acknowledge one another for having done so successfully. Reaffirm your commitment and enjoy the intimacy.

To develop anger skills, practice is crucial. If you have difficulty getting angry, rehearse until you feel more comfortable with it. You can pay a therapist a lot of money for this practice, but many people can do it for themselves. First, study the principles of intimate anger. Second, list specific situations at home or work in which you have difficulty communicating anger. For example, you might recall a situation in which you were hurt and felt angry but couldn't express yourself. Then, write specific statements you might make incorporating the elements of constructive anger. Fourth, practice aloud your delivery of that communication. You may feel foolish at first, but with practice, you'll be able to feel genuine anger and express it more positively and under control. If you have difficulty using new responses in an actual situation, that's okay; just give it thought and reenact what you might have done differently. Mastery comes from a willingness to acknowledge and learn from your mistakes. You are more likely to use these skills when the next difficult situation arises if you have rehearsed intimate anger dialogues before a real confrontation.

Of course, there is no one "proper" or "psychologically correct" style of anger communication that fits every love relationship. For example, some love partners seem to thrive on dispute; it keeps the passion flowing. We know a married couple who frequently heap insults and verbal abuse upon each other. Even in public, these well-educated, highly successful individuals will sometimes yell and call each other "jerk," "son-of-a-bitch," and worse. In the presence of these seemingly hostile and bitter attacks, most friends and associates cringe with embarrassment. This particular couple, for the thirty-two years of their marriage, however, has positively relished these verbal battles. In fact, both find the anger catharsis to be stimulating. They enjoy doing battle with one another and often direct that energy into passion in the bedroom. They have discovered how to make their expression of anger an intimate and constructive form of play.

Common Anger Traps

Many arguments have little to do with the issues or ideas being discussed. For instance, you and a loved one may quarrel over finances, the children, politics, home remodeling, or even your reactions to a recent film. The anger and heated words are often less about the issue and more about the frustration that ensues from a failure to listen to each other's feelings and acknowledge each other's points of view. In reviewing case notes over the past decade, we have identified ten maladaptive communication habits that cause most of the problems. We call these habits anger traps, because couples fall into them time and again.

Look at the descriptions below and see if you or your love partner are stuck in any of these emotional traps:

Anger Trap 1 *"I'm right; you're wrong."* Human beings can be incredibly self-righteous. In an argument, it is easy to know how right you are and how wrong the other person is. Neither side wants to give in, and both sides feel misunderstood. There is always a Greek chorus of like-minded friends and relatives who unequivocally support how right you are and how obviously wrong your lover is.

When both lovers are defending "I'm right and you're wrong" positions, a simple discussion of a specific issue can evolve into a powerful struggle of wills. You may think you are arguing the merits of an issue, but you wind up responding emotionally as if you are fighting for the survival of your basic self-worth. Families are notorious in this regard. How often have you heard a simple discussion at the dinner table evolve into a loud argument with everyone feeling uncomfortable?

The "I'm right" syndrome can make it difficult if not impossible to accept valuable feedback from your lover. If your lover criticizes a cherished belief, you may feel so put down that you resist whatever your lover says, to the point of adamant defiance. Even if that criticism would invite little argument, such as a suggestion that you stop smoking, some people caught in the "I'm right" trap interpret it as an attack on their emotional survival. Well-intentioned criticism is vital to a healthy love relationship, and overcoming the "I'm right" trap is crucial to allowing such healthy communications between lovers.

If you stop reactively insisting how right you are and try instead to listen receptively, you'll allow your love partner to be right as well. A key to nurturing every love relationship is to set aside your own self-righteousness and both acknowledge and value your lover's opposite point of view. Remember that reasonable people disagree about important matters all the time without becoming emotionally inflamed. If a simple discussion leads to a quarrel with your lover, the "I'm right" anger trap is probably the cause. The antidote is to recall that when it comes to sharing feelings, no one is wrong.

Anger Trap 2 *Win/lose.* Trying to "win" when you and your lover disagree is a futile endeavor. The urge to win is associated with the need to be one up and force your love partner to be one down. This competition inevitably leads to both lovers losing. Even if you "win," your lover feels resistant, defiant, and resentful for being turned into the "loser," and you will soon pay for it in diminished affection or the next round of quarreling. A variation of this anger trap is to fight over who is being "fair," and it is this petty, self-defeating bickering that leads to both lovers feeling cheated because neither gets what he or she really wants. In any dispute with your lover, you must aim for a resolution in which you both win, you both are right, and you both get your wishes and needs fulfilled. While this resolution cannot always happen in business, it can happen very often in a healthy love relationship. Disagreements between lovers have to do with priorities, recollections, choices, judgments, values, opinions, and other purely subjective perspectives. Consequently, there is usually no absolute standard for measuring who wins or what is fair.

To find creative solutions to disputes with your lover, you need to begin by accepting each other's points of view as valid. For example, your husband shouts, "You should do more of the dirty work around the house; I slave to earn us a living." Trying to convince him that his feelings of working so hard are inaccurate or that you already do most of the "dirty work" won't get you very far. Striving for a win-win solution means assuming that if you are in your love partner's shoes, you might feel exactly the same way. From that perspective, the effective response might be: "I understand how hard you have been working. I work awfully hard too, and I want to make things better for us. Let's discuss how we can make some positive changes." That doesn't mean that you must bow down three times and meekly scrub the kitchen floor or iron the laundry. Rather, you communicate respect for your lover's feelings, and then together examine practical solutions that serve you and your lover. The more you can truly empathize with your lover while maintaining your own dignity and self-worth, the more he or she is likely to move from a rigid position and empathize with you.

Anger Trap 3 *Double bind.* A communication is called a "double bind" when it contains two contradictory messages. For example, your lover says, "Come here, darling," with hostility and venom in her voice. Do you come over or don't you? You feel ambivalent because you are getting a double bind message. Here is another example: He says, "Why do you have to do everything I tell you?" In this situation, what is the love partner to do? By complying with his demand, she is doing as he tells her, but by ignoring it, her behavior continues to irritate him. Another double bind is to demand behavior that can only be spontaneous: "Show me how much you love me," or "I want you to respect me more." Even if you cooperate with these messages, you will do so with resistance as opposed to genuine love and respect. Double bind messages almost always leave you in conflict and your partner dissatisfied.

The solution to the double bind message is straightforward. Beware of putting your lover in such a trap, and if your lover trips you up with a double bind, don't try to figure out what he or she really wants. Ask instead. Often the real problem is wholly unrelated to the initial confusing message.

Anger Trap 4 *Either/or thinking.* Many people assume there is only one right answer to every question. In relationships, there is almost always more than one right answer, and the truth usually lies somewhere between the two extremes. Nevertheless, many couples create hours of needless quarrelling by taking the position that statements are either right or wrong.

Consider a typical domestic battle between lovers who think in all-or-none terms:

WIFE: You're always hassling me, always putting me down, and always finding fault with the way I raise the children and spend the money. I can never do anything right as far as you're concerned.

HUSBAND: That's not true; I never do that.

WIFE: Yes, it is.

HUSBAND: No, it's not.

WIFE: See, there you go again; disagreeing with me.

HUSBAND: I'm not disagreeing with you.

WIFE: Oh, yes you are.

HUSBAND: No, I'm not.

WIFE: So, then, you admit that you always find fault with me!

This anger trap can grow beyond what either lover may have initially intended and can result in serious problems. All too many marital clashes hinge upon either/or thinking. Couples adopt opposite positions on money, sex, relatives, personal habits, the right way to discipline children, and so on. The result is a never-ending power struggle.

The antidote is to recognize that when it comes to beliefs and perceptions, there are multiple right answers and compromise is to be highly valued. It should not be looked upon as a sacrifice of some high moral position. The more you incorporate words such as "sometimes" or "often" and avoid terms such as "never" or "always," the more you will avoid this anger trap.

Anger Trap 5 *Assumptions*. A common anger trap is assuming that you know better than your lover what he or she is "really" feeling and thinking. It is not unreasonable for you to perceive your lover's behavior differently than your lover perceives his or her actions. It is unreasonable, and a breach of trust, for you to deny your lover's report of his or her feelings, thoughts, and experience. Assuming you "know" what is true for your lover better than he or she does demonstrates absence of respect and sensitivity. It also leads to accumulating resentments and a potentially serious crisis when one lover finally "has enough" of being pushed around.

Misuse of the word "we" is the classic expression of this anger trap. Many couples say, "We feel that," "We disagree with," or "We would like to" when all that is really being said by the dominant figure, usually the male, is "I feel that," "I disagree with," or "I would like to." The more submissive and compliant love partner is not even asked for his or her beliefs, opinions or point of view. Such behavior inevitably results in diminished self-esteem and a hidden resentment. If you assume too many "we's," some day your lover will rebel with venom in his or her eyes. The solution to this anger trap is very simple. Ask your lifemate how he or she feels and accept the response as true. Also, do not speak for your love partner unless you've asked his or her opinion first.

Anger Trap 6 *Disapproval, judgments.* Excessive need for approval is a major anger trap. People with this need tend to avoid criticism at all costs and invest other people's opinions and judgments with unreasonable value: "What will the neighbors . . . your mother . . . your lover think?"

Trying to please everyone all of the time is simply impossible. No one in the history of the world has received 100 percent approval. Some people, and that will occasionally include your lifemate, are bound to dislike something you say or do no matter how hard you try to please them. You and your lover may respect each other very much, yet you are going to have some traits or behaviors that you each disapprove of. Rather than feeling hurt or angry when you face such disapproval, it is best to recognize that some criticism is healthy in any love relationship. The more you accept it as feedback and not reject it, the more you will create a sense of self-approval and learn from such criticism.

To overcome the "approval trap," distinguish between "facts" and "judgments." For example, "I work as a full-time housewife" is a fact. "I am *only* a housewife" is a judgment. The judgment may proceed further as follows: "I should have gone to college and taken up a profession. My failure to do so is a shameful disgrace. My spouse looks down on me and so does everyone else." Thus, people apologize for their backgrounds, jobs, or homes and go through life feeling ashamed. When you live in fear of judgments, you constantly punish yourself and naturally feel angry measuring yourself against other people's standards.

Every effort should be made to become less judgmental toward yourself and others. This is especially critical in a love relationship because you train your lover how to view and treat you. If you believe you are unworthy because you are "only a housewife," then it is possible your love partner will reflect this image to you, leaving you feeling rejected and insecure. If, however, you feel great about being a "housewife," "mother," and "domestic engineer" and recognize your work as one of the most important and vital professions in the world, then you will train other people to see you and what you do with great dignity. As Eleanor Roosevelt said, "No one can make you feel inferior without your consent."

Anger Trap 7 *Stress.* Under stress, there is a tendency to revert to old habits. With increasing pressures and demands outside the relationship, it is more than likely that arguments will occur. No relationship exists in a vacuum, and everyone experiences periods of intense stress. If, for example, in addition to the usual demands, you find yourself having to move, just as you are planning for the arrival of your second child, and your mother-in-law is arranging a visit, you are likely to feel irritable and more prone to arguments. It helps to be as compassionate as possible with both yourself and your love partner when going through a high-stress period.

If, in spite of your intention to stay calm, you find yourself irritable and angry when you or your lover are under stress, ask for a time-out. The purpose is not to avoid a necessary discussion but rather to take some time for each of you to relax and regain composure. You might say, "This argument is out of control and destructive. Let's take twenty minutes to cool down and unwind. Then we'll be calmer and more receptive to working it out." You also have the right to say, "Thanks for your input. I'd like to give it careful thought during a twenty-minute time-out and talk about it later." This time-out is useful in exorcising rage privately and safely, whether you go for a brisk walk or sit down to meditate and relax. In any case, a time-out will help avoid adding fuel to feelings of self-righteousness or indignation. Your time-out is an opportunity to look at both sides of the issue and consider how you may have contributed to the problem, perhaps by repeating some negative pattern or unfairly venting your frustration on your love partner.

From the following list, select the area(s) in which you and your lover experience the most frequent conflict and tension:

1. Finances
2. Child rearing
3. Extended family, in-laws, ex-spouse
4. Career versus home
5. Time management
6. Sex, quality intimacy
7. Personal habits—such as alcoholism or drug abuse versus exercise, a healthful diet, and meditation.

At a time when you are most relaxed, creatively brainstorm, looking for alternatives and choices that will reduce stress and eliminate the risk of a destructive argument. For example, you may choose to go out to dinner one less evening per week, and apply the savings toward a housekeeper. Or, take turns having special time with your child or children, freeing your spouse to explore leisurely interests—athletics, music, or reading.

Most people assume they can accomplish more in a given period than actually possible. You and your love partner would be wise in setting goals and deadlines to allow an extra 20 percent for things to go wrong. It can also avoid unnecessary stress by setting personal and relationship priorities. In that way you can effectively plan which choices and commitments will take precedence in your lives.

Anger Trap 8 *Accusations*. These expressions can range from subtle body language—raised eyebrows, a wagging finger, "tsk, tsk," or shaking the head—to an out-of-control verbal attack: "What the hell's wrong with you?" Suppose your lover said to you in an accusing tone, "You don't love me." Your reaction would probably be defensive. "Sure I do. How can you say that? I tell you I love you all the time. What's the matter with you?" You don't really want to know about your lover's accusations or what he or she expects; you just want to talk him or her out of it because you feel so uncomfortable. You might even want to make him or her ashamed of the accusation. A lot of us are critical of our love partners for criticizing us! Unfortunately, this leads to a cycle of accusations —what you resist, persists.

Accusations are a way of life in many relationships. Many people sincerely feel their lovers could improve by changing, so they berate continuously out of the misguided belief that such criticism is helpful. An accusation such as "Damn it; do you have to be such a slob? Who do you think I am, your mother?" is rarely met with "You're right, honey, from now on I'll put my clothes in the hamper." A common retort would be "Get off my back and stop acting like such a bitch. You're always so uptight." When you and your lover get caught in escalating accusations, remind yourselves that mutual love is more important than determining who's at fault or who started the argument.

When you strive to be compassionate and understanding, you will ask questions with tenderness and curiosity. First determine whether your perception of the other person is correct: "I'd like to know more about what I've done that upsets you," or "You must have good reasons for feeling as you do. Please trust me with your anger or pain," or "What do you want that you're not getting now, that would give you the experience of being loved more deeply?"

When your lover is accusatory or angry with you, try to listen to the message of hurt and restrain the temptation to be defensive. This takes great strength, but once you understand your own anger and tendency to criticize, you can better accept your lover's anger and accusations. You can make constructive statements even if your love partner doesn't know how. Ask what you did to cause the hurt, what you can do to change, and what is necessary for the anger and accusations to subside.

An angry statement that begins with "You" often makes the listener feel accused and defensive. Something is being directed personally at *you*. Most if not all "you" statements are really camouflaged "I" statements. "You are selfish" really means "I think that you are selfish in this situation." "You" statements make it easy to blame the other person, ignoring your own responsibility in the situation. For example, "You should be more affectionate" sounds as if all your friends and indeed the whole world agree with this "fact." On the other hand, saying, "I wish that sometimes you could be more affectionate" makes it clear that this statement is made in the context of the relationship and is an expression of need as opposed to a personal attack. An "I" statement is much more likely to be received constructively.

Anger Trap 9 *"Shoulds," "have tos."* A love relationship built upon "shoulds" feels like a prison with a never-ending series of demands and duties. Tight, raised shoulders are often the result. Burden your lover with shoulds, and you create resistance and resentment, rather than joyous freedom to love and serve. For a love relationship to thrive, it is best for each partner to feel as if there are 90 percent "want tos" and only about 10 percent "shoulds" and "have tos." Learning to say "I would prefer it if" instead of "You should" or "It would be nice if" as opposed to "You have to" is a critical lesson in encouraging your lover to meet your needs. Shoulds and have tos trigger old resentments from childhood toward a critical parent.

Most people often criticize in a lover the things they can't accept in themselves. For instance, if your love partner accuses you of being lazy or sloppy, there is a good chance your actions have triggered a response of disapproval toward your lover's own laziness. Your lover is saying, "How can I possibly tolerate in you what I criticize myself for all the time?" You may be inspired to improve your housecleaning habits, or you may be satisfied that you are already sufficiently hard-working, clean, and orderly. In either case, the more you recognize that your lover's demands reflect his or her own turmoil, the less likely you are to take those demands personally. In your love relationship, you are mirrors for one another. Instead of reacting defensively with "You're never satisfied with what I do around the house," empathize with your partner by saying, "A clean house is important to me also. Let's discuss what arrangement would be most satisfying for both of us." With this statement you are not out to make your partner wrong, but rather to look for a happy resolution that keeps the "mirror" clear.

Anger Trap 10 *Hitting below the belt.* Partners in an intimate relationship know each other's most vulnerable points and levels of tolerance. Threats, warnings, and punishments (e.g., "If you do, I'll leave." "You'd better stop crying now.") produce fear and invite further retaliation and sabotage. Belt lines differ with each individual. Some lovers feel devastated by yelling and screaming; others cannot tolerate swearing or hostile silence.

Another low blow consists of invalidating your lover with an inappropriate personality attack.

"You're just hostile to men."

"You're a resentful mama's boy and woman hater."

"You're saying that because you're a manic depressive."

"You're crazy."

"You're a pathological liar."

"You must have done something to create that."

Such "psychobabble" arouses further anger and defensiveness, because these comments are neither helpful nor therapeutic, just barely veiled hostile name-calling.

If you resort to low blows, you will have to live in a hostile climate. The tendency to strike below the belt is another habit usually learned from watching parental arguments. We have outlined many alternatives to such destructive behavior.

Now that you have identified the anger traps that trouble your relationship, focus on making specific changes. A simple program of reminders can be very helpful. For example, one client placed copies of the following list on the nightstand, the car dashboard, and a kitchen bulletin board to help correct faulty tactics for dealing with conflict:

Anger Traps to Work On

1. Don't "mind read," never assume you know what your love partner is thinking or feeling. Ask instead of tell.
2. Avoid "you are" messages and instead use "I feel" messages. For example, say, "I feel ignored and unappreciated when you don't call and come home late." Don't say, "You are a hostile and selfish s.o.b. for always being late."
3. Don't blame, complain, accuse, label, or attack. Do listen, praise, compliment, and forgive.

Go through the list of points under intimate and destructive anger and review the section on "Common Anger Traps." Make up your own list to carry in your pocket, place by your bed, and put on your refrigerator door to assist you to learn new positive habits in the way that you handle anger and communicate your needs. These reminders will help you improve communication skills on a daily basis.

Lightening Up

One final tip on lessening anger in your love relationship is to keep your sense of humor and, paradoxically, have fun with anger. For instance, your husband may come home after a rough day at work and take out his frustrations by yelling at the kids or you. Instead of becoming angry and miserable, try to create some humor and fun. Imagine your husband, sitting in front of the television being grouchy and irritable, as a warm and cuddly bear in need of a hug and a kiss. Hear him saying he needs your help because he has had a difficult day at work. Do not take his grumpiness seriously, because what he really needs is your care.

After you have concocted this funny image, ask yourself if your husband's tension is such a big deal that you need to confront him, yell, and set about ruining your weekend. Ask yourself if there's any reason to let it bother you since his distress has nothing really to do with you. We are not saying that his irritability is not a problem for you, particularly if it occurs repeatedly. If it only happens occasionally, however, your willingness to be compassionate and have fun will be contagious. Instead of getting caught up in an angry melodrama, slip into some slapstick comedy in your own head and loosen up. Humor and good jokes, well timed, can lighten almost anyone's burden.

Another great "exorcise" is to spend ten or fifteen minutes doing a "war dance." Put on some upbeat music, then picture the person or situation that you feel rage toward and aggressively dance out the anger. Release your hostility by yelling or screaming, jumping, punching, and kicking the air. The more uninhibited your war dance, the fuller the release. For maximum results, it is best to do this exercise until you are psychologically spent or physically exhausted.

Here is another way to lighten things up. When you are *not* tense and angry, show one another your meanest face—complete with growl and menacing look. Also, show each other your most bitter and resentful faces; be sure to look in the mirror. One way to release repressed feelings of bitterness and hostility is to create and release these feelings in an atmosphere of fun. Now finish by showing each other your looks of joy and love. This exercise is literally showing each other the "worst" and the "best" parts of you. The more you can comfortably and consciously show each other the faces of your "dark" side, the more you and your love partner will lighten up.

Another way to ease tension is the "Yes, No, Get Off My Back" exercise. If you come home tense and your spouse says something awful like "Hi," making you irritable and annoyed, it's time to *safely* release your anger and tension. Stand side by side; then jump up and down at least three times, yelling "Yes, no, get off my back." When doing this exercise, picture the situation that has been bothering you and move your arms as if to throw the burden off your shoulders. This exercise may seem silly, but try it just for fun. Both you and your spouse will feel much lighter. You can then more easily talk about what's been bothering you and have a playful, relaxed evening.

You can also significantly reduce irritability with a few mental exercises. If you think destructive, angry thoughts, you become more anxious and enraged. To lighten up, refocus your mind on positive, healing images. Visualization and guided imagery are effective tools in reducing the symptoms of chronic anger—headaches, clenched jaw, muscle spasm, tension. Experiment with each of the following visualizations:

1. Close your eyes. Imagine your body and emotions filled with lights. For example, red lights for anger and blue lights for peace and relaxation. Visualize the lights changing from red to blue, and from blue to red, and notice your physical sensations. Gradually, change all of the lights in your body to blue and experience feeling lighter.

2. Close your eyes and focus on the physical sensations in your body as you experience anger: jaws clenched, face flushed, shoulders tense, heart pounding, stomach in knots. Experience this for a minute. Don't resist . . . pause. Now, imagine finding your way out of this tense, dark place to a safe and beautiful retreat—the beach, a lake, a mountaintop. Experi-

ence the tension in your body dissolving as you move into the light. You are safe. You are relaxed. You are comfortable.

3. Close your eyes. Be aware of the anger and rage filling your mind and body . . . pause. Now go underneath your anger and hurt to visualize your love-filled heart—powerful, radiant, healing, alive. Imagine your heart able to withstand all challenges, sending renewed love to every part of your body and beaming light all around you. Your anger is merely a creative challenge, a courageous opportunity to love and be loved even more deeply. Close your eyes and return to the safety of your eternal heart whenever you need rest and renewal.

One of the major causes of anger and irritability is chronic fatigue. Remember how you feel about yourself on days when you wake up feeling refreshed and vital. You enjoy everything more, including your love relationships. If you're tired, however, even small problems can seem insurmountable. You are more likely to pick a fight or feel hostile.

On the basis of our own experience as well as scientific research, we feel that the best daily means for achieving concentrated rest and peace of mind is the Transcendental Meditation (TM) technique. TM is a reliable method you can practice anywhere; it's easy, effortless, and highly enjoyable. It is a very potent means of psychological housecleaning. Regular meditation leads to becoming less reactive and volatile. By systematically reducing stress levels you will be far less likely to carry a chip on your shoulder and turn a minor incident into a frustrating dispute. TM is especially wonderful for lovers to practice together, and for long-term growth of the heart.

The Anger Athlete

Becoming a successful anger athlete is perhaps the greatest challenge of the Love Fitness program. Intimate anger is a source of power to keep your love vibrant and your relationship healthy. Intimate anger needn't be feared and shouldn't be suppressed. The paradox of anger is that when you become comfortable with this intense emotion, you can transform it into a power that deepens love.

Every person and every couple, including ourselves, sometimes has a destructive fight. None of us is perfect at anything, including sharing and receiving anger. When you've had an argument, acknowledge your mistakes and work through them. Forgive your lover and yourself, and learn from it. Review ways in which you could have handled the situation more effectively. Intimate anger is a series of habits that you can improve upon through care, attention and practice. The more fit you become at handling your own and your love partner's anger (remember, it's a process), the greater your capacity for a vibrant relationship with your lifemate.

Chapter 6

Healing the Hurts
of Love

Emotional wounds often heal slowly. If left untreated these hurts, whether inflicted in childhood or in adult relationships, can develop into emotional scars that undermine relationships and impair the ability to love. The pain caused by rejection, betrayal, humiliation, neglect, and loss can be even more severe than that caused by physical injury. Although the body is capable of tolerating intense physical pain, the loving heart has little protection other than to lash out in rage, plunge into depression, or suppress that pain in the deep recesses of the psyche.

The natural response to an intense emotional injury is to feel overwhelmed with alternating feelings of rage and dark depression. For example, if you discover that your spouse has had an affair, it is just as common to have murderous thoughts ("I want to kill him/her . . ." "If I see them together, I'll . . .") as to have suicidal thoughts ("How could this happen . . ." "I can't go on . . ." "This hurts so much I want to die . . ."). Unless a person takes specific steps to heal a fresh emotional wound, the mind soon adapts to these unacceptably violent feelings by forcing them below the surface of consciousness. The problem is that buried feelings rarely disappear. Trapped within the psyche, they tend to fester until the original emotional wound has an opportunity to heal fully.

The impact of emotional wounds on the ability to love is broad. A fresh wound can fill the heart with so much pain as to paralyze the ability to love. That is why relationships begun on the rebound usually go nowhere. With a broken heart you may find comfort in a new relationship, but loving is almost impossible until some healing occurs. The pain of a severe emotional wound can also be turned inward to cause a variety of physical symptoms including headaches, muscle tension, loss of appetite, overeating, insomnia, gastric upset, and loss of concentration.

When the mind finally suppresses the intense pain associated with a slow-to-heal emotional injury, obvious symptoms lessen, but new, subtle, and potentially more damaging consequences occur. Emotionally, there is a tendency to fear new commitments. Scars develop that make it difficult to trust or show affection to a new lover or yourself. Painful memories may reappear from time to time, causing an upsurge of anger or a flare-up of depression. Resentments also develop and tend to seep out as poisonous, spiteful comments that transform a relationship into a nightmare of verbal abuse. Physically, suppression of pain from unhealed emotional wounds can contribute to drug abuse, obesity, high blood pressure, and more serious illnesses such as cancer and heart disease.

Few people have managed to avoid accumulating some deep emotional wounds that remain active sources of turmoil and pain. For some people, childhood hurts are a significant issue; for others, divorce, death of a spouse, rape, physical violence, or betrayal of a love is a trauma; and for still others, an emotional crisis may be triggered by ending a long-term relationship or discovering that a lover has not been faithful.

Healing the hurts of love and permanently releasing the associated emotional pain is essential to the Love Fitness program. This chapter provides a series of Love Fitness workouts designed to help you heal old emotional wounds safely and effectively.

Hidden Resentments

Denial is a natural emotional response to the hurts of love. The mind automatically responds to intense emotional pain by trying to shut off feeling. Couples often mistakenly deny their hurt feelings in the hope of maintaining stability in their relationship. The result is an accumulation of hidden pain and bitter resentments that add substantially to the normal tensions of living together. For many people, denial works so effectively that they are not aware of how painful memories and old resentments are disabling their feelings of self-worth and their ability to love. Following are the warning signs of unhealed emotional wounds and hidden resentment. Do any of the following apply to you?

- You explode in rage over small matters and later regret what you said.
- You feel left out, overlooked, unappreciated, or taken for granted at home or at work.
- You suffer frequent head, neck, back, stomach aches, or other physical complaints with no attributable physical disorder.
- You poke fun at, make spiteful comments to, or often feel like telling off or getting back at those you love.
- You abuse alcohol or drugs or go on an eating binge whenever you are emotionally upset.
- You lack confidence in your ability to sustain an intimate relationship.
- You are uncomfortable with or unaccepting of your sexuality.
- You suffer from fears of rejection, disapproval, or abandonment.
- You create an "arm's-length only" intimacy for fear of being trapped in a committed love relationship or marriage.

- You are frequently disappointed by or bitter about your family, work, the world, life, God, or other people.
- You feel as if "nobody ever loves me" and try to make other people feel sorry for you.
- You often hold back feelings of hostility and are restricted in expressing love.
- You are afraid of marrying someone who may later begin to resemble an ex-lover or parent you resent.
- You have started to act "just like" the person, parent, or spouse you may hate.
- You treat your spouse the way your ex-lover treated you.
- You find yourself experiencing the same career or money conflicts your parents had.
- You find yourself reenacting upsetting events or upheavals of a previous marriage or love relationship.
- You re-create in your adult life emotionally upsetting situations similar to the unresolved incidents of your childhood (only the characters and settings have changed).
- You feel like giving up at love.
- You feel estranged, emotionally isolated.
- You believe you never received the support or love you needed when you were younger.
- You repeat mistakes you made in love or still regret opportunities you missed years afterward.
- You feel like a victim or martyr.
- You worry that your lover will grow tired of you.
- You are afraid your career will suffer by making a commitment to settle down.

Most people recognize one or more of these signs of buried emotional wounds. A primary objective of depth psychotherapy is to uncover these old hurts and painstakingly work them through to resolution. In no way do we imply that the pain of such traumas can be resolved in one chapter or with one technique. However, by demystifying the process of healing and understanding how these old wounds affect your current psychology, you can do much to heal old emotional traumas. For the basically healthy person who is well motivated, the emotional workouts in this chapter can assist in resolving resentment and discovering a deeper capacity to love and be loved.

Childhood Struggles

We began this book with an illustration from our own lives about how the emotional trauma from exposure to our parents' constant conflict affected our love relationship. Is your parents' marriage an ideal model of what you want in a love relationship? Most people answer no; they desire much more. The fact is, however, that the state of your parents' marriage is among the most important factors in determining the quality of your own love relationship.

Many people cringe at this idea. Don't worry—you are not doomed to have a love relationship no better than your parents' marriage. Although all of us have an innate tendency to repeat our parents' mistakes, we can also avoid them. What is needed is an understanding of how your parents' relationship affected you, what bad emotional habits you may have developed, and how to change them.

A lover or even a very close friend can be enormously helpful in healing emotional traumas from parental conflict. We have devised a list of questions designed to help you recognize and change emotional habits internalized from your parents' battles. Discussing these questions with your lover or a friend can help you acknowledge hidden conflict and resentment and loosen the grip of poor parental modeling upon your adult love fitness. Take your time with each of these questions, and don't hold back. Let your feelings surface whether you are angry, sad, humiliated, enraged, or embarrassed. Accepting your feelings is part of the healing process.

1. How did your parents behave toward each other? Were they approving, loving, and happy with one another, or were they hostile, angry, or emotionally distant from each other? Was your father or mother in a dominant or submissive role? Describe the feelings, tone, and behavior between your parents. Give concrete and specific incidents.

2. What was the atmosphere like in your home when you were growing up? Was it tense, serious, and bitter, or lighthearted, excited, and relaxed? Was it very different at different stages? Why? Did your parents show physical affection for each other in front of you, such as hugs, kisses, or intimate talks? Did you sense that your parents were covering up conflicts around money, sex, alcoholism, or other issues? Be specific.

3. Over what issues did arguments arise in your family: jealousy, work, friends, values, etc.? Did you fight over dating, eating, drinking, cleanliness, household chores, schoolwork, neatness, curfew? Recount a concrete incident from childhood and from adolescence.

4. How did each of your parents treat you? Did either make degrading comments that left you feeling inferior? What specific statements did they make that you've never forgiven them for? Was there any physical or sexual abuse?

5. How did you deal with rejection from either of your parents when you felt put down, humiliated, controlled, or rejected? Did you get angry or have a temper tantrum? As a child, were you withdrawn or rebellious? Did you scream and yell? Did you try harder to be a "good boy" or "nice girl" at all costs? Did you go quietly to your room and cry and feel sorry for yourself? Share specific memories.

6. In what ways are you like your mother or father? In what ways are you different from them? What are the specific regrets and resentments you have about each of your parents? If a parent was angry and criti-

cal, do you also tend to react that way? How do you feel about having some of the negative traits your parents had? Would you like to change that behavior?

7. How have your childhood arguments and power struggles affected your adult love life? How do you act out these old patterns and power struggles? Give specific examples from your current and past love life.

These questions may provoke emotional responses that surprise you. Also, you will probably find that in one sitting, you can at best work through one set of questions. That is to be expected. This workout is best undertaken over five or six one-hour sittings. With patience and care, you and your partner can support one another in very deep healing.

The Photohistory Exercise

Here is another exercise that you and a lover or very close friend may use to heal hurts from childhood. Within everyone, no matter how adult, is an inner child who still carries unresolved hurts, needs, and pain. Photographs or home movies of both you and your partner as children can be very helpful in uncovering those unresolved feelings. The key is to find a series of photographs from your childhood as well as subsequent eras. This exercise is much more than simply reviewing an old family album. The following instructions will help you use these old photographs as a tool for self-discovery and, ultimately, self-healing.

As you look through the old photos or home movies of you or your love partner as children, consider: What was I/he or she feeling then? What insecurities and pressures were controlling that small child? How did that child feel about himself/ herself? What unresolved conflicts affected his/her moods? Were your parent(s) stern or loving?

Look at the expressions of each family member—

the way they sit or stand, the body language that is visible in the photographs. What pressures were put on the parents' shoulders? What were the relationships like between you/your love partner as a child with siblings? Were they competitive, supportive, loving, or cold? What victories, achievements, losses and deaths in the family have affected you/your lover since that photograph was taken? Photos are taken in specific situations. What specific memories can you recall in connection with each of the photos or movies?

Old photos are also a way in which to appreciate the traditions, religion, national origin, and family struggles that make an individual unique. It may be important to ask about and understand the social, political, and economic forces (such as what it was like emigrating to another country, what it was like during the counterculture sixties, what it was like growing up with various hardships) that affected you and your love partner. Through old photos and by talking to relatives and friends, you may discover difficulties that later were played out with you. As Santayana said, "Those who fail to learn from the past are doomed to repeat it." Sharing each other's childhood pains and struggles is deeply healing.

The Crisis of an Affair

Just as a love partner can be very helpful in healing childhood traumas, he or she can be terribly destructive in inflicting emotional wounds through betrayal and deceit. The injury resulting from a marital affair can rarely be healed by mere expressions of anger. A marital affair often produces a severe crisis of mistrust and rage. This is true whether the couple is in a committed love relationship or already married. Once two people feel coupled, outside affairs usually impair the love bond severely. One party feels as guilty as the other feels betrayed. Unless the resentments are healed, the love relationship is likely to become filled with bitterness or fall apart.

Mark and Nina illustrate the challenge of overcoming an affair and rebuilding a marriage. An attractive woman in her late thirties, Nina has been married to Mark for ten years. Mark had gone out of town for a business convention, and when he returned, Nina relates, "When Mark got off the plane, he seemed unusually quiet as we were driving home. Suddenly he blurted out that while he was gone, he had a fling with Camille, a saleswoman at the convention. I was in shock. He immediately said he had practiced 'safe sex,' as if that would appease me. It was just impulsive and that I had nothing to worry about; the whole thing was 'no big deal.' "

That night Nina felt as if her husband of ten years was a stranger. Mark kept apologizing and assuring her that it had only been a one-time thing. She, however, felt numb, unable to get angry and yet so hurt that she wondered whether or not to walk out. Over the next few weeks, Nina began making increasingly sarcastic remarks to Mark, while trying to restrain most of her anger. She developed headaches and stomach pains and had difficulty falling asleep. Their emotional distance grew while their sex life diminished. It was at this point that Nina felt like a "volcano about to burst" with no safe outlet. She sought counseling from us. We felt deeply for Nina's hurt and bitterness. We also emphasized the psychological importance of working through painful resentments; if she did not release suppressed feelings of hurt and anger, she would remain imprisoned by them.

In many love relationships, one or both partners have a tendency to collect resentments that they are afraid to face. They store memories of abuse, betrayal, and rejection, in part due to repeated hurt, and also because they don't know how to change the relationship. Some resentments, such as infidelity or physical abuse, are major. Others result from little annoyances and minor irritations that are part of daily living.

In both instances, resentments pile up over the life of a relationship to poison the underlying love.

Paralyzed by feelings of betrayal, Nina was initially unable to confront Mark and the deep hurt caused by Mark's affair. We told Nina that if she wanted to stay with Mark, she would have to acknowledge her resentment and pain so that the healing process could begin. We worked with Nina over a three-month period during which we recommended a variety of Love Fitness workouts. Here are the exercises she found most useful.

"Writing" the Wrong

We suggested Nina set aside private time to make a list of her resentments and describe each painful memory or hurt as specifically as possible. Once she started her list, tears and anger began to pour out. Here is a partial list of Nina's resentments:

"I hate you for screwing Camille."

"I hate you for your betrayal and the pain you caused me."

"I hate you for humiliating me."

"I hate you telling me it was 'safe sex' and I had nothing to worry about."

"I resent your sexist, 'no big deal' attitude; if I had had a fling, you'd be crushed."

"I hate you for expecting me to immediately be understanding when I needed to cry."

"I resent you for making it sound like you're now the suffering one."

"I hate you for blaming our diminished sex life on me."

"I resent you for continuing to stare at other women on the beach and at parties."

"I resent you for getting upset whenever I ask you for reassurance."

"I resent you for trying to be 'all smiles' and your 'Everything is wonderful!' attitude."

"I resent you for telling me to 'get over it' and not to be 'so angry.' "

When Nina completed the Writing the Wrong exercise, she felt as if a load had been lifted from her shoulders. The purpose of this exercise is not to punish anyone or wallow in pain but to release bitter feelings safely. Once you let go of your bitterness and feel more at peace, you will be in a better position to initiate a constructive dialogue with whoever betrayed or hurt you. By first completing your own psychological housecleaning, you will be better able to share your hurt, your anger, and, when appropriate, your love.

Exorcising Rage

Earlier we discussed the difference between intimate and destructive anger. One subject we didn't broach is the difference between anger and rage. The difference is more than one of degree. Anger can be a constructive energy to facilitate communication. Rage is a destructive energy of overpowering force. While anger is the natural response to ordinary hurts of love, rage is an automatic, emotional response to threat of survival, severe rejection, betrayal, or physical abuse.

It is essential to have a safe means of releasing rage. For this, we suggest using the "Love Bat," a durable cushionlike bat with a handle for gripping. Nina found the Love Bat to be a perfect tool for pounding out rage with no damage to herself or her belongings. While Mark was at work, she closed the door to her bedroom, took the phone off the hook, and found a comfortable chair. She then closed her eyes and visualized the act of betrayal; her pain at seeing Mark with another woman. At first, she felt inhibited, but once she began to give herself permission, she found a tremendous release of pent-up rage. Love Bat in hand, Nina pounded the bed mattress angrily and shouted, "You bastard; you whore; I hate you both for what you did!" Nina visualized Mark's face as she did this. "How dare you give someone else your passion and give me a boring weekly sex routine. How would you like it if I went out and had a wild affair? You selfish sleaze; I hate you." Nina gave herself permission to do all the vicious and vengeful things she had secretly been fantasizing, but did not know how to release. After about forty minutes, she felt completely spent and drained. Later she commented, "My throat got sore, but after lots of yells I was able to have a good cry and release my pain. I also felt lighter and much more in control of my rage."

Rage, which is characterized by the intention to destroy, must be appropriately and safely discharged. As long as you remember that you will not act out your rage on actual people, this exercise causes them no damage. In fact, in the long run, it will contribute to their well-being as well as yours. Everyone has some suppressed screams of rage, but usually these feelings are so powerful and unacceptable that most people hold their pent-up rage inside. This repression of violent feeling can be damaging to your health and well being, while safely releasing rage can give you back your self-esteem and power.

The first step in healing your own rage is acknowledging the existence of this violent energy within. Accepting this dark side of yourself can be frightening. To test whether you may be harboring buried rage, think back on those incidents where you may have been betrayed or abused by a friend or lover, or humiliated by a parent or a teacher. If the rage is there, the memory alone may cause your jaw to clench or your heart rate to accelerate.

In order to release pent-up rage safely and constructively, like Nina, you can use the Love Bat or a large pillow, while imagining the painful incident or the negative aspects of the person who hurt you. Beat the mattress or couch until you are exhausted, as you scream out all your resentments. Our clients also enjoy the Squeez'em for wrenching out their frustrations. This plastic troll-like character has a face you love to hate. The Squeez'em snaps back into shape no matter how hard you pound, punch, or crush it.

Jogging, brisk walking, aerobics, dancing, swimming, competitive sports, and other forms of vigorous exercise are additional ways to let off steam. Beware, however, of using sports as a means of escaping from rage. In order to release rage, you must get in touch with the memories of your injury. For example, you can play a game of tennis where you picture the tennis ball being the negative aspects of the person you wish to destroy. Or, you can deal repeated blows to a punching bag while you envision the former lover who hurt you terribly.

Another important reason to discharge rage safely and appropriately is to avoid a long debilitating depression. For some, depression is, in part, resentment turned inward. As you release your rage through these techniques, you will likely experience these benefits:

1. A reduction or elimination of the stress symptoms, including headaches and muscular tension.
2. An increase in sexual vitality.
3. Reduced feelings of depression, including the reduced desire to escape through drugs, alcohol, or binge-eating.
4. Increased ability to forgive and to direct your attention on healing your love relationship.

A Heart Letter

If you try to deal with a recent betrayal in a Heart Talk, you may not get very far. The issues are too volatile for effective communication. Your lover may easily get angry and interrupt you. Even if your lover has agreed to say only "Tell me more," the intensity of your rage may very likely provoke a defensive response which prevents you from working through your feelings. One way to overcome this barrier to heart-to-heart communication is through a "Heart Letter."

This exercise is very simple. You write a letter in which you disclose to your lover the full intensity of your hurt, rage, and pain. By first writing your pent-up feelings in letter form, you give yourself and your lover an opportunity to hear and acknowledge hostile feelings in a structured, safe manner.

There are additional benefits to composing a Heart Letter. Deep hurt is often accompanied by an overwhelming desire to take immediate action, and writing a Heart Letter meets this need. Describing your emotions on paper establishes a beginning, middle, and end, reducing inner chaos and giving you a renewed sense of control and power. Following a Heart Letter, you will find yourself in a more positive frame of mind to elicit a meaningful Heart Talk with your love partner. The Heart Letter can also prevent further outbursts of hostility by emphasizing responsibility for the results in your relationship, allowing the shift from victimization to accountability.

To begin healing her marriage, we suggested to Nina that she write a Heart Letter to Mark. We explained that for most married couples, underneath anger there is hurt, and underneath hurt there is love, even when the anger rises to the level of rage. To be effective, a Heart Letter must express the rage, hurt, and love. We gave Nina the following instructions in composing her Heart Letter:

1. Describe the full intensity of hurt and rage, but beware of merely dumping accusations on your love partner. Be specific about the injury and the pain. Express pain with "I" statements, such as, "I felt betrayed when . . ." "I still feel unresolved about . . ." or "I felt angry about . . ." Take responsibility for your feelings, and avoid accusatory "you" statements such as "You did this" or "You should've . . ."

2. Acknowledge that you both can grow from the incident. Be willing to admit that you might have contributed to marital tension and miscommunication. The issue is not to place blame but to learn how to improve and rebuild the love and trust in your relationship.

3. Express love and the desire to rebuild trust and intimacy. Your Heart Letter is not complete until you have written about forgiveness and love. You don't have to pretend you don't love your lifemate to punish him or her. In fact, the more you express feelings of tenderness, the more easily your lover can acknowledge your pain. Forgiveness doesn't mean forgetting or whitewashing what has happened, but rather letting go, moving on, and favoring the positive.

The purpose of a Heart Letter is both to convey your point of view and to express emotion. First and foremost, write a Heart Letter for yourself. Allow yourself to express and work through your anger, hurt, fear, and sadness until you experience a new sense of love and understanding. The process of releasing negative feelings and coming to a genuine state of love and forgiveness is essential to personal growth. When you stop loving, it is you who suffers the most. When you hold on to rage, resentment, and bitterness, it is your flow of love that is blocked. When you are willing to work through your negative emotions and re-create love, then you are the winner.

In each Heart Letter, begin by expressing your rage, and allow yourself to progress through each emotional level until you reach your love. The following lead phrases may help if you have difficulty moving from one stage to the next:

Level 1: Rage. Express your rage, resentment, and hatred: "I hate it when . . ." "It makes me furious when . . ." "I'm disgusted with . . ." "I resent . . ." "I'm fed up with . . ." "I can't stand. . . ."

Level 2: Hurt. Express your hurt, disappointment, and pain: "It hurts me when . . ." "I feel disappointed that . . ." "I feel rejected when . . ." "I feel jealous when you . . ." "It's devastating to me when you . . . ."

Level 3: Fear. Express your fear, anxiety, and insecurity: "I feel scared when I . . ." "I am frightened when you . . ." "I'm afraid that . . ." "I feel tense and anxious when you . . ." "I feel insecure about. . . ."

Level 4: Sadness. Express your sadness, remorse, and responsibility: "I'm sorry that . . ." "I feel awful when I . . ." "I feel sad that I . . ." "I feel sad that you . . ." "I feel guilty because. . . ."

Level 5: Wishes. Express specifically your wishes, goals, and wants, not your demands: for example, "It would be helpful for us to have at least two sessions with a competent therapist," or "I'd like for each of us to do another Heart Letter during the next week." "I wish I felt . . ." "I wish you had . . ." "I want . . ." "I hope. . . ."

Level 6: Love and forgiveness. Express your love, understanding, and forgiveness: "I love you because . . ." "What I love most about you is . . ." "Thanks to this relationship I . . ." "I'm proud of you for . . ." "I forgive you for . . ." "I forgive myself for . . ." "I love it when . . ." "I understand that . . ." "What I have learned is. . . ."

Nina gathered her courage and followed the above instructions. After several days of thought she composed the following Heart Letter:

Dear Mark,
 Out of my love for you and the commitment to our marriage, there are some deep feelings I need to share. I bring up this unfinished business out of the sincere

desire to complete it, and to be more loving. I did both of us a disservice by being so nice and understanding right after you told me about the affair. I'm glad you told me, but inside I was burning up, so I need to share all of my feelings with you.

I despise you for having that affair. It makes me sick to think of you having sex with another woman. I hate having to worry about whether or not I am now in danger of AIDS, herpes, or other sexual diseases. I'm disgusted by your big, insecure, sexual ego. I hate picturing you flirting with that little bitch. I felt hatred when you asked me to put a smile on my face and forget about it. I resent you for not giving me the opportunity to share my anger with you.

I feel so hurt by what you did my heart is breaking. I feel disgust when I imagine you laughing and joking with her while I sat home alone. I feel betrayed and deeply rejected. I feel so sad and distant from you. I want to feel close to you again. It hurts me that you gave so much attention to another woman, yet your sex drive with me has decreased.

I'm afraid our marriage is over now and you'll leave me. I'm afraid I'll never be able to trust you again. I'm afraid you aren't in love with me anymore. I'm scared you find other women more attractive than me and I'm no longer what you want. I'm scared I can't handle the competition out there. I'm afraid this affair will always come between us. I'm scared of losing you and being alone.

I'm sorry I wasn't there to give you what you needed, and you went to get it elsewhere. I'm sorry that all of this has happened. I'm sorry I'm so jealous. Please understand my pain. I need you to hold me, accept all of my feelings, and make me feel special again.

I want us to be intimate lovers again. I want to trust you again. I want to forgive you. I want to have more fun with you again. I want to heal this trauma and rededicate ourselves to each other. I want us to be happy together again. I don't want to feel threatened when we aren't together all the time. I want to love you and feel more passionate toward you.

I love being with you, Mark. I love the way you listen to me and really care about what I feel. Thank

you for being understanding about my fears and insecurities. You are the most wonderful man I know, and
I know you feel as terrible as I do about this. I know
we can make our marriage work. Thank you for being
so honest with me and being willing to work on healing this together. I want us to learn from this experience and love each other more fully. I cherish our life
together.

I love you,
Nina

After Mark read this Heart Letter, they talked and
wept for several hours. As Nina shared, "This was a
huge breakthrough because we had been walking on
eggshells ever since the affair. Mark told me he felt
relieved to finally talk about what had been hurting
us. Mark still felt very guilty and blamed himself for
our emotional distance."

Nina and Mark continued marital counseling to improve heart-to-heart communication and begin moving
forward. As we explained to them, in an intimate
relationship both people are constantly changing and
evolving as individuals and as a couple. Regular Heart
Letters, in addition to Heart Talks, are another way of
encouraging communication of intense feelings that
you may be afraid to face. The "I love yous" don't
sound insincere and veiled with resentment, but remain clear, bright, and honest. Through their commitment to communicate heart to heart, Nina and Mark
turned their severe marital crisis into an opportunity
to become closer; they achieved a real breakthrough.
In a follow-up session one year later, they reported
their sex and love life had reached a higher level of
intimacy than ever before.

As emphasized in Chapter 3, there is no innocent
party in an unhappy love relationship. Emotionally
there are no victims. Both partners contribute to whatever happens. Yes, Mark had the extramarital affair,
but when Nina took responsibility and looked back,
she realized that she too had been ignoring problems
in their relationship. They had lost some of the inti-

macy and emotional connection that made their relationship vibrant. Nina and Mark allowed their lives to become so busy that there was no time for a romantic weekend together. This does not excuse Mark for his actions, but it is valuable to ascertain each person's part in creating the problem.

No love relationship has a martyr. Taking responsibility means recognizing how you participated (at least indirectly) in setting up a problematic relationship. Similarly, no relationship has an absolute tyrant or dictator. No one can make you feel inferior or subservient without your permission. Mark acted out of the emotional distance and sexual boredom that both he and Nina created. A marital crisis can lead to a breakdown or breakthrough. Once Mark and Nina assumed joint responsibility for the situation, they were able to make substantive, positive changes for the future.

Forgiving from the Heart

Learning to forgive from the heart has been advocated by the greatest spiritual and religious teachers since the beginning of recorded history. Modern psychological research confirms the importance of forgiving fully and completely for the health and vitality of love relationships. To forgive does not mean to forget, but it does mean to let go and move beyond.

Holding on to rage and resentment may easily cause cynicism and bitterness to predominate over love. Intimacy remains clouded with venom and fear: "I'm still terrified of that rotten s.o.b.," or "I feel such hatred and still want revenge." The price of withholding forgiveness is your own peace of mind, which impedes your capacity to love and be loved.

Earlier in our counseling, we asked Nina, "Do you want to let go of your resentments or do you still want revenge?" We explained that if she remained committed to revenge, her energy would remain bound in bitterness and defenses. If she chose to forgive, the release and the relief would free her to resolve the conflict. She finally chose to forgive.

We then suggested the following "Forgiving from the Heart" exercise.

This visualization exercise is designed to heal lingering hurts. Find a comfortable spot and make sure you will not be disturbed for thirty minutes. Close your eyes, relax, and visualize you and your love partner (or whomever you are working on forgiving—a parent, a friend, an ex-spouse) in an appropriate setting, perhaps your current home. If for some reason you find it difficult to visualize, try expressing your feelings while looking at a photograph of him or her.

With that image in mind, say in your own words, "Out of the love I have for you and the love you have for me, there are some things we need to clear up, from my heart to yours." For the next twenty or so minutes, continue to visualize your love partner and fully express the resentments you harbor. Imagine you have complete permission to say whatever is in your heart. Throughout, picture your lover giving you the support, respect, and love you deserve.

To end the exercise, take a few deep breaths and imagine a healing light sweeping over both you and your love partner. The light can be seen as emanating from any source comfortable to you—God or the universal spirit of love. Just as warmth and light can assist the healing of a physical wound, this inner light can assist in healing the pain and bitterness in your heart. Relax for five or ten minutes in this inner light to complete your workout. If you experience a lingering pressure in your head or some irritability, be sure and take additional time to rest and let go.

After doing this exercise, you may feel a release of tension or you may feel emotionally fatigued. Lie down, take a few deep breaths, and let yourself unwind. Practice this technique at least three or four times following a major trauma. Repeat the exercise until your "heavy" resentments lose their intensity and become "lighter."

Nina found the Forgiving from the Heart exercise extremely powerful. As she described it, "I pictured Mark and myself sitting in our den, and all sorts of feelings came up—anger, revulsion, sadness. For the first time I could fully express myself; I didn't have to defend myself against Mark's resistance or angry tirade. After ten minutes of visualization I felt tears streaming down my face. I was so relieved to get the negativity out of my system."

After several sessions, Nina experienced a release from resentment and a reopening of her heart. She and Mark went on to fully renew their bond of love and intimacy.

Rx for the Hard-Hearted: Appreciation

Why do relationships get boring? One reason may be that you no longer give attention to what attracted you to your lover in the first place. In fact, you may have gone so far as to focus on the unpleasant experiences you've had together, disregarding the pleasant ones you share. How does this happen?

You may have exaggerated images of your lover's bad habits. Perhaps you remember all the hateful things said in every hostile argument you've ever had. As this dialogue is played over and over again in your head, resentments grow deeper and soon it becomes impossible to see any positive qualities in the person you once loved so dearly. If you only pay attention to resentments and to the negative, those aspects will grow stronger in your life. What if, in the middle of a heated argument, you remembered your partner teaching you something, a time when your lover did something really special for you, or even the first time you passionately kissed and made love. This could have a great impact on how you treat the person you love and the outcome of your argument.

In long-term love relationships, there is a tendency to take each other for granted and give less and less acknowledgment to your lover's best qualities (such as warmth, affection, consideration, the ability to cooperate and compromise). Lovers who take each other for granted often criticize each other for becoming hard-hearted, selfish, and unfeeling. This process becomes self-fulfilling as criticism begets criticism. Part of the solution involves asking yourself, "Is this what I want in my life and in my love relationship? Is this really what I want to see happen?" Now is the time to examine the effects of your perceptions and make the changes necessary to prevent a situation you would rather avoid (divorce, boredom, apathy).

Many problems among couples arise from a lack of appreciation. Without being consciously aware of it, lovers resort to blaming and complaining when denied what they really seek, which are positive expressions of appreciation. If you do not get the respect and affection you need, you are likely to ignore and/or feel victimized by your lover's demands. Some people would rather leave than ask to be appreciated. They say, "I shouldn't have to ask or beg for love." Although it may seem uncomfortable at first, if you see your lover taking you for granted, it is *your* responsibility to request the expression of the love and appreciation you deserve. You shouldn't have to wait for occasional compliments or hint about your needs. You deserve to be consistently and lovingly appreciated.

It is a serious mistake to underestimate the need for and power of appreciation in a love relationship. Our experience indicates that consistent expression of appreciation can make enormous differences in revitalizing a relationship that has gone stale. It takes practice at first to stop taking your lover for granted, but the rewards are well worth it.

Here are some suggestions to start expressing more mutual appreciation:

- Spend time at the day's end to acknowledge each other for all you have done. Take turns using a few Heart Talks: "Something I appreciate about you is . . ." "Something I'd like to be appreciated for . . ." "The best thing about our love relationship is . . ." "The things I love most about our marriage are. . . ." No one ever tires of hearing how much they are loved. By telling your lifemate that you love him or her, you are not merely conveying information, you are renewing your love through appreciation.

- Each of us thrives on different kinds of appreciation. For example, a beautiful woman may receive frequent attention for her physical attributes, but what she may really need is acknowledgment for being competent, intelligent, and effective. On the other hand, a person who is highly successful may get enough acknowledgment for his or her career performance, but what he or she really needs to hear is that the love will be there whether he or she succeeds or fails. Someone who is constantly acknowledged for being strong may also need acknowledgment for those times when he or she is willing to be open and vulnerable.

- Due to childhood experiences, you may have difficulty in graciously accepting attention and appreciation from your love partner. You may jump in to "even the score" ("I love you, too. You're wonderful, also.") or brush aside compliments as undeserved. If this pattern is true for you, practice accepting the love instead of keeping yourself love starved. Remember, there is a simple, appropriate response to a heartfelt compliment: "Thank you."

- Appreciation is a two-way street. Expressing your gratitude will inspire others to acknowledge their gratitude for you. Tell your lifemate why you love him or her. For example: "That was an excellent dinner you made." "I like that outfit you are wearing." "Your efforts to exercise have paid off. You look great." "You are so much fun to be with." "I really enjoy it when you sing and play the piano for me." "Our love means a great deal to me." "Having you by my side gives me such strength." "I admire how honest and straightforward you are in business." "You have an excellent memory." "Your enthusiasm is contagious." "Thank you for being available to listen when I have something on my mind." "I love how you parent our children."

A relationship characterized by emotional generosity is one of fulfillment, respect, and caring. Five specific acknowledgments a day keep the marriage counselor away. If you have fallen into the habit of arguing or taking each other for granted, try listing five positive qualities about your lifemate and tell him or her at the very next opportunity. Take note of his or her responses. You will see the power of appreciation firsthand.

Mending a Broken Heart

Not all love relationships are meant to last. Sometimes it doesn't work out; it's just not meant to be. Loss is an inevitable part of love, and there is no denying that the pain of a broken heart can be emotionally devastating. To avoid emotional distance in future relationships, you need to heal a broken heart completely and learn what you can from the past.

Sandra, a thirty-two-year-old, highly successful rock-and-roll promoter and manager, felt devastated when Elliot, her lover of four years, wanted to begin dating other women. Sandra thought theirs was a fulfilled relationship that would eventually lead to marriage. Instead, one evening Elliot announced that he wanted to feel independent, so he was going to move out.

Unwilling to lose him, Sandra struggled to save the relationship. When she came to see us, however, she lamented, "I can't stand the thought of what he might be doing on nights when I'm on tour. He desires other women and only wants us to be friends. I can't believe it. We're breaking up." Sandra cried, "Our apartment, all the memories, remind me of him. I want to call him but I know it won't do any good. I'm enraged that our love doesn't mean more to him, that he could be so unfeeling. I guess it's really over. I can't go back."

Sandra was suffering intensely, unable to resolve her feelings of loss and rage. She began having tension headaches and early-morning awakening. To help Sandra heal the pain of her broken heart, we provided some specific suggestions to care for herself during the mending process. Here are the essential points:

- *A broken heart requires at least as much care as a broken bone*. With proper care you can be confident that you will heal. The same powerful forces that mend a broken bone will heal your emotional pain, but a wounded heart needs time to heal.
- *A broken heart goes through four stages of healing*. First, you will experience shock and denial ("I can't believe it." "This can't be happening." "It's not over." "He/she will be back."). Second, you will experience anger ("How could he/she do this to me?" "I want to tear her/him apart." "I hate him/her for leading me on."). Third, you will go through sadness and depression ("I can't live without him/her." "I'll never find anyone else again." "Now I'm alone and it hurts." "I'm afraid of what is happening."). Finally, you will reach understanding and forgiveness ("We had some good times together." "Our lives were going in opposite directions." "It is too bad we made such mistakes, but our lives must go on." "I have gained a lot from knowing him/her."). These four stages are inevitable. Each stage may last a few days or weeks or months. Have faith that healing will occur. Others have gone through these stages of healing a broken heart, and you will too. All the

remaining suggestions will help you get through each of the stages of healing.

• *Be with the pain.* Admit you're hurting. You may be struggling to believe and to disbelieve what has happened. You must face reality. Feeling the pain and desolation of emotional trauma is a normal sign of healing. It bears proof that you are alive. Although you may find the emotional upset chaotic and even frightening, be with the pain. Let it heal and it will end.

• *The greater your hurt, the more time required to heal.* In this era of instant gratification, many people are unwilling to give themselves the time they need. Time may be a luxury, but it is one you deserve. Be careful not to rush the healing. What you resist persists. Take care of your emotional needs now to avoid chronic pain years from now.

• *The healing process is not smooth.* You're going to experience ups and downs. One day you may feel the pain is almost over; the next day you seem to hurt twice as badly. You may feel positive and hopeful, then find yourself besieged by guilt or sadness. Birthdays, anniversaries, and holidays can be especially taxing. Depression is often worse upon awakening or when coupled with physical illness. You can expect to be more vulnerable, and your moods will fluctuate. These ups and downs are signals that healing is underway.

• *Get more rest.* The number one prescription for an injury, physical or emotional, is rest. Extra sleep will help, especially if you wake up exhausted. Set aside extra time in the morning and afternoon for meditation or relaxation. Pamper yourself with a soothing whirlpool bath, massage, or a weekend visit with family or friends.

• *Keep to a regular routine.* Healing is most rapid when rest is balanced with dynamic activity. Too much rest will encourage self-pity and even lethargy. Quality activity is the best antidote. Keep to

a regular schedule at home and at work, and plan
daily exercise.

- *Remember you are not alone.* "Misery loves company." You have plenty of company. You can't be
human without experiencing emotional suffering.
Think of all the people you know who have suffered terrible losses. Like them, you will recover.
The pain will pass and you will be stronger.
- *Disappointment is a blow to your self-esteem.* No
doubt about it. No one suffers a major setback
without also experiencing some self-doubt. Guilt,
worry, and self-depreciation are symptoms of your
hurting. Don't give them prime-time status by
paying them too much attention. They have only a
temporary reality, nothing more.
- *Your judgment may be clouded.* You'd be wise to
postpone important decisions, such as changing
your job or residence, until you're further along in
recovery from hurt. Nor is this the time to look
for a new love relationship. If you must make a
major decision, seek helpful advice from trusted
friends.
- *Beware of the rebound.* Following a broken heart,
everyone feels empty. Just as nature abhors a
vacuum, so does the human psyche. You're likely
to feel an intense desire to seize the very next
opportunity to ignite a fiery new romance. Falling
madly in love after a traumatic loss may feel terrific at first, but romance on the rebound is usually doomed for more emotional hurt.
- *Critical dos and don'ts.* A first aid kit of dos and
don'ts includes the following:

Dos	Don'ts
1. Do stay calm.	Don't panic.
2. Recognize and accept your injury.	Don't deny the hurt.
3. Be with the pain.	Don't blame yourself.
4. Take time to heal.	Don't dwell on the negative.
5. Rest, nurture yourself.	Don't abuse alcohol or drugs.

Dos	*Don'ts*
6. Allow yourself to be cared for by friends and family.	Don't stay isolated.
7. Stick to a routine.	Don't create more chaos.
8. Take care in making important decisions.	Don't make impulsive judgments.
9. Accept understanding and support.	Don't be afraid to ask for help.
10. Anticipate a positive outcome.	Don't lose faith.

• *It's okay to feel angry.* Whenever you experience hurt, anger is inevitable. Some people hide it, others have difficulty controlling it. It's healthy to get angry under the right circumstances and in the right way. Anger can be a positive, even satisfying experience when used to express your hurt and as a vehicle to improving your relationships.

• *Feel depressed?* That is natural! At any given time, millions of people feel depressed because they have suffered a major hurt or disappointment. There's nothing shameful about depression. When you suffer an emotional blow, the hurt isn't all in your mind. Biochemical changes occur in your brain that produce feelings of alarm and depression. Now is the time for grieving. Everything else can wait. By denying your loss, you postpone the healing process and may find yourself plagued by attacks of depression for months. Do your mourning now.

• *Have a good cry.* Don't try to pretend that it doesn't bother you. Crying is a natural response to a hurt or disappointment. If you hurt and the tears are coming, let them flow and feel your pain fully. Crying is an important part of cleansing the pain.

• *Suicidal thoughts?* You are not alone; most people are unhappy enough at least once in their lives to have a suicidal thought. This feeling of intense despair is symptomatic of your pain. A thought of suicide is just a thought; it does not require action. If suicidal thoughts persist and you are afraid you might act on them, seek help immediately. You can always telephone the operator and ask her to connect you with the local suicide prevention agency. You can also contact family, friends, a minister, or your physician, or go directly to a hospital emergency room. Suicidal thoughts may signal intense anger over being hurt. Instead of accepting the anger and releasing it, you are turning it against yourself. This is a mistake. The anger needs to find appropriate expression. Safely venting your anger with a Love Bat or Squeez'em is an important step to healing.

- *Thinking of him/her?* If you have suffered a divorce or romantic breakup, you may be tempted to rekindle the relationship. Imagining that you can renew a relationship once it's over is a predictable path to self-punishment. It's like tearing off the scab on a wound trying to heal. The only result is a lot more pain. Accept the reality; let yourself mourn. That's the best way to help yourself develop a greater capacity for love in the future.

- *Heal at your own pace.* Friends or relatives may tell you, "It's about time you got over it," or "That's enough crying; now you should get on with your life." This advice is well intended, but remember that you have the right to experience your hurt and heal fully. Telling yourself, "Who cares?" or "I'm fine now" when you don't feel that way is a false attempt at acceptance and understanding. If you've suffered a major loss, it may be a year or more before your grieving is complete. Not that your life has to stop in the interim, but it does mean you have the right to take it at your own pace.

- *Indulge in positive rather than negative addictions.* Now is a good time to start running, swimming, playing tennis, meditating, or hiking in the woods. These are intrinsically healing activities and naturally pleasurable—positive addictions. Beware of your self-abusive tendencies. Alcohol may temporarily numb the pain, but in the long run will only prolong the suffering. So, too, will marijuana, cocaine, uppers, downers, and any other "recreational" drugs. Momentary highs mask the pain; what you need to do is be with it. If you're a calorie junkie, take special care to avoid putting on unwanted pounds. Any solace you get from food will be offset by the drop in your self-esteem as your waistline increases. The only drugs to be taken are those prescribed by your physician.

• *Be willing to let go of your pain.* There is a time for being with your pain and a time to let it go. Though it may seem paradoxical, pain can become a friend. You may be tempted to hold on to it longer than is necessary. Staying distraught, sullen, and withdrawn is no proof of love. The unconscious thinking goes something like, "I've lost something important, so at least I'm going to savor my bittersweet tragedy." You need not be a Byron to become romantically attached to your pain.

A Farewell Heart Letter

To further help Sandra heal her deep hurts, we asked her to write a "Farewell Heart Letter." As described earlier, a Heart Letter addresses six emotions in this order—rage, hurt, fear, sadness, wishes, and forgiveness:

Level 1. Rage. (I hate . . . , I'm furious that . . . , I'm angry because. . . .)

Level 2. Hurt. (I'm hurt that . . . , I feel pain because . . . , I'm disappointed that. . . .)

Level 3. Fear. (I'm scared that . . . , I worry that . . . , I'm terrified. . . .)

Level 4. Sadness. (I'm sad that . . . , I'm sorry for
. . . , I regret. . . .)

Level 5. Wishes. (I wish I had . . . , I wish you
. . . , I hope? . . .)

Level 6. Love and forgiveness. (I understand that
. . . , I forgive you for . . . , I forgive me for. . . .)

This exercise was a breakthrough for Sandra, enabling her to acknowledge the negative aspects of her
ex-lover and open fully to the anger, hurt, and loss.
Here is the letter Sandra wrote:

Dear Elliot,

I'm angry at you because I couldn't control you and
because I couldn't win you over. I hate you because
you rejected me. I'm angry because all my friends are
either married or in good relationships and I am alone
again. I'm furious because we had so much in common
and I really wanted this to work. I'm angry because I
was not important enough to you. I'm angry because
marriage could have been so great. I'm angry that
when you said you loved me, I usually answered that I
didn't feel like you did. I pushed so hard for what I
wanted that I didn't appreciate what you were able to
give. I'm angry because you would rather be single
and alone than be with me.

I'm hurt because I started off in this relationship so
powerful and strong, but as I gave in to love I became
so weak, and vulnerable. I'm hurt that you wanted to
be with me only when you felt like it, not all the time.
I feel pain because I cannot give up anything in my
life; I hold on to everything. I feel pain because I
allowed this to happen to myself. I'm disappointed
that you couldn't open up and allow yourself the joy
of loving me. I'm disappointed that our relationship
started with so much hope and ended with so much
resentment, pain, and hurt. I'm disappointed that I
have another failed relationship.

I'm afraid that I will be alone forever. I'm scared
that men won't find me sexy and attractive. I'm scared
that a man that I fall in love with will never love me.
I'm scared that I won't find a husband. I worry that I
am getting too old to have children.

I understand that I must forgive you. I understand

that I must love and forgive myself for my mistakes. I understand that you are also in pain.

I wish you and I could have met when we both were more mature. I want to heal this pain and move on in my life. We cannot be friends now because I couldn't bear to see you with another woman. I don't want to see or hear from you until I heal myself. I forgive you for wanting to be on your own instead of being with me. I thank you for the love you gave to me and I forgive you, Elliot, for not being in love with me.

Good-bye,
Sandra

It took Sandra several hours to compose this letter detailing her feelings. By the time she came back to our office, the impact of this letter was already evident. She had made the transformation from a woman crippled by anger and hurt to one who had learned substantially about her own needs after having gone through an intense relationship. This exercise did not lessen the intensity of Sandra's loss, but it did help to unlock her pent-up emotions and begin the process of healing.

Letting Go of Your "If Onlys"

After working out the anger and depression, it is possible to begin transforming your emotional hurt into forgiveness and personal growth. A lingering obstacle can be regret over what might have been. In healing hurts of love, it is crucial to let go of the "if onlys" and allow that remorse to pass.

To heal completely, Sandra needed an opportunity to let go of her "if onlys"—the memories and wishes about what she did or failed to do that left her with regrets. Also included in Sandra's list of "if onlys" were circumstances beyond her control, but ones that nevertheless left her feeling remorseful.

Following our instructions, Sandra prepared for this

exercise by allotting for thirty minutes of complete privacy. She sat down with a box of tissues, a pen, and a pad of paper and began writing down her regrets and wishes about what might have been. Later she described this exercise as creating "a great release. Tears were streaming down my face and I just kept writing."

Among the "if onlys" Sandra wrote were the following:

If only you hadn't been so recently divorced and on the rebound.

If only your mother and I hadn't had such an awkward first meeting and liked each other more.

If only I had expressed more faith in our relationship and hung in there when you had doubts.

If only I hadn't thrown a temper tantrum at your birthday party.

If only we had gone to see a good therapist earlier, at the first sign of trouble.

If only I hadn't been so bitchy.

If only we had made more time together and not let work dominate our lives.

If only I had understood what you wanted from me.

The more specific the "if onlys," the more this exercise will release the pain you feel. Your goal is not to dwell on remorse or criticize yourself. Instead of continuing to punish yourself inappropriately, this exercise will help you to forgive yourself and your ex-lover, and further accept what was meant to be. When you truly forgive and let go of your "if onlys," you will feel wiser and much more alive. You will be ready to love again.

In addition to the If Onlys exercise, here are some additional suggestions for releasing regrets and remorse:

• *Forgive the other.* After working through your anger and pain, you are in a better position to truly forgive. Whether your lover left you, your friends betrayed you, your boss fired you, or life has dealt you a bad break, you gain strength by forgiving that person or the "fates" as soon as you can. The act of forgiveness is for your benefit, not theirs. It is for your peace of mind and the quality of your future love relationships. Remember that to forgive means to let go and move beyond. Only then are you free. Use the Forgiving from the Heart exercise.

- *Forgive yourself.* Yes, perhaps you made a stupid mistake and have regrets. But you made your choices based on your awareness and information at that time. Speculation is useless and debilitating. Forgiving is an act of self-acceptance and a major step toward wisdom and love.

- *Accept your memories.* Letting go of pain doesn't mean you must never look back. On a quiet Sunday afternoon you may reminisce about your ex-loved one. This is normal. It doesn't mean you're slipping further into a black hole of depression. Without tragedy, the life experience would become flat and unchallenging.

- *Appreciate your hard-won lessons.* You've learned something more about yourself. Perhaps you were naive about the difficulties of a long-term love relationship or how ruthless the business world can be. You now have an opportunity to transform that hurt into a step toward personal growth. Examine your loss to see how you can avoid making the same mistake in the future. The lessons you've learned may not be apparent yet, but learning *is* going on at deeper levels. You may find that your emotional sensitivity has grown, allowing you to empathize more with others. You may feel different, even a bit strange. That's okay. It's all part of the unfolding of a greater, enhanced capacity to love.

How to Choose a Psychotherapist

While the Love Fitness workouts described in this chapter can heal deep hurts, you may also consider seeking professional help to assist your growth. Seeking psychotherapeutic help is a very personal decision. Certainly most of life's difficulties or emotional crises do not require psychotherapy. Nevertheless, professional assistance may be necessary or useful in the following instances:

- If your love relationships are repeatedly frustrating.
- If you and your lover are caught in bitter conflict.
- If you don't feel good about yourself most of the time.
- If you seek solace in a liquor bottle, drugs, or binge eating.
- If you feel perpetually out of control and under strain.
- If you and your lover have sexual problems that you haven't been able to resolve on your own even after making a sustained effort.
- If you fear actually doing damage to yourself or someone else.
- If you're in a severe emotional crisis, and the support of family and friends is not enough.
- If you are afraid that you may act on your suicidal thoughts or rage.
- If you are increasingly isolated emotionally and socially withdrawn.
- If you may be suffering from a serious mental or physical illness.

Another reason to get professional help is to change a recurring and a self-defeating pattern in your love life or career. This is particularly important if you find yourself frequently falling for lovers you later find repulsive. Some common examples of repetitive patterns in which you keep finding the wrong person are as follows:

- You are easy prey for the expert seducer. Initially you are overwhelmed by his or her charm and ability to fulfill your desires, especially in bed. However, you soon find the seducer is bored and must go on to the next "love 'em and leave 'em" victim. The seducer is terrified of genuine intimacy.
- You are attracted to someone who is defiant and "challenging," only to find this person's hostility eventually directed at you. You were fascinated by his or her sharp tongue and acerbic wit, but now you are the target of insensitive jokes and verbal attacks.
- You chose an insecure partner knowing he or she won't leave you, but later find this person so insecure you're claustrophobic and want to leave yourself. At first you liked how "comfortable" you found this person, but soon discovered that increasing familiarity breeds boredom and then contempt.

Most people spend more time buying a car than searching for the right psychotherapist! There is nothing mysterious about psychotherapy, and no therapist can perform magic. Any psychotherapist, no matter how brilliant, can only assist you in discovering how you can solve your problems; he or she cannot solve them for you. If your therapist is a psychiatrist, he or she can also prescribe medication as necessary.

Let's assume you have decided to seek psychotherapeutic assistance. According to a survey by the National Institute of Mental Health, over 130 different psychotherapies are now being practiced. Despite the apparent conflict over what works and what doesn't, here are some guidelines to help you choose a method of therapy and the right therapist.

Research indicates that the empathic ability of a therapist, rather than his or her theoretical persuasion, is critical in determining whether you benefit from counseling. Therapeutic strategies and techniques can be very powerful when used by a therapist who is inherently helpful and genuine. Other characteristics to consider are authenticity, nonpossessive warmth, and sense of humor.

The importance of carefully choosing a psychotherapist cannot be overemphasized. Seek referrals from your family physician, mental health agencies, and trusted friends. Visit two or three licensed therapists with the intention of determining who would be most suitable. It can be helpful to include a close friend or family member in these evaluations for additional input.

When making your final decision, consider the following questions:

1. Is he or she a licensed psychotherapist who is respected by the professional community and general public?
2. Does the therapist have a pleasant disposition, a sense of humor, and appear to be functioning well in his or her life?
3. Do you feel safe, comfortable, and at ease with the therapist?
4. Is the therapist honest, nondefensive, and empathetic?
5. Is the therapist willing to explain his or her approach to your problem, including strategies, goals, and length of treatment?
6. Is the therapist very rigid in his approach or flexible and open to your input?
7. Does the therapist treat you as if you are foolish, flawed, or defective, or treat you as an equal?
8. Does he or she just listen silently like a blank screen, or do you feel you are getting some sensible and generally helpful input?
9. Does the therapist answer your questions and concerns directly rather than always asking what you think?
10. Is the therapist willing to apologize when he or she was mistaken or inconsiderate?

11. Does the therapist give appropriate feedback, or are you left with constant doubts about how the therapist perceives you?
12. Does the therapist seem more like a consultant or as a controller?
13. Do the therapist's strategies and techniques show care and concern for you as well as others?
14. If you are interested, is the therapist willing to see your love partner or other significant people in your life?
15. After the session, do you feel more hopeful and empowered with higher self-esteem?

The therapist should be willing to explain his or her assessment of your case, strategies, and treatment goals. It is also reasonable to ask for an estimate of how long treatment will take. Significant benefit can often be obtained in a short number of sessions. The Chinese symbol for "crisis" also means challenge and opportunity. At its best, psychotherapy is an opportunity to face the challenges of life and convert them into opportunities for emotional growth and spiritual renewal. The therapist should strive to preserve a client's self-respect, dignity, and privacy by maintaining a safe and trusting atmosphere for disclosure.

The therapist should be understanding of your problems and your pain. The therapist should be accepting, never finding fault or condemning you for your mistakes. The therapist should be honest, caring, and kind. The therapist should absolutely avoid romantic or sexual involvement with you. The ideal therapist is a teacher, guide, and friend who acknowledges that ultimately it is *you* who must become your own best therapist.

When considering the necessity of professional assistance, bear in mind that depression is the most common of all psychological illnesses. Depression is an inherent part of the human condition that everyone suffers to some degree at one time or another. For some people, however, depression may be so severe that psychotherapy alone may yield few positive results. In these cases, a psychiatrist can prescribe antidepressant medications which make severe depression a highly treatable illness.

Most people are unaware that low energy, lack of sexual passion, and an inability to love and be loved can be the biological result of severe depression. Almost as painful as being severely depressed is being the mate of someone suffering from this disorder. No matter how hard you try to be intimate and stimulate passion, nothing seems to work. Both people tend to blame themselves and each other. All too often, people suffering symptoms of severe depression fail to seek help and appropriate medical treatment because they fear the stigma of "mental illness." This is an unfortunate irony because severe chronic depression is a highly prevalent and well-recognized medical disorder, one as treatable as diabetes or hypertension.

The primary symptoms of severe depression are anhedonia (reduced enjoyment and pleasure), boredom, loss of concentration, difficulty in decision making, neglect of personal appearance, early-morning awakening, low self-esteem, outbursts of rage, exhaustion, insomnia, reduced sexual activity, feelings of guilt, worthlessness or stupidity, suicidal thoughts, and a diminished capacity for love and affection.

Severe biological depression results from a biochemical imbalance in the brain. Antidepressants, taken as prescribed by a psychiatrist, are non-addictive and highly effective. Some people resist taking antidepressants because they are "drugs" and therefore perceived as "unnatural." This is unfortunate because antidepressants restore a natural biochemical balance.

Proper medication used in conjunction with psychotherapy can bring immediate relief and in most cases, an effective end to severe depression. If you or someone you know suffers from the symptoms of depression, consult your general practitioner or a psychiatrist for help.

Convincing Your Lifemate
to Join You in Therapy

In therapy, as with this book, your relationship will benefit most if you can persuade your lifemate to participate. Men in particular are often resistant to working on a relationship. They either lack the time, patience, or interest, or at least that is what they tell themselves until a major crisis like impotence, threat of divorce, or an affair arises. Here are our suggestions for encouraging your lifemate to join you.

Prepare. Before broaching the subject with your lover, get a clear idea of what you want to achieve and why. Beware of making your lover wrong with statements such as, "You've got a problem." Instead, rely on "I" statements such as, "I am unhappy with certain aspects of our relationship, in particular how often we fight and I suggest we [get professional help or try some Love Fitness workouts] to change matters." Know in advance what therapists you might consider and be ready to explain how you propose to choose a therapist.

Select a time and place. You may think that a restaurant or some other romantic setting might be a good time and place to suggest work on your relationship. We don't recommend it—too many distractions and wrong associations. Rather, we suggest you pick a quiet evening at home when neither of you is excessively tired, pressured, or stressed. Choose your time and place carefully. You need time to talk without fear of interruptions.

Be brief. Avoid complexity. A simple statement of one or two objectives is best. Make clear that you intend to find a therapist who advocates brief treatment that both of you value. Review the five "Myths of Personal Growth" in Chapter 1. Be prepared to debunk the myths that may quite reasonably dissuade your lover. Emphasize the goal-oriented approach you intend to follow and the specific benefits you hope to share.

Establish deadlines. Explain that you don't want continuing problems in your relationship. Propose that you work toward resolution of the issues within a specific number of days. If your lover then postpones and puts you off, don't simply wait for him or her. Start working on the problem yourself and let him or her know you have done so. If need be, make an appointment with a therapist for yourself.

Don't give up. Even if you start working on the relationship alone, give your lover several chances to follow. Point out that he or she can benefit as well from changing the relationship. Set an example by making those changes he or she might like to see in you or in the relationship. Tell your lifemate that you intend for both of you to get more out of the relationship than ever before. If you have started seeing a therapist, continue to suggest that your partner try an easy-level Love Fitness workout such as the "Mutual Appreciation" exercise.

Affirm your intention to change. If you start making progress but your lifemate continues to resist, you must ask yourself what you really want. Will you hold on to an unsatisfying relationship, perhaps out of fear of being alone? Or will you make your needs clear? We are not suggesting that you pack your bags, but you must let your lover know that a refusal to grow could have painful consequences. Don't be afraid to talk about how you both may be hurting and how important it is for the relationship to change.

Respect yourself and your lover. Once you have initiated the process of change either through the Love Fitness program or therapy, you must continue to respect yourself. To retreat out of fear will have consequences you will regret. At the same time, trying to force your lifemate to change will be equally futile. By respecting your lover's right to make his or her own decisions, you strengthen yourself and the integrity of your relationship. Sometimes, in communicating such respect for your lover, you will inspire your lover to reciprocate. The last thing you want to create is another "should" that your lover will resent as one more burden. Create mutual respect and you may be surprised to find your lifemate soon asking how he or she can start working with you to improve the relationship.

Chapter 7

The New Love Contract

When it comes to love relationships, two halves do not make a whole. The single most damaging assumption you can make about a love relationship is that you and your lifemate are supposed to make each other happy. This assumption makes no more sense than if you thought you could exercise for your lover to keep him or her physically fit. Individual happiness arises from personal growth—developing your own skills, achievements, capacity for intimacy, friendships, success, peace of mind, and spiritual insight. A healthy love relationship can add marvelously to that growth. Severe problems in your love relationships are inevitable, however, if you allow your love to blind you to your fundamental responsibility to create your own happiness.

Becoming Fit for Love Together

You may acknowledge intellectually that you are primarily responsible for your personal happiness, and you can't expect someone else to "make you happy." The difficulty arises in taking this concept to heart. How do you acknowledge your needs without becoming needy? Is your sense of self-worth dependent on your love partner's attitude or feeling toward you? How do you develop and express your strengths without threatening your lover? How do you handle your own frustrations without succumbing to the natural tendency to blame? How do you get what you want from a relationship without getting caught in self-defeating efforts to change your lover? The answer lies in creating a new love contract: becoming fit for love together.

By love "contract" we are not referring to a legal written document. Rather, we mean the unspoken psychological promises that lovers make to one another. In the business world, conflict arises when people make promises they can't keep. They wind up breaching their contracts. So, too, lovers are often tempted to make emotional promises they can't keep. When lovers unconsciously enter into an unspoken agreement that each may look to the other as a primary source of personal happiness, lovers make psychological promises they are bound to break.

It is in many ways easy to understand how and why lovers wind up assuming that each should be responsible for the other's happiness. Lovers naturally want to please each other and to earn each other's approval. Out of mutual commitment to each other, lovers desire to meet each other's needs. Living together involves some divisions of labor, whether one person cares for the home and the other works outside the home, or whether all these duties are shared. This sharing of responsibility encourages a feeling of responsibility for the other's well-being and happiness. While all these reasons explain how lifemates assume each is responsible for the other's happiness, a simple fact remains: Personal happiness depends on your own personal growth, not that of your lover.

The Old-Style Love Contract: Co-Dependency

Some of our clients find this analysis unsettling. We explain that the underlying assumption of the old-style love contract is, "I am responsible for your happiness and you are responsible for mine." They tend to say,

"Of course, that is what love is all about." We then suggest more careful examination of how the old-style love contract gets played out. Does it focus each person on what each can add to the relationship, or does it focus each lover on what each wants to take from the relationship?

Since happiness stems from within, a relationship based on the old-style love contract usually winds up with lovers feeling disappointed with one another. How couples handle a business failure and economic setback typically illustrates the problem. When economic crisis hits, one lover may try to be understanding but secretly feels let down. Illness also tends to highlight the problem when one lover isn't there for the other, causing resentment to build behind a facade of tenderness.

More commonly, when you feel bored, moody, or frustrated, you may be expecting your love partner to magically boost your spirits. Unfortunately, no matter what your love partner has to offer, what often follows is a tirade of complaints and blame, such as, "My life would be terrific if you would . . . [do what I say, take care of household chores, lose weight, stop spending so much money, etc.]."

Such co-dependency can also inhibit you from pursuing your own goals. Couples caught in the old-style love contract tend to allow one partner to pursue personal achievement while the other assumes a supporting role. For some couples, this arrangement works wonderfully, but for others, time passes, children grow up, and the care-giver who now feels unfulfilled, may blame his or her mate for denying him or her an opportunity to experience the satisfaction of a career. Even where both partners work, it often happens that one will take a "safe job" so the other can pursue his or her dreams. The one who fails to reach for his or her personal star winds up frustrated and resentful.

Taking unreasonable responsibility for your lover's moods also results in enormously unproductive guilt and worry. If you believe you are responsible for your lover's happiness, it is quite natural to feel guilty about your lover's distress and to worry that his or her frustration is somehow your fault. We see this pattern of guilt and worry quite typically among care-giver women, terrified of abandonment, who will do anything to keep a relationship from dissolving. Unfortunately, no matter how much they try to "help" or please, they cannot make their love partners happy. In almost cruel fashion, they are confronted with a dissatisfied, emotionally unavailable lover who fantasizes that another woman could make him happy. These women also become subject to fantasies that a Sugar Daddy or Prince Charming will come along and give them the romantic bliss they have been craving. The result is that both people subconsciously wait for someone else to make them happy and resenting that no one does.

Though every person must ultimately take responsibility for his or her own happiness, it is quite natural to wish for a magical lover who can do it all for you. Romantic infatuation is usually so glorious that even the most ordinarily sensible person can be heard to say, "I have finally found the one who can make me happy." Unfortunately, when the romance and infatuation wear off, it is all too easy to begin wondering if you have found the right person after all. Romantic distortions inevitably lead to anger and disappointment.

Love fitness requires letting go of the assumption that someone else can make you happy. Instead, you must commit to choosing satisfaction in your own life and love relationship on a moment-to-moment basis. The more you resist choosing satisfaction, the more likely that complaints and antagonism will grow. A quality love relationship is not made up of half-full partners trying to rescue each other or become whole by merging. Only when both partners are striving to be full and complete within themselves can love and happiness overflow.

Choosing to be satisfied doesn't mean that you settle for less or become complacent. Rather, it means that you look for concrete ways to develop your aspirations in harmony with those of your lifemate. It means identifying your most important goals, keeping yourself fit, and taking charge of your life. We don't pretend that it is easy for you and your lover to seek your own happiness and remain in harmony. What if you desire children at different times? What if you get important career opportunities in different cities? What if one of you wants to go back to school? These issues challenge your love fitness, and certain emotional work-outs provide important help.

Part of taking responsibility for your own happiness is learning how to support yourself when fears and doubts arise. How often have you used fears or a victimized expression to induce your lover to make critical decisions for you? How often have you pretended you couldn't face an issue when in fact you could have but didn't want to? How often have you waited for external forces to make your decisions for you?

Though you may know that you are responsible for your choices, and that you cannot abdicate responsibility for your happiness to your lover, knowing and doing something about it are quite different. For many people, the habit of looking outside themselves for support and happiness are deeply ingrained. They often revert to avoiding major decisions and instead wait anxiously to be rescued by a lover.

Exploring Your Love Contract: A Quiz

The following quiz is intended to help you assess the degree to which you take responsibility for your own happiness and well-being in a relationship. Read each of the thirty-three statements as if you were speaking to your lifemate, or, if you are not currently in a relationship, the person with whom you last had an intimate involvement. On reading each of the statements, ask yourself whether it applies to you rarely, sometimes, often, or always. Score 3 for rarely, 2 for sometimes, 1 for often, and 0 for always.

1. I struggle to be more of an individual person in our relationship.
2. I try to guess what you need and feel frustrated when I am wrong.
3. I expect you to know what I want and to give it to me without asking.
4. I feel guilty saying no to your requests for fear of making you unhappy.
5. When I want something from you, I feel hurt when you say no.
6. I don't feel happy unless you are happy also.
7. I feel I cannot live without you.
8. I feel guilty if you are not sexually satisfied.
9. I feel used rather than loved and appreciated.
10. I feel pressured to change my thoughts, feelings, or behaviors.
11. I feel as if you complain or nag about my failure to make you happy.
12. I tend to blame you when things go wrong.
13. I tend to blame you when I'm not feeling good about myself.
14. I regret giving up professional career goals for our relationship.
15. I place responsibility for my life's happiness on you.
16. I hold myself back from expressing my full abilities, competence, and intelligence.
17. I find myself playing the role of Prince Charming or Cinderella, trying to rescue you and make you feel happy.
18. I feel our love for one another can solve all problems.
19. I don't need friends; I need you.
20. I don't need family; I need you.
21. I feel I have to be strong and responsible so you won't feel scared or disappointed.
22. If you are not happy, I feel guilty.

23. I feel if you don't need me, you won't want to be with me.
24. If I make myself happy, I'm afraid of being considered selfish.
25. I fear you will outgrow our relationship and leave me.
26. I have to give up my desires in order to make you happy.
27. I feel that I need to protect, defend, and save you.
28. I feel that our love is a prison; I've lost my freedom and happiness.
29. If I am happy and successful, I won't need anyone, including you.
30. I count on you to make major decisions when I am unsure of how I feel.
31. If you love me, you will do what I say to make me happy.
32. I wish I could take more financial responsibility and were less economically dependent upon you.
33. I feel responsible when you are hurt or upset.

Now add up your score. For each of the above, "rarely" signifies that you feel free to be yourself and enjoy taking responsibility for your own happiness. An "often" response suggests that you relinquish responsibility for your personal happiness and are prone to excessive dependence on your love partner. The following analysis of your overall score will help you to calculate the level of freedom and autonomy in your relationship:

80–99 You experience an abundance of freedom in your relationship. You are a whole individual who enjoys interdependence and understands that the source of personal happiness lies within.

60–79 You enjoy above-average autonomy in your love relationship. You know how to meet your needs and don't make your love partner responsible for your personal satisfaction.

40–59 Although you have enough independence to hold your own in a relationship, you may often feel "If you really love me, you would . . . ," causing you a good deal of unnecessary frustration. The emotional work-outs in this chapter will be useful in gaining a new perspective on the price you pay for these expectations and how to increase your independence and self-sufficiency.

29–39 You tend to be excessively dependent and look to a relationship as a prime source of happiness. If you have difficulty sustaining a love relationship, your expectations may be excessive or demanding. The Love Fitness exercises in this chapter will help you expand your satisfaction and self-reliance.

0–19 If you are in a relationship, you are probably locked in the old-style contract of co-dependency where you and your love partner look to one another for personal happiness. Freedom to take responsibility for your own emotional well-being is probably limited. You and your lover blame each other for your frustration and lack of happiness. There may be problems in your relationship that could benefit from professional consultation.

Pay particular attention to statements on which you scored 0 or 1 and ask yourself how those attitudes and beliefs have an impact on you and your relationship. If possible, have your lover complete this quiz as well. When reviewing the results together, beware: Don't use the quiz to blame, but rather to learn. Be sure to acknowledge yourself and your lover for the courage and commitment it takes to look honestly at the hidden assumptions in your love contract.

False Assumptions

One terribly destructive offshoot of assuming that you are responsible for your lover's happiness is believing that love is a license to change your lover. What lies behind such efforts is usually a desire to make your lover fit your expectations and meet your needs. Below are examples of individuals who created disasters in their relationships in this way:

- Melanie and Bradley lived together for three years. Although Melanie wanted to get married, Bradley kept putting it off because he wasn't "ready." The more Bradley resisted a commitment, the more Melanie coaxed him to "overcome his fears and grow up." Melanie had spent her lifetime trying to "fix" unavailable and uncommitted men. She found unstable lovers to be challenging, unpredictable ones mysterious, immature ones demanding—and all of them in need of her understanding, support, and advice. When asked about her suggestions, Bradley declared, "Melanie is always trying to 'help' me be more intimate, but that just makes me feel like running away."

  By assuming the role of therapist and rescuer, Melanie was trying to force Bradley into fitting her expectations of the perfect lover. What she had to recognize is that no man wants to feel scrutinized and badgered. Her efforts to understand and enlighten him were actually manipulative and controlling. Through counseling, Melanie discovered that this desire to "help" was really an effort to force Bradley to provide the unconditional love that she so desperately sought. Melanie had to learn to accept a man as he is, not as she hoped he would be. Only by understanding her own needs and how to fulfill them could she really love—that is, accept her lover as he is.

• After a six-month whirlwind romance during which Dana, a professional chef, often prepared gourmet meals that took days to plan, Matthew, a stockbroker, proposed to the only woman who he said, "cooks better than Mom!" Yet five months into marriage Matthew was seriously troubled by Dana's new "attitude." "Things were better before we got married. Dana used to take such good care of me, but now she never has time," he lamented. Dana, on the other hand, felt abused as Matthew became increasingly demanding and angry.

Like so many men, Matthew confused love from his wife with motherly love—which comes only once in a lifetime. He sought from Dana the special quality of nurturance received from his mother, which included fixing all his meals, cleaning up after him, and indulging him during illness or difficult times. When Matthew began berating Dana for not being more caring like his mother, Dana blew up.

Through counseling, Matthew saw that he was expecting a superhuman effort from Dana, one that she could not fulfill. We asked Matthew to recall the ways in which his mother pampered him, and then to recognize how he tried to make Dana assume the role of caretaker. Matthew also realized that he was still tied to his mother's apron strings by always seeking her approval of major decisions, such as his choice of spouse, changes in lifestyle, and when to start a family. We assisted Matthew in taking more responsibility in the relationship and helping to increase the amount of quality time he and Dana were able to share. Because she was no longer forced to take care of Matthew in addition to her other responsibilities, Dana once again experienced joy in creating an occasional special dinner for him. Matthew stopped trying to force Dana into a mother/child role and instead joined her in creating an adult/adult relationship. In time, Matthew and Dana learned to function as a team. Becoming true partners is a key to becoming lifemates.

- Lita was a twenty-nine-year-old charming and vivacious sales executive who was deeply troubled about the breakup of her eighteen-month relationship—her longest love yet. She asked, "I've got so much going for me; why do men leave me?" The issue for Lita was a powerful need to control and manipulate men by using sex appeal, flirtation, and charm.

Throughout her youth, Lita's father was unaffectionate toward her and rarely vocal of his feelings. Consequently, Lita's experience of rejection was internalized in the message: "I'm not lovable or attractive; I can never have what I really want." As a teenager, Lita had romantic fantasies of idols from Clint Eastwood to Mick Jagger and Joe Namath. Lita kept hoping her Prince Charming would appear; in the meantime she grew increasingly bitter, cynical, and full of despair. She so feared losing at love that the intense efforts she made to seduce and sexually addict her lovers eventually led them to feel suffocated, controlled, and imprisoned. This was especially true because Lita was attracted to highly independent, powerful types who, like herself, enjoyed their careers.

Feeling controlled by a woman, for many men, is akin to bondage, not love. Men, like women, need to feel free to love, not obligated to meet emotional demands. Ironically, those lovers who gave in to her need for control were treated with contempt. Lita viewed these men who were once strong and powerful as weak pushovers not worthy of her attentions. Lita was addicted to "I'll be happy when . . ." Since she could never enjoy what she had. She liked to seduce men with power, but eventually no lover could live up to her expectations. Lita lived with a two-horned dilemma: a fear of being less or else settling for less. Either way she lost.

In therapy, Lita had to confront her own need for control and her lack of self-worth. Only then was she able to sustain a relationship with a man who felt comfortable with her strength and whom she could respect. Lita also had to come to grips with the fact that, just as there are no perfect men, the idols in her fantasies might, in the long run, bring her misery rather than fulfillment. In therapy, Lita examined the needs behind her fantasy and what she really wanted in a relationship. By learning to identify and attend to those needs, Lita was able to let go of her romantic fantasies and to find a man who was genuinely caring, successful, and able to commit.

A Relationship Isn't "It"

Part of taking responsibility for your own happiness is recognizing that just being in a love relationship doesn't bring an end to personal frustration. No one can possibly meet all your needs, and the search for such a person is like the search for the Holy Grail. It will doom you to despair. Therefore, to create a new love contract in your relationship, you have got to make a new love contract with yourself.

First, you must recognize that a paradox of unconditional love is that we all have conditions. No relationship is "perfect." The more you accept that no partner will ever fit all your pictures, the more you can make a realistic, mature choice and appreciate whom you are with. A relationship isn't "it"; your experience of love, joy, and satisfaction will always rest primarily within you.

Second, you must realize that you cannot please everyone. If you have fallen in love only to be bitterly disappointed, you may question your self-worth. By attempting to be a "pleaser" you've discovered that no matter how much time and energy you give to your love partner, he or she will still complain and make demands.

The lesson here is to stop looking for approval and to put your own needs first. As you do so, you must also learn to accept your lover's occasional criticism. Do not resist, justify, or apologize. Simply go about your self-nurturing activities. Your talents, well-being, and happiness are the greatest gifts you can give yourself—and your love partner. The new love contract means you do not develop yourself for someone else's love. Taking responsibility for yourself gives great freedom to your lover and to your children to equally develop themselves. In the old-style contract a love partner and children are often left feeling guilty and responsible for your unhappiness, and, as a result, suffering and manipulation abound.

Third, you must give yourself the freedom to be exactly who you are. You do not owe it to your spouse or your children to be anyone other than who you are. With this attitude about yourself, you empower your love partner and/or your children to be themselves and to develop their abilities and happiness without excessively worrying about you. Just as seeing a parent suffer causes a child to feel responsible for easing the pain and turmoil, so seeing a parent joyous and embracing life gives the child a model as well as permission to do the same. All relationships become easier and happier.

Fourth, you must accept that no matter how committed your love relationship or marriage, you are still, and always will be, "single" as well as part of a couple. Love is a special, intense connection, but it is not an answer to all or even most individual problems. If you have old emotional wounds, you must take responsibility for healing. Your lover can provide support but he/she cannot perform your Love Fitness exercises for you, just as your lover cannot exercise or lose weight for you.

Finally, you must learn to accept your lover exactly as he or she is; not as you hope or wish him or her to be. A change that you think is in your love partner's best interest may not seem that way to him or her. Certainly you can be candid, make requests, and give feedback, but manipulation of your lover to meet your needs is a prescription for disaster. Change only comes about because your lover wants it. Mature love means accepting your lover's flaws and respecting that which is unique and lovable.

Habits of the Heart

The psychological assumptions that govern love relationships can best be thought of as habits of the heart. Ordinary habits such as sleep or eating patterns tend to be difficult to change. Habits of the heart are no different. In order to break habits of the heart that support an old-style love contract, substantial personal effort is required. The Love Fitness workouts to make these changes can be practiced on your own. The rewards are worth the effort, as our client Valerie now enthusiastically tells her friends.

Valerie, a thirty-one-year-old single parent of a four-year-old daughter, felt devastated because her fiancé of six months, Jake, was threatening to leave her. Valerie didn't know much about being loved, but thanks to a childhood with a very critical and withholding mother, she knew a great deal about trying hard to please and then being rejected. Her first marriage was to a man who ardently pursued her. Once married, however, she found him condemning and super-critical. Despite the romantic courtship, Valerie felt little affection in her marriage; sex was a struggle to win her husband's approval rather than an expression of intimacy. Their eight-year marriage failed, further convincing Valerie of her inherent unworthiness.

Valerie repeated the same self-destructive pattern with Jake. She believed that no man would leave someone so willing to try to give, please, and sacrifice.

Valerie wanted to do everything together with Jake twenty-four hours a day, until he began to feel claustrophobic. She read women's magazines and self-help books on "how to win your man." Valerie would call Jake at work several times a day and cook gourmet meals for him every night. As a result of this pressure, Jake developed a growing sense of guilt and resentment, to the point where he felt he had to leave.

In her initial interview, it became self-evident why Valerie had such difficulties maintaining an intimate relationship, as we particularly noted in her attitudes toward love:

"I try not to do anything to hurt or upset my love partner's feelings, but I always seem to fail."

"I let my boyfriends put me down, partronize me, or call me cutesy names."

"When someone I love is unhappy, I feel guilty and worry it's my fault. I'm afraid of being selfish or saying no."

"I try very hard to please so I won't be rejected."

These unrealistic attitudes about love relationships caused Valerie to sacrifice her self-confidence at great emotional expense. Once again, Valerie was "looking for love in all the wrong places." To feel self-worth, she sought her man's constant approval. On the one hand, Valerie was desperate for love; on the other, she was unable to receive the love Jake freely wanted to give. Valerie felt compelled to manipulate and control him, looking to Jake for what was missing in her.

Valerie had to develop a fit-for-love relationship with herself before she could relate in a more healthy way to a man. She had to experience for herself that the more she commanded respect, the more love she would actually receive. Valerie had to put her own growth first and learn a new set of fit-for-love habits. We recommended a key Love Fitness workout to transform her habits of the heart.

Valerie was surprised to discover her power to re-shape her emotional responses. Together we identified those messages, beliefs, attitudes, and expectations that led to the problems she was having in her love relationships. The premise behind this exercise is to contrast those internal messages antithetical to love fitness and replace them with habits of the heart that support a truly loving balanced relationship.

Unfit	*Fit for Love*
1. It is selfish and wrong to put your needs before the needs of your love partner.	Each love partner is primarily responsible for his or her own happiness. Your primary responsibility is to take care of your needs first. Only then will you be genuinely able to give more of yourself to others.

No one knows your needs and wants better than you. The truth is, no one else has, or ever will have, as great an interest in seeing your desires fulfilled as you. Your happiness is your responsibility. Being "selfish" means you are accepting that opportunity for growth and achievement. As you respect your own needs more, you will radiate confidence and grow more attractive; this in turn will affect how others perceive and treat you.

Unfit	*Fit for Love*
2. I need love. Somewhere there is a perfect lover and a perfect relationship.	I want love very much but I can survive and feel reasonably happy without it. It's up to me—not a relationship—to make me happy. There is no perfect lover or relationship.

Those who subscribe to the ideal of eternal romance inevitably find that no relationship fits the bill. Do unto you as you would do unto others. Learn to see and serve the beauty in yourself. The less you resist the fact that no lover will ever meet every single one of your expectations, the more fully you can appreciate whomever you are with now. Only when you work to become more whole of heart does a healthy and long-lasting love relationship become possible.

Unfit	*Fit for Love*
3. If someone is to love you, you must be perfect in all that you do. You cannot make mistakes.	No one is perfect. You need not feel guilty about mistakes that affect your life and your love relationships.

A sense of failure, self-blame, and diminished self-confidence is the result of believing you must be perfect. It's okay to make mistakes, as long as you can take responsibility, forgive yourself, and learn from them. The more accepting you become of yourself, the less critical you will be of your love partner.

Unfit	*Fit for Love*
4. You should go to great lengths to please your love partner or he/she will abandon you. You should always be sensitive to the needs and wishes of others even if they don't tell you what they want.	You have a right to not anticipate your love partner's needs and wishes. You are not a magician or mindreader. You cannot possibly know what others really want and need —unless they tell you.

The more you can be who you really are, the more you create an atmosphere where others can be who they really are. They can take it or leave it, but if people are responding to the real you, you don't have to worry about slacking off or not being on your best behavior.

Unfit	*Fit for Love*
5. You should never hurt a love partner's feelings; people are fragile.	You are ultimately not responsible for your love partner's feelings, no matter how much you respect him or her. Whether you allow yourself to feel hurt or not is primarily up to you.

If what you need or want seems to hurt or deprive your lover, withholding information about your desires merely creates guilt, frustration, and anger. Continuous efforts to communicate with clarity, openness, and honesty will result in a relationship capable of negotiating needs and creatively integrating one another's desires.

Unfit	*Fit for Love*
6. Being alone is painful. Happiness and pleasures can only flourish in the presence of your love partner.	Being alone can be a wonderful experience and a great pleasure. It refreshes and renews your ability genuinely to enjoy and love your mate. A love relationship also needs room to flourish—time together as well as time apart.

Joy and self-worth can be experienced alone as well as with your lifemate. Being alone regularly enhances personal growth and is important to psychological well-being. You have a right to be alone and refresh yourself. You can simply say, "Thank you; I've already made a previous commitment [to yourself!]."

Unfit	*Fit for Love*
7. To have a good relationship you should focus on mutual sacrifice	You have a right to say no. A love partner has a right to ask, and you

Unfit	*Fit for Love*
and giving. It is always better to give than to receive.	have a right to say no graciously.

Relationships are best when they consist of 90 percent want tos and 10 percent have tos. A high percentage of have tos causes dissatisfaction and frustration. The habit of self-denial, of always saying yes, can result in bitterness and resentment.

Unfit	*Fit for Love*
8. It is easier to sidestep a confrontation. Avoid disagreement and difficulties whenever possible. Peace is worth any price.	Love guarantees some degree of hurt and anger; it goes with the territory. If your inner voice says you need to confront something your love partner has done or said, you can learn to do so effectively.

Unfortunately, avoiding confrontation usually results in the problem getting worse. A truly destructive emotional explosion can be the consequence. Chapter 5 provides some anger workouts that can help you use disagreements to grow closer.

Unfit	*Fit for Love*
9. I am unattractive; I have love handles/tiny breasts I can't accept. No more-attractive woman/man would want to stay with me for long.	A great irony of sex appeal is you don't have to be a model to be considered handsome or beautiful. If you possess an inner glow of confidence you will be perceived as energetic, intelligent, and sexually attractive.

If you judge your body and appearance harshly, you send out messages that say, "Don't notice me," or "Without makeup I'm a mess." Such self-criticism spurs others to see you as unattractive; your self-criticism becomes in essence a self-fulfilling prophecy. On the other hand, you don't have to be young, gorgeous, or pencil-slim to radiate sex appeal. When your posture, eye contact, facial expressions, clothing, and attitude reflect self-confidence, a lover will also feel good about your appearance. There is no barrier other than your belief to experience yourself as beautiful or handsome.

Unfit	*Fit for Love*
10. I constantly compare myself to others and I often feel inferior. I am afraid that someone who has his/her act really together will find out how insecure and weak I am and pass me by.	I recognize that I am a wonderful, unique, and special person. If someone really gets to know me, he/she will discover how much I have to offer.

Many times the feeling of inadequacy is so familiar that, ironically, you may feel uncomfortable living without it! The key to breaking this pattern is to develop a more loving attitude toward yourself. Beauty may be in the eyes of the beholder, but the person who determines how a lover will judge your worth is you. Pay more attention to your strengths and attractive qualities, and remember no one can make you feel inferior except you.

• • •

Sometimes it is difficult to recognize unfit internal messages because thoughts move at lightning speed. You will rarely conceive an unfit thought as a complete sentence stamped across your forehead. Once you begin to examine the habits of your heart, however, you will find unfit messages appearing in a millisecond shorthand: "ugly," "no good, "afraid," "better not." These self-deprecating thoughts must be fully challenged and changed. Other clues that suggest negative habits of the heart include self-criticism, a negative self-image, remembering a traumatic love scene, or tension and anxiety.

The habits of the heart described above identify not only Valerie's but also perhaps some of your unfit internal messages. These assumptions are likely to be a major source of unhappiness in your love relationship. In the coming weeks, whenever you are experiencing self-doubt, fear, or oppression in your love relationships, refer to this list and see if you can identify your unfit habits of the heart. Then intentionally shift your attention to the fit-for-love habits by reading, writing, and incorporating them into your behavior as much as possible. Remember, repetition is the key to mastery. The more you review and visualize appropriate situations in your life where you can apply these Love Fitness habits, the less you will be at the mercy of old unfit patterns. This is a fundamental aspect of love fitness—learning to trust your ability to recognize and modify your habits of the heart and to support yourself in meeting the challenges of love.

The Mirror Exercise

You deserve to feel attractive. Society, advertisements, and publications tend to reinforce a general dissatisfaction with appearance and image. More than just "looking good," a truly beautiful person radiates energy and excitement, and a feeling of being genuinely comfortable alone or among others.

To further help Valerie feel more self-confident, attractive, and sexy, we suggested she do "The Mirror Exercise." Learning fully to accept and appreciate how you look isn't easy. Whenever you look in a mirror you make a basic choice to feel either satisfied or dissatisfied. To get into the habit of self-validation and praise, practice The Mirror Exercise as follows:

1. Set aside ten minutes in which you will not be disturbed. Stand nude or semi-nude in front of a full-length or bathroom mirror.
2. Stand up straight with your shoulders back and breathe deeply. With conviction affirm, "I am attractive." Notice whatever negative judgments come to mind (for example, flabby thighs, breasts too small) and go back to affirming, "I am attractive."

It may seem quite confrontational to look at yourself in the mirror and practice self-praise. In fact, many people feel embarrassed, foolish, and self-critical at first. Keep focused on being more accepting rather than self-conscious. It takes determination to make this a habit, but the rewards are so great that it is worth going through any early discomfort. In addition to these "beauty treatments," commit yourself to no longer complaining about your looks. It took years to develop and recognize your insecurities, and you won't unlearn them overnight. The Mirror Exercise can be done when you start your day or before going to bed. This practice will also make sticking to a diet or physical-fitness program easier. Whenever you eat a meal, go for a job, put on swimwear, or get ready for a date, say to yourself, "I am attractive." When you disrobe in front of your lover, thinking and believing "I am attractive" will enhance your sex appeal and self-confidence.

In addition to her mirror workouts, Valerie used a second exercise to turn her what ifs into so what ifs:

What Ifs	*So What Ifs*
What if I have wrinkles?	So what if I have a few lines; they represent the wisdom I've gained.
What if my breasts are too flat?	So what if my breasts are small; they're sensuous and attractive.

What Ifs	*So What Ifs*
What if my hips and thighs are too big?	So what if my thighs are heavy; they make me more voluptuous and sexy.

Valerie used these emotional workouts to become more fit for love. Instead of underrating herself, she felt more confident, assertive, and attractive. The more positive Valerie felt about herself and her looks, the more Jake wanted to be with her.

Here is a shorthand list Valerie made that she found particularly useful in reinforcing her gains.

Unfit	*Fit for Love*
I try to control.	I, Valerie, relax and let go.
I am poor.	I, Valerie, am abundant.
I feel afraid.	I, Valerie, am strong and self-confident.
I feel disappointed and stuck.	I, Valerie, go with the flow.
I have self-doubt.	I, Valerie, trust my inner voice and intuition.
I take life too seriously.	I, Valerie, have lots of fun and enthusiasm.
I am dissatisfied with my appearance.	I, Valerie, am sexy, attractive, and take care to look my best.
I feel needy.	I, Valerie, love fully.
I am self-critical.	I, Valerie, talk to myself gently, with approval.

Valerie put copies of this list by her bedside, the refrigerator, and the dashboard of her car. She also carried the list in her purse. Valerie took a few minutes three or four times daily or whenever she felt stuck, to review her new habits of the heart. Her commitment paid off. Just as dissatisfaction with yourself is contagious, so is enthusiasm.

As Valerie became better able to nurture herself, paradoxically Jake no longer felt a need to leave. As Valerie became less needy, Jake felt more free to reciprocate with love. He no longer felt trapped, controlled, or smothered by the relationship. To the contrary, as Valerie became more fit for love, Jake found her much more exciting and attractive.

Nine months later Valerie and Jake were married. Valerie learned the special joy of fully taking responsibility for her health and happiness and not looking to Jake to bolster her self-esteem. A follow-up three years later found Valerie pregnant, with a sparkle in her eyes that radiated self-confidence and inner power. Valerie and Jake had forged a new love contract.

Beyond the Blame Game

When you were a young child, the responsibility for your happiness rested with your parents. An infant cannot feed, comfort, or clothe itself. A small child cannot survive, physically, or emotionally, without the consistent help of others. As a result of such dependency, you learned to behave in ways that would get others to do what you could not do for yourself. You discovered how to cry when you were hungry, to pout when you were upset, and to throw a temper tantrum when you didn't get your way.

As adults, we retain basic psychological needs for affection, support, and nurturance. Many people assume that the responsibility for satisfying these needs is still outside of them, still primarily up to others. When we feel frustrated at work, we blame our boss or office politics. When we see a character trait in ourselves that we don't like, we blame our parent(s) for making us that way. When we are bored or in a lousy mood at home, we blame our mate.

Your lover is the most convenient person to blame for your flaws, failures, and flops. How often have you shrugged your shoulders, pouted, or complained in order to manipulate your love partner into doing something you could have just as well done for yourself ("Where's the butter?"; "I can't find my pants")? How often have you blamed your lover for your own shortcoming ("How could you pig out in front of me when I'm trying to lose weight?"; "Why don't you make the kids behave")? How often have you told your love partner to make a decision for both of you and then complained about the outcome ("Why did you pick this lousy movie?"; "This Chinese restaurant is awful")?

Blaming and complaining are insidious emotional traps that spring from excessive dependency needs and can severely undermine a love relationship. It is so easy, almost natural, to blame your love partner for your own problems and failures. People tend to unload personal frustrations on whoever is nearest and dearest. Blaming and complaining is the adult version of the whining temper tantrum.

"Poor Me": Tears, Tantrums, and Threats

Twenty-six-year-old Shane runs a small business out of her home in the country, while her husband Keith is a lawyer in a neighboring town. Shane and Keith each had a long list of complaints that threatened their marriage. Shane said, "I have no time for myself. I work on my business at home and take care of the three children. I feel I have nothing exciting to get up for in the morning." Keith declared, "When I get home from seeing clients, Shane is miserable, the kids need my attention, and I feel very neglected. If this is all marriage is, let me off at the next stop, please.''

Shane felt that Keith had no sympathy for her and the pressures she faced daily. Even though Keith did help out with the children while she worked in her office at home, she felt he did so resentfully. She complained about the odd jobs around the house that Keith put off completing. Consequently, Shane began to resent giving Keith attention and instead felt upset with him most of the time. She lamented, "I hate being a nagging bitch, but Keith doesn't help the situation at all."

Keith felt agitated because Shane did not appreciate that he took care of the children in the evenings while she was working. He cooked dinner, tucked them into bed, and tidied up the house. Keith resented that Shane paid more attention to what he didn't do, and failed to acknowledge all the responsibilities he assumed around the house. As a result, Keith found himself seething with anger and making sharp, derisive comments.

In a love relationship that deteriorates into blaming and complaining, each partner feels like "poor me." Rather than work through the challenges of their situation, Keith and Shane would resort to emotional weapons to manipulate each other. Each would attack by sulking, yelling, and withdrawing love. The problem is that when you and your love partner are each trying to change the other, it's a no-win situation. By pushing against the other, all that happens is an increase in disappointment and resentment. The more you persist in proving each other wrong, the greater the resistance.

Here is an exercise we asked Keith and Shane to perform to break the blaming and complaining cycle. Each listed specific complaints about the other on a sheet of paper. We then showed them how remarkably polarized their complaints had become when set side-by-side:

Shane	Keith
1. You always want things your way.	You never make decisions.
2. You are so predictable and compulsive. You don't take time to have fun.	You are too impulsive, outrageous and silly. You always want to play.
3. You are always worrying about business and money.	You don't think about where the money will come from.
4. You are too secretive.	You pry too much.
5. You are too insensitive.	You are overly emotional.
6. You are so opinionated; you can never be wrong.	You are too nice, always letting your friends influence you.
7. You always interrupt and never let me talk.	You withdraw and punish me with silence.
8. You are cold.	You are too needy.
9. You act sometimes like a stranger to me.	You don't respect my need for more space and privacy.
10. You aren't open; emotionally you're tight as a clam.	You just want to talk about your feelings; you're so self-centered.

This exercise was useful in two respects. First, it helped to get frustration out in the open. For Shane and Keith, however, this exercise had the additional benefit of showing them how each was failing to acknowledge the other's point of view. They matched each other point-for-point in the blaming and complaining game, but they weren't resolving the problems in their relationship. Fortunately, Shane and Keith were able to laugh at how they had been poking at one another out of frustration. They shared enough love and motivation to learn to put into practice the following solutions.

The 200 Percent Relationship

Love fitness requires taking responsibility for your choices, experiences, and feelings without blaming your love partner. Many people have a tendency to pay lip service to the concept of responsibility while really feeling, "but in this case it really is his/her fault." Being fit for love means recognizing that partners are equally responsible for what transpires in their relationship. Old-style relationship contracts were a 50–50 division of responsibility; new-style love contracts are 100–100. Rather than feel victimized and miserable, each partner must take 100 percent responsibility for creating problems and finding solutions. If you and your partner each make such a commitment, you can create a 200 percent relationship.

This next emotional workout is designed to help you stop the tendency to blame and complain and to take full responsibility for your relationship. When your lover becomes upset, ask yourself the following questions:

1. What reason does my lover have for thinking, feeling, or behaving this way?
2. Why do I allow it to affect me negatively?
3. What am I doing to elicit, provoke, or maintain my love partner's hurt, anger, or frustration?
4. What expectations or assumptions underlie my feelings of being hurt, threatened, or irritated?
5. What care and compassion is my lover really seeking through his or her distress?
6. How might I choose to react to elicit a positive response from my lifemate?
7. What can I say to acknowledge my lover's good points?
8. What can I do to convey more love, understanding, and acceptance to my love partner right now?

What these questions boil down to is quite simple. Whenever you and your lifemate feel hurt, angry, or irritated, ask, "How can I create more love, acceptance, and appreciation right now?"

Many people complain that their lovers always criticize them when in fact, they criticize their lovers for criticizing them. You can break the blaming habit by acknowledging what your lover does right most of the time, not just when he or she irritates you. Shifting your attention from nagging to acknowledging is a powerful relationship-changing love fitness skill.

Some love partners secretly feel that once they stop complaining and arguing, they will have nothing left to talk about. First of all, you have to recognize that problems will always come up in your relationship. Second, you now possess new love fitness skills to handle these challenges. Here are some further suggestions to change a relationship that has gotten stuck in blaming and complaining.

Even more painful than tirades of criticism and complaints is suppressed love. You can break through years of negativity and conflict by honoring your highest intention to share love. Don't be afraid to say, "I love you," no matter how many times you have suppressed these words in the past. Keep in mind that arguments are a signal that your love partner needs care and understanding from you. Be willing to give a warm hug from your side instead of waiting for your love partner to take the first step. It may feel awkward and risky, but the rewards for being open with your positive feelings are enormous.

When you say or do something loving for your lifemate, don't be surprised if he or she has some difficulty responding immediately. Your love partner may be changing the habits of a lifetime— and that takes time. Just as you have felt unloved at times, he or she may have been acknowledged too infrequently or with too many strings attached. Complaints build because of a failure to love and be loved. Now it is up to you to bring in more love! Send a love note and flowers when they are least expected. You may have to initiate not just the first step, but the first ten. Give your love partner a few moments to accept the loving things you say or do. Part of saying "I appreciate you," "Thanks," and "I love you" is waiting patiently for your lover's defensiveness and cynicism to fade and to realize your sincerity. Act from that position of strength and power, and you will no longer need to be afraid of sharing your love.

Rephrasing with Love

Here is a Love Fitness exercise, "Rephrasing with Love," to shift from blaming and complaining to acknowledgment and intimacy. You can rephrase a complaint into a caring statement that calls for a responsible and mutual solution. The key is to describe the problem in terms of your own behavior. This is the exact opposite of blaming, because you identify what you can and will do to make the relationship work better. The following emotional workout between Shane and Keith will allow more insight into the mechanics of this process.

The items on the left-hand side are a list of their blaming and complaining statements. On the right are the same sentiments rephrased with love:

Blaming and Complaining	*Rephrasing with Love*
1. You never give me credit for how hard I work to provide a lifestyle you enjoy.	When I need acknowledgment for being a good provider I will say, "Sweetheart, I've had a rough day and when you get time I need some hugs and understanding."
2. You never do anything with the kids; you're tired and don't have any time for me.	The kids really enjoyed going with you to dinner and to a movie a few weeks ago. I'd appreciate your spending time with them this weekend.

Blaming and Complaining	*Rephrasing with Love*
3. You yell and bitch when I come home at night; I wish you'd be more fun.	I've been unresponsive to your needs, causing you to be upset with me. I'd like for us to have more fun. I've gotten a baby-sitter and have arranged a surprise evening.
4. Why don't you ever create a romantic, erotic, and adventurous evening for me? I'm always the one to plan them.	I really love it when you create excitement in our love life, like the time you . . . (specific example). Let's do it again.
5. How could you be so stupid? It's your fault! If you'd listen to me, these problems would never happen.	I need to be more assertive and give you my input on major decisions. I have a tendency to hold back my opinions and then say, "I told you so."
6. You're always breathing down my neck and finding fault; quit telling me how to run my life.	I have a right to make my own decisions. I value your input, but even if you think I'm making a mistake, please respect my choice.
7. You let yourself get overweight and out of shape and don't care about looking good for me.	I get turned on when you feel good about yourself and make an effort to stay in shape. Why don't we start jogging or going to the gym together?

Try this exercise yourself. Make an uncensored list of the five biggest complaints you have about your lover. Then, take each complaint and rephrase it to reflect your responsibility for the problem, and how you can talk about these issues with greater intimacy.

Rephrasing allows you to avoid the frustration of waiting for your lover to change. As a result of practicing these Love Fitness skills, Shane and Keith were able to restore intimacy and support to their relationship without "giving in" or "giving up." Remember, Rephrasing with Love is not primarily for your lover, but for you, your personal satisfaction, effectiveness, and power.

Transforming Expectations into Preferences

As you take responsibility for developing love fitness, you will be less likely to expect the impossible or seek to control your lifemate. Nevertheless, you may already be carrying unrealistic expectations that cause significant dissatisfaction in your love relationship. If your parents argued either too much or not at all, you may have unrealistic notions about whether or how often you and your partner should argue. If an ex-lover catered to your every whim and desire, you might be expecting your current partner to live up to an impossible standard.

Some expectations, of course, are appropriate. If your lover abuses alcohol or drugs, has a history of infidelity, or is unable to make a living, you are right to be cautious.

Some of the demands and expectations you carry into your love relationship, however, might usefully be converted into preferences. We define an expectation as something you need from your lover in order to feel happy, secure, and whole. In contrast, a preference may be defined as something you want from your lover but don't need so desperately that your happiness or well-being depends upon it. Almost all expectations can be transformed into preferences, and the process of transformation contributes to greater autonomy, increasing intimacy, and better communication.

The following are some expectations we've heard from clients whose relationships benefited by converting these demands into preferences. Take an honest look below to see which of these common expectations you bring to your love relationship.

"If you love me you would . . ."

Like my friends and want to socialize with them.
Make family priorities more important than work.
Have no expectations of me.
Include me in all your activities.
Do what I tell you.
Want the same things I want.
Never do anything that upsets me.
Be on time; never be late.
Make love to me whenever I desire.
Never interrupt me or walk away when I am speaking.
Lose weight and stay in shape.
Stop watching TV when I'm talking to you.
Agree with me.
Make more money for a better lifestyle.
Be more affectionate and attentive.
Always have an orgasm.
Wait for me to have an orgasm.
Never attend conferences or go on vacation without me.
Always look attractive.
Never be attracted to anyone else.
Call me every day when you are away on a trip.
When we argue, be the first to make up.
Do all the things around the house I don't like to.
Do lots to make me happy.
Never fantasize about old lovers.
Stop being friends with people I don't care for.
Make sacrifices for my parents and family.
Never do anything that hurts or aggravates me.

Now review the statements you have checked and consider the following questions:

- How realistic are your expectations?
- What is it that you are looking for from your partner?
- What could you do to create more of what you want and impose fewer expectations on your partner?
- Why are these expectations important to you?
- Why might these expectations not be important to your partner?
- What additional expectations do you have that are not on the list? A useful stimulus is to say, "If you love me you would . . ." or "I expect you to . . ." and then write down whatever might follow.

It is important to recognize that no lover could possibly live up to most of these expectations. As you develop yourself, you will be less likely to demand the impossible or seek to control your love partner. Even for those expectations you consider realistic and appropriate, it is helpful to express these as "I would prefer it if you would . . . (lose weight and stay in shape, be more affectionate, wait for me to have an orgasm). Remember, it is easier to respond with enthusiasm to a request rather than a demand. As you accept more responsibility for your fulfillment and happiness, the need to extract unreasonable promises from your love partner will lessen, and the more spontaneous, free-flowing love you will experience.

Love Fitness: A Brief Summary

A serious issue in writing a book about love and relationships is that it can never be complete. We have provided certain Love Fitness workouts to help develop personal qualities, emotional strengths and communication skills that contribute to a strong and passionate relationship. It is impossible, however, to reduce love fitness to one neat package. We thought it might be helpful as a summary to present what our clients and seminar participants have said about love fitness. Here are some of their thoughts:

- Love fitness means being 100 percent responsible for your experience of living, to not be a victim or a martyr, to be 100 percent accountable for the quality of your life, which includes the amount of love, joy, and growth you create in your relationship.
- Love fitness is the ability to remain strong, stable, and committed through difficult times, changes, and challenges. Being fit for love means being gentle, kind, and supportive of your lifemate's potential, goals, and aspirations.
- Love fitness is recognizing that you may choose at any time to experience joy and satisfaction, and therefore to be able to share your love. Whatever the circumstances or difficulties, you assume responsibility for your happiness and can turn within to regenerate satisfaction and overcome any obstacles in the relationship. Being fit for love entails a willingness to risk being hurt, rejected, and even at times feeling unloved. It is recognizing the need to be vulnerable and open on the level of your heart and spirit.
- Love fitness means sticking it out and solving problems that arise instead of running away. Love fitness means acknowledging that disagreements are inevitable and that problems are mutually created.
- Love fitness means accepting your lifemate's blind spots and shortcomings with no expectations or illusions. Love fitness is agreeing that no one and no relationship is "perfect."
- Love fitness is an opportunity for you both to grow and express yourselves as whole yet inter-

dependent individuals, committed to a relationship of love, equality, unity, and respect.

• Love fitness is operating under the assumption that your lifemate loves you, even when his or her behavior, feelings, or thoughts may at times seem otherwise. The commitment to love means seeing your partner's love for you even when he or she can't see it. Your awareness and faith can see through walls of anger, hurt, and fear, and by so doing help reconnect your love partner to the love inside him or her.

• Love fitness is utilizing a painful situation to further develop yourself as a person and lover. Rather than invalidate the relationship or negate your partner, a personal or relationship crisis is an opportunity to expand your fitness for love. Your courage and skill allow you to get through to someone's heart. Love fitness is understanding that a relationship is a learning experience for you and your partner. Any difficulties are to serve your path of the heart and growth as a human being.

• Love fitness is a commitment to creating an atmosphere where both people can share their opinions, thoughts, and ideas without becoming argumentative or defensive.

• Love fitness means continually discovering pleasure in the hidden aspects of your lifemate (as well as within yourself) that emerge as your heart unfolds and challenges emerge.

• Love fitness includes at times letting go when your lifemate desires freedom, but also knowing how to hold your partner close when he or she needs security and nurturing. It means wanting the best for your partner even if it may mean giving up some advantage or desire on your part, even if it means negotiating and compromising. Love fitness means wanting your partner to become all that he or she can become without feeling threatened by the changes, successes, or challenges that this might incur.

- Love fitness means respecting, valuing, and appreciating what your lifemate has to say and feel. It is acknowledging that openness and intimacy make a relationship special.

- Love fitness is recognizing that not only are you committed to the responsibilities of love and perhaps marriage and family, but also to the spontaneity, playfulness, and fun of being together.

- Love fitness is embracing differences and discovering ways in which to build a common lifestyle, share in decision making, and take equal responsibility for the results.

- Love fitness is realizing that you can only have power or manipulate another human being as long as he or she is willing to be a victim or martyr. Being fit for love is recognizing that you are powerless to control your love partner. All you can do is take responsibility for yourself.

- Love fitness is accepting your lifemate as he or she is without trying to change him or her through threats, screams, sulks, withdrawal, or hassles. Being fit for love is knowing that attempts to coerce a partner through intimidation will produce negative results. Even if he or she does comply, change occurs at the expense of pride and mutual respect.

- Love fitness is assuming at all times that your lifemate is good and loving and lovable at his or her essence, and that any negative behavior is learned and a challenge to further understanding.

- Love fitness is recognizing that each human being needs nurturance and support. Everyone needs someone who cares, encourages, and believes in us, especially when we sometimes don't. Love fitness is the ability to assume the responsibilities and challenges that arise when a lover is sick or unable to take care of financial commitments,

and being there through difficult, if even tragic, circumstances.
- Love fitness is admitting that you cannot burden your lover with all of your needs. The more self-sufficient you can be, the less pressure you put on your relationship. You will always have a need for professional self-esteem, friends, and self-actualization and growth that no relationship can make up for.
- In a fit-for-love relationship, lifemates recognize that they are together by choice and not because they have to be, or for the children, or because they are terrified of being alone. In a fit-for-love relationship, both parties respect the skills, competencies, strengths, and weaknesses of each other without regard to rigid sex-role stereotypes. A fit-for-love relationship means being able to ask directly for what you want, as well as being able to accept no for an answer.
- Love fitness is a willingness to express your deepest feelings, desires, thoughts, and opinions, without needing approval or agreement—where your partner can disagree or disapprove without you becoming defensive or needing to justify.
- Love fitness means you define problems that come up in the relationship in terms of your own behavior rather than blaming your partner. Being fit for love means working together as a team without competing or putting the other person down. Being fit for love is a willingness to make key decisions together, making the most of what each love partner has to contribute.

Love guarantees some degree of anger, hurt, and frustration. Love fitness is realizing that to experience joy and love more deeply, you must eventually become vulnerable to hurt, not dwelling on it, not paying excessive attention to it, but recognizing that pain inevitably comes with love.

These Love Fitness principles are worth rereading from time to time, especially during a difficult period in your relationship. You may be surprised to find yourself challenged by different Love Fitness principles at different periods in your relationship. Also, be sure to add other principles you have discovered to be effective in your relationship. Insight alone, however, is never enough. Repetition and practice is the key to mastering the Love Fitness program. Above all, acknowledge both your own and your lover's commitment to keep learning lessons of the heart.

Survival of the Fittest

Love fitness brings deep personal satisfaction, but also something more. It changes your perception of yourself and your relationship to the world. As you develop more love fitness, your appreciation of your interdependence with every other human being grows as well. The more love you feel, the more love you want to share. Personal growth and social contribution become woven into one strand.

The techniques and strategies we've developed have emerged from commitment to the belief that human beings are capable of enormous personal transformation. To whatever extent you put these suggestions to use, you will break through old barriers and past resistances to new levels of emotional strength and honest communication. You will overcome old negative habits and experience more love and pleasure in almost everything you do. You will become more attuned to your loved ones and discover your power to create the life you want. With this experience of love fitness, your perspective is also likely to grow from "me" to "we," and you are likely to become more concerned about making the rest of the world a better place.

The more conscious you become of your own emotional strength, the less possible it becomes in the face of human suffering to deny the inner query: "What can I do?" When you experience your power to change your own life, it becomes difficult to justify inaction with a stock phrase such as, "One person can't make a difference," "It's someone else's problem," or "I don't have time; I'm too busy." Once you make the Love Fitness program a part of your existence, it becomes impossible to turn your back on other people and world problems.

With the growth of love fitness, you come to appreciate that life is one; an outpouring of love flows through you toward your fellow human beings and all creation. Love fitness becomes a way to experience unity amidst diversity, the mystery and beauty of life. Large numbers of people acting upon their power to love can herald a new era of human relationships. An idealistic speculation? Perhaps, but a possibility worthy of consideration.

A new vision of social institutions that nurture individual and relationship growth is gathering momentum. No longer are people willing to put up with needlessly circumscribed lives defined by stifling jobs, joyless consumption, personal anxieties, and unhappy relationships. In the past decade, many have become aware that their lives can be richer, deeper, fuller, more pleasurable, and satisfying.

During the very early stages of this social awakening, the interest in personal growth appeared to be an exercise in withdrawal from social involvement. Tom Wolfe coined the phrase "the Me decade" to describe the sudden explosion of interest in the inner self and personal growth techniques. The pursuit of inner growth, say the critics, is a naive, narcissistic attempt to achieve peace while all around society is crumbling— like Nero playing his fiddle while Rome burns.

Now it's becoming apparent that the critics are wrong. As people practice personal growth programs, they are not turning away from others, but toward them.

They are not shunning social problems but becoming involved in the search for new solutions. They believe that the individual can make a difference and that major social problems will yield to answers based on a new vision of human capacities. Love Fitness signals an end to the Me decade mentality and the birth of a sense of greater community.

Our culture is in mid-life crisis. We are moving from the machine age to an age of discovering the spirit in the machine: the sacred within the secular. As psychotherapists, we see everyday what happens when stressed, fearful individuals spend the majority of their energy in defensive modes of behavior: there is less energy for love and creativity. Nations are collections of individuals, and the collective consciousness of the nation reflects the consciousness of its citizens. Presently, the nations of the world spend trillions on defending themselves while millions of children continue to die annually from starvation. As a result, there are fewer resources to solve the most serious world problems.

Love Fitness raises fundamental questions about the human spirit and political will. Are we to remain culturally conditioned and exhaust our resources in psychological conflicts, struggles between the sexes, and individual fear? Or can we human beings change such ingrained habits and become more fit for love? So, too, are we to remain politically conditioned by economic conflicts, ideological battles, and global paranoia? Or can we politically lessen fear and solve the pressing problems of potential environmental disaster, nuclear confrontation, and worldwide economic crisis?

An individual becomes a lover of life not just by taking a philosophical stance, but through a passionate commitment to a positive career and social endeavors. Once aware, the worst evil may be to remain passive. Everywhere there are problems that call for individual and political action. For example, storage of nuclear weapons, dumping of toxic waste, the greenhouse effect, and acid rain leave no country and no person unscathed. Inadequate schools remain an impediment to progress even in some of the most developed countries. Defense spending continues to exceed health care spending by several hundred percent.

We are hopeful that by becoming more psychologically fit, more people will join hearts, minds, and hands with others to form a spirited love conspiracy (*con-spire*, meaning, "to breathe together") to shift resources away from defense and toward constructive investment in our collective future. There is much each individual can do. You may choose to participate on a local land use board in support of environmental impact laws to ensure those natural rights for future generations. Support charities and organizations that reflect your world vision and values. Volunteer your services at shelters for the hungry and homeless, hospices, centers for abused children or the physically disabled, to name a few. Most importantly, in all arenas be one who listens, learns, and shares without self-righteousness. We are all in this together, so let us humbly support one another in becoming more fit for love.

We regard the Lifemates' Love Fitness program as part of a global shift among people more openly accepting their desires for caring, intimacy, cooperation, and worldwide friendship. The dream may be large, but its fulfillment begins with heart-to-heart communication, person by person, family by family, and eventually nation by nation. In an age of potential nuclear war and environmental catastrophe, love has become the master key to survival of the fittest.

REFERENCES

Bloomfield, Harold H., with Leonard Felder. *Making Peace With Your Parents*. New York: Random House, 1983.

Bloomfield, Harold H., with Leonard Felder. *Making Peace With Yourself* (formerly titled *The Achilles Syndrome*). New York: Random House, 1985.

Bloomfield, Harold H., and Robert B. Kory. *Inner Joy*. New York: Wyden, 1980.

Cologrove, Melba, Harold H. Bloomfield, and Peter McWilliams. *How To Survive The Loss Of A Love*. New York: Bantam, 1977.

Cowan, Connell, and Melvyn Kinder. *Women Men Love, Women Men Leave*. New York: Clarkson Potter, 1987.

Goldberg, Herb. *The New Male-Female Relationship*. New York: William Morrow, 1983.

Keen, Sam. *The Passionate Life*. New York: Harper & Row, 1983.

Lazarus, Arnold. *Marital Myths*. San Luis Obispo, California: Impact, 1985.

Leonard, George. *The End of Sex*. Los Angeles: Tarcher, 1983.

Norwood, Robin. *Women Who Love Too Much*. Los Angeles: Tarcher, 1985.

Paul, Jordan, and Margaret Paul. *Do I Have To Give Up Me To Be Loved By You?* Minneapolis: CompCare, 1983.

Robbins, Anthony. *Unlimited Power*. New York: Simon & Schuster, 1986.

Rogers, Carl. *Becoming Partners*. New York: Delacorte, 1973.

ACKNOWLEDGMENTS

We wish to thank Anjani Kory for her editorial assistance and her contributions throughout the book. Not only did she work long and hard hours reviewing every word in each draft, but she did more. She added music to the manuscript.

We also wish to thank those from whom we have drawn deep inspiration, especially Arnold Lazarus, Abraham Maslow, Carl Rogers, and Maharishi Mahesh Yogi. Our heartfelt appreciation to Bernard Baars, Don Baptisite, Leo Buscaglia, Suzanne Caldwell, Bobby Colomby, Norman Cousins, Ken and Karen Druck, Lenny Felder, Bill and Anita Fitelson, Mike and Donna Fletcher, John Gray, Susie Gomez, Trudy Green, Crystel Hammed, Michael Jakes, Judy Jean, Rabia Jibri, Natasha Josefowitz, Norman and Lyn Lear, Barnet Meltzer, Bonnie Mills, Jordan and Margaret Paul, John and Judy Phillips, Ali, Sybil and Phyllis Rubottom, Paul Sanford, Gay Swenson, Diana and Paul Von Welanetz, Oprah Winfrey, Nikki Winston, and all our friends and clients in Del Mar, California.

For their guidance, commitment, and friendship, we wish to acknowledge Elaine Koster, Michaela Hamilton, Judy Courtade, Pat Doyle, Lisa Berkowitz, Janet Schnall, Mary Siegel, and the staff at New American Library.

We also wish to thank Barbara Terrell-Washington, Elizabeth Norment, Ann McWilliams, and June Marshall for their help in the preparation of the manuscript.

Much appreciation to our daughter Shazara and Sirah's sons Damien and Michael for their love, support, and remarkable Heart Talks. Mother Fridl, Nora and Gus, Dorothy and Lou Vettese, Virginia and Ross Kory, and Hilda and Robert Thomas provided us with love and nurturance.

Index

Harold H. Bloomfield, M.D., and his wife and associate, Sirah Vettese, Ph.D., are among the most sought-after keynote speakers and seminar leaders in the nation for public audiences, corporate spousal programs and institutions. They have produced audio and video cassettes demonstrating Love Fitness exercises. For further information regarding personal appearances and to order additional products, please call or send a self-addressed envelope to:

Harold H. Bloomfield, M.D.
Sirah Vettese, Ph.D.
1011 Camino Del Mar, Suite 234
Del Mar, California 92014
(619) 481-1369

There's an epidemic with 27 million victims. And no visible symptoms.

It's an epidemic of people who can't read.

Believe it or not, 27 million Americans are functionally illiterate, about one adult in five.

The solution to this problem is you... when you join the fight against illiteracy. So call the Coalition for Literacy at toll-free **1-800-228-8813** and volunteer.

Volunteer Against Illiteracy. The only degree you need is a degree of caring.